Cary Tennis

Since You Asked

CARY TENNIS BOOKS, LLC
San Francisco

These columns first appeared on Salon.com

FIRST EDITION

Tennis, Cary.
Since You Asked / by Cary Tennis.

ISBN-13: 978-0-9793270-0-1
1. Self Help—Advice. 2. Essays—Advice.

Printed in the United States of America

10 9 8 7 6 5 4 3 2 1

Book design by Norma Tennis

2007905550

To the 94 anonymous correspondents
whose letters are answered here

Acknowledgments

I WOULD LIKE to thank, first of all, the 94 anonymous correspondents whose letters are answered here.

Next I would like to thank my wife, Norma Tennis, who gave her gift of design to the book. It is a great pleasure to work with someone you love on something you love.

I thank my friend, attorney and business partner Dave Crow, who, strangely intrigued by our notion of forming a publishing company, decided to join us at a crucial time. We could not have published this book without him.

In allowing a writer like me to write an advice column in the first place, Salon.com displayed rare journalistic courage. In fact such courage is so rare today it almost looks like foolishness. But if it is foolishness, it is foolishness of the most brilliant sort.

Everyone at Salon deserves thanks. Initial attempts to do so properly, however, caused this page to grow to such lengths as to raise our printing bill substantially. So let me first say I love and admire everyone at Salon and I am indebted to you all. Then we'll see how much room there is left for names. (After working many years in the medium of the Internet, it seems strange now to be constrained to a page of this archaic material we call ... *paper*!)

Caricaturist Zach Trenholm deserves special thanks for the charming and apt illustration that graces the book's cover and has graced every column since the beginning in October 2001. (See more of Zach's fine work at zachtrenholm.com.)

Special thanks to writer and radio host Garrison Keillor, whose Mr. Blue column preceded this one and showed what an advice column could do.

Gail Williams, director of communities at Salon, came up with the title "Since You Asked." Much thanks, Gail.

Thanks to Mark Faber for proofing galleys late into the night. In the long gestation of this book we at Salon have benefited from the advice of various professionals including literary agents Diana Finch and Sloan Harris. I personally have benefited from the advice of Elise Cannon of Publishers Group West, Dawn Cusick of EarlyLight Books, Brad Grochowski of AuthorsBookshop.com and the inimitable Bucky Sinister of Last Gasp Press, who tried with little success to talk us into doing something sensible—like not trying to distribute each and every book out of our garage.

I would like to thank my parents, who taught me to write. I would also like to thank all family and friends without whom daily existence would be impossibly bleak.

Well, it looks like there is a little more room here, after all. So let us thank by name those at Salon whom we can thank before running out of room: David Talbot, Joan Walsh, Karen Croft, Gary Kamiya, Scott Rosenberg, Michael O'Donnell, Ruth Henrich, Michal Keeley, Karen Seriguchi, Max Garrone, Jeanne Carstensen, Kevin Berger, Mignon Khargie, Bob Watts, Jennifer Ormerod, Lori Leibovich, Lauren Sandler, Joy Press, Sarah Karnasiewicz, Walter Thompson and Jennifer Sweeney, all of whom have had a tangible and positive influence on the column. Others in and around Salon whose generous, creative spirits have helped in ways they themselves may never fully realize include King Kaufman, Bill Wyman, Chris Neimeth, Elizabeth Hambrecht, Paul Lesniak, Douglas Cruickshank, Chris Colin, Amy Standen, Melissa Baron, Mark Follman, Jim Fisher, Katharine Mieszkowski, Andrew Leonard, Farhad Manjoo, Amelia Nash, Ewald, Maria Russo, Sheerly Avni, George Kelly and Sue Shor.

Finally, I thank all the readers and writers of letters without whom the column could not exist.

Well, we have to stop now. If your name got chopped off, I am sorry. The web of aid and inspiration is nearly infinite.

Cary Tennis
August 2007
San Francisco, California

Introduction

Dear Reader,

THANK YOU FOR opening this book and looking inside. Here you will find 94 advice columns chosen by Salon.com's readers as their personal favorites out of the more than 1,000 I have written since taking over as advice columnist in October 2001 from the writer and radio host Garrison Keillor.

I think that most of the advice columns I have written are pretty good but these are the really, really good ones, the ones that made you finally move to Seattle or move out of Seattle to Paris or stay in Paris and file for divorce or sell the restaurant and buy a dog or finally insist that your boyfriend tell you where he actually, truly lives. These are the ones you tacked up on your cubicle wall or pasted into a journal. These are the ones that crystallized the real but frequently vague constellations of joy, doubt, worry, frustration, hope, grief, hilarity and longing that we blithely refer to as our emotional lives.

But why the book, if these columns are already on the Internet?

First of all, this book is intended as a gift. It is a gift to the many readers of the column toward whom I feel great affection and admiration.

This book is also for those potential readers who appreciate good writing but do not read Salon.com either because they don't read the Web at all or because they have not yet discovered the fine nonfiction and reporting available daily on Salon.com.

This book is also for people who thought they would never read an Internet advice column in the first place. I am one of those people myself. So let me say this about that:

To my great surprise as a writer, I have found the advice column to be an almost perfect literary form. It poses the writer a daily riddle to solve with literary concision and vision. It also offers great freedom. I have found happiness working within it. As has been suggested by my friend at Salon Kevin Berger, I am at heart an improvisational literary artist. I use readers' questions as instances of inspiration and places of departure.

Also, this must be said: I am somebody who knows what midnight looks like from underneath. I stand with the underdogs, with the bewildered and suicidal, the alcoholic, depressed and grieving, the confused and recently abandoned, the war-torn and peace-scarred and drug-addicted and all the rest who do not fit and do not expect to fit and do not even know what it might feel like to wake up one day miraculously cured of idiosyncrasy and purged of tragic nature.

This is for us. We know who we are.

There are many other things I wanted to do in this book but now it looks as though there isn't time. I wanted to tell you how some of these stories turned out. I wanted to include some essays and drawings and poetry. I wanted to talk a little about self-publishing, and how the business of book publishing is changing.

But that will have to wait until the next book. Making this book was more work than we thought. I have to finish this introduction now and go to bed.

A note about the Table of Contents: There isn't one. But please, do one thing: Check out the index! It's very fun.

And remember: This book can be safely read wherever you like, in places where it would be quite ill-advised to bring a laptop. It will fit into most backpacks and large jacket pockets and, unlike a laptop, if it is ever lost or stolen it can be replaced for a relatively modest price.

So please enjoy these columns. They are truly among the best pieces of writing I have ever done.

Cary Tennis
August 2007
San Francisco, California

Since You Asked:
The Columns

I'm married with kids—and in love with a prostitute

I know it's crazy, but she's the woman of my dreams.

Dear Cary,

I AM GOING through what is a classic midlife crisis with a bit of a twist. I'm in my early 40s and have a great wife and two great young kids, all of whom I love dearly. I've been with my wife for over 20 years. Everyone tells me how lucky I am to have the perfect marriage. But, of course, I don't feel so lucky. Instead I feel burdened, trapped by the overwhelming obligations of family and of keeping up appearances. The way I've tried to deal with these feelings is by seeing prostitutes.

About eight months ago, I met and paid for the woman of my dreams. She's beautiful, a sexual dynamo, smart, funny and sweet. She's not a typical prostitute; she's more like the girl next door who wants to get paid for her great looks and abundant sexual talents.

I soon went from being her client to being her friend and confidant. Her presence in my life does two things for me. First I get to feel those incredibly strong emotions that I haven't felt in years about my wife (lust and longing), and more important, I feel so free during the few hours a month I get to see her. Not only do we explore sexual fantasies that would be completely out of bounds with my wife, but more important, I can completely relax around her and joke around and talk frankly, and not have to worry about things like who's picking up whom from school.

1

Of course, I know that this whole thing is incredibly stupid and immature, but I can't figure out how to unring the bell and go back to a life without this woman. Do you think it will be possible to not see her and forget about the pleasure, love and passion that we had? I've tried for a few weeks at a time, but I've always felt the need to see her again—the urge for release, both literally and metaphorically, was too strong. I have a hard time imagining life without her, but at the same time, she could never be a part of my "real" life—I have too much invested in my marriage and family to break it up.

So the question boils down to this: How do I give up sexual (and emotional) nirvana for the sake of my family?

Lost in L.A.

Dear Lost in L.A.,

IMAGINE THIS: In 15 or 20 years, when the kids are out of the house and you and your wife are adjusting to a new life in which the focus is less on the daily grind and more on gauzier, more philosophical questions, when you're both less easily shocked by the rank perfidy and incompetence of man, when you have faced some of the early questions of mortality and senescence and have learned not to be thrown too hard by the occasional sucker punch, you sit down over coffee and tell her about an episode in your married life that you'd kept secret until now, an episode a long time ago that almost brought everything crashing down.

There's no telling how she might respond. She might deck you. She might walk out and not come back. But imagine if she were to tell you, much to your surprise, that she had known all along, if not the details, at least the rough outline, and that by saying nothing she had knowingly protected you from the breakup that she could easily and quite innocently have precipitated had she chosen to confront you and demand all the sordid details. She might reveal that she had thought long and hard about what to do and had decided to continue with marriage and motherhood, betting that you would eventually resolve this devastating personal crisis on your own and come back to her.

Such a future is certainly not guaranteed. But it is only even possible if you can find a way to end this unconscionable indulgence and put it behind you. Even if you do everything right, things have a way of going wrong. But consider the alternative. Imagine where you will be in 15 or 20 years if you blithely continue along this path and are discovered in flagrante delicto, or, what might seem more honorable but could in a practical sense be worse, if you decide to come clean about this and throw yourself at your wife's mercy.

My bet is that you then go through an ugly divorce. And 15 or 20 years in the future my guess is that the kids have still never forgiven you for destroying the marriage; they have never been able to understand how their father could have hurt their mother so, could have done such a stupid, selfish thing, could have, basically, destroyed his own life and theirs. The affair and divorce have become the pivotal trauma of all your lives. You never really get over the loss, never again really feel whole and untroubled. Nor perhaps do you ever really get over the rejection by your "girlfriend" who, pleasure being business, must regretfully decline your proposed promotion from paying client to permanent lover.

No matter what your wife would do if told 15 or 20 years later, the news couldn't possible be as tangibly disruptive to her life then as it would be now, when its revelation would threaten everything she has—her marriage, her children, her self-esteem, her identity, her trust in others. While your letter mainly spells out your own concerns about the effect all this might have on you, it is the effect on your wife that must determine your course of action.

So, for your wife's sake, I think your best course of action is to end this affair immediately, put it behind you and never say a word about it.

> Protect those
> you love
> from your
> own tragic
> weaknesses.

3

There are problems with ending it and keeping it a secret, of course. Even if you're capable of doing it—and we'll get to how in a minute—some might argue that as an adult with free will she deserves to know the truth so she can choose whether to stay with you. Others might argue that the psychological damage done by keeping this secret would be greater than the damage done by revealing it. Some might say that a relationship based on less than complete disclosure is morally or psychologically inferior to one that includes full disclosure, and that it's your duty to be forthcoming, whatever the practical effect.

But in weighing the known ill effects of revealing this effrontery—the probability of divorce and ignominy—against the hypothetical evil of keeping it concealed, I find in favor of the perhaps impaired but still functioning relationship. That is, I sentence you to live in your own private hell instead of dragging everyone else into it.

So, as you so astutely observe, what this all boils down to is that you need to give up this sexual nirvana and put this whole episode quietly behind you. The question is how?

I would submit that you replace this sexual nirvana with a more compelling vision: the hero's quest to protect those he loves from the effects of his own tragic weaknesses. That is, you undergo a transformation of your fundamental orientation toward the world from one that is self-centered and narcissistic to one that is quest-centered and classically heroic. You move from a hedonistic extended adolescence in which you feel entitled to pleasures that threaten your marriage, to an adult role in which protecting your wife and children from your own imperfect character is your life's guiding principle.

But what's the fun in that? you ask. Well, frankly, it isn't much about fun. It's about right living. But there is something in it for you: self-worth, and the secret pride of knowing that you have done the best for others whether they know it or not. It's the kind of thing you can take to the grave with you and die happily. If lived with sufficient vividness, this sort of renunciatory role can have an almost erotic allure—like the priesthood. OK, so maybe I exaggerate a little. But my basic take on it is that your only salvation from this god-awful mess is to pass into a new stage of manhood in which sacrifice and not pleasure is the goal.

Colloquially, this is known as "being a man," or "stepping up" or "doing the right thing"—dealing with this quietly, on your own or more likely with the help of some confidential aide such as a spiritual counselor, 12-step sponsor or psychotherapist.

Again (and again and again) I'm not saying I think keeping secrets from your wife is a good idea. It's a terrible idea. I'm just saying that confessing to her that you've fallen in love with a prostitute is an even worse idea.

You won't have as good a marriage as you could have had if you had never allowed this situation with the prostitute to come up. But that's tough. Something bad has happened. It's your fault. Somebody has to take the fall. That person is you. You take the fall for the good of your wife and your kids. You shut up and be unhappy and uncomfortable for a while. That's a small price to pay, I'd think, to protect the lives of your wife and children.

My friend married a dud

He seemed OK when she was checking him out, but once she got him home he turned out to be a lemon.

Dear Cary,

I HAVE A very good friend—swimming lessons together when we were 7, shared birthday parties, close enough to fight with each other's siblings, college roommates, etc.—who married last August. Her husband, T., appeared to be the nicest guy in the world. He's outdoorsy and takes my friend (a nature child in her own right) camping, hiking, rock climbing, biking and backpacking all the time. He was friendly, sweet and sincere to her while they were dating and impressed me and our other roommates at the time as being one hell of a catch. We just couldn't figure out why someone so great was single after so many years.

Well ... nine months later, it's pretty apparent to all of us what was and is wrong. My friend, A., has hinted that life with T. isn't so great. He's insanely jealous of her time and accuses her of not loving him, talking about him behind his back and plotting to leave him—all statements that are patently and ridiculously false. At a recent dinner with several other friends, A. and T. at my house, he pouted the entire evening and said nothing more than a few acerbic, sarcastic sentences while we tried desperately to engage him and make him comfortable. He rarely wants to hang out with A.'s friends, and seems to be trying to make her miserable when we're around. He torments her, saying things he knows will deliberately annoy her, and he frequently makes hurtful jokes at her expense.

This past weekend, they came camping with me, my husband, another college roommate and her boyfriend. The tension on the trip was intense and troubling to all of us. T.—by far the oldest member of the group—acted like a 7-year-old child. He needed constant coddling, reassurance and placating. We all had to do what he wanted all the time or he threw a fit. One night, when someone made an offhand remark about camping, he took it as a personal dig on his hobbies and spent a few hours alone in his truck listening to music while the rest of us sat around the fire chatting.

My friend is a mellow, nice woman who deserves better treatment. I think her husband needs medication, therapy or more time to grow up without damaging her. I don't want her to be unhappy, as she has told us she is now. However, I don't want to meddle in her marriage. T. poisons every interaction between us, but I don't want to cut off our friendship and leave her with a man I think could hurt her in many ways. How can I help?

Worried in the West

Dear Worried in the West,

HOW CAN YOU help? You can be a good friend. Sometimes a good friend will just be very honest and say: You know I love you like a sister, but that husband of yours is an exploding Pinto, an old bag of spoiled peaches. He's a frown magnet, a disappointing afternoon. He's a bad gasket, a supermarket go-back, a failed experiment, a wilted head of lettuce. He's yesterday's jacket and tomorrow's bad shoes rolled into one. He's a divorce lawyer's meal ticket and that's about it. You could tell her that.

But something tells me it might not work out so well.

You see, I was sitting among a handful of reasonably civil people, women included, just yesterday, and I posed the question why a woman can't tell another woman that her boyfriend or husband ought to be put in a childproof container and removed from the shelves. I posed it as a serious question. But I wasn't able to get an answer. I don't know if there is an answer. I suspect that it's nearly impossible for women to tell women certain things. Still, I say if you're a good friend, you provide her with the name of a divorce lawyer with a smooth head of hair and a way with judges.

Not all jerks are wife beaters. Even still, once you marry a guy who acted fine before the wedding and then turns out to be a sulking, angry, brooding, disconsolate piece of bad fish left in a hot car on a busy street, what do you do? You divorce him. That's what people do.

You could try to fix him up. Some jerks need medicine. Some need more exercise. Some just need to be out in the wilderness cooking trout in a pan—they aren't happy except when squatting in front of a tiny little fire, blackening the bottom of a perfectly good piece of Calphalon. And if he needs to be out in the forest, you're doing him a favor by cutting him loose. Catch and release: That's a humane practice.

I'd do one or the other. But just tell her you think she's getting a raw deal. See what she says. If she asks you what she should do, tell her. Tell her to maybe set a deadline. He's got to shape up or he's out. No sense sticking with him and being miserable and then having kids and having them be miserable. And then the kids have kids and they raise their kids to be warped and the whole thing spirals out of control into the next millennium. What's the sense in that?

> Tell your friend the truth: She married a bag of old, spoiled peaches.

Why can't my boyfriend say, "I love you"?

It's just three little words, but they won't come out of his mouth.

Dear Cary,

MY BOYFRIEND OF over two years, who I know cares about me deeply, cannot say those three words that I always thought were a necessity. My boyfriend cannot say to me, "I love you." I know he loves me. So why can't he say it?

I know that when he was a teenager, something (many things?) happened in his first relationship that shook his vulnerable, depressive, overly sensitive self and left him unable to enter into another. It's hard for me to understand because I don't know why he hasn't been able to construct a different narrative for himself about events that happened more than 10 years ago. Why can't he tell himself a new story about that relationship, one that allows him to put it in the context of the overly dramatic, unreasonable teenage years?

A lot of people would like to make this into a simplistic case of "he must not really love me as much as he should." But I know differently. I know that we're both word nerds who like the preciseness of language, who share a fascination with the movies, music with thoughtful lyrics, books, theory, photography, art, travel, a certain West Coast city, long conversations, sushi, cooking, coffee and quiet mornings, among other things. We've had many discussions about this "love" thing. And everything he says and does seems to suggest that he holds the feeling those words express. And yet.

My family raised me to say those words, and I grew up to be an extremely passionate person. My family says it a lot. I tell my friends—my kindred spirits—that I love them. Because I do. I can't keep the words inside me. And I tell my boyfriend that I love him. But he can't say it in return.

It scares the crap out of me. I feel like I'm building up the beginnings of some strange resentments and fears and insecurities. No one seems to be able to know what to say when I tell them about this. Maybe you'll have a few words for me? I'm a literature major. I live on words. I breathe them, dream them, eat them for breakfast. What should I do?

English Major Seeks Three Little Words

Dear English Major,

PICTURE IT LIKE this: At birth everybody gets a sweater. Our sweaters keep us warm and they're very colorful. But while we're growing up they get snagged on things.

Your boyfriend's sweater got snagged on a girl a long time ago and he can't get it untangled. He'd like to if he could but it's not easy and plus you are growing impatient and your impatience is making him nervous. That's how it is when you're trying to untangle your sweater from a teenage girlfriend. You get nervous because someone is waiting. Sometimes in desperation you just shrug it off and the sweater rips a hole. (You sometimes meet people who claim that no sweater was ever issued to them and hence was never snagged. But go through their closets. You'll always find one, snagged and full of holes.)

Anyway, he's owned up to what happened to his sweater—it got snagged on a girl. As a result he claims he is unable to pronounce a certain phrase to you. It does seem unlikely, the connection, but there are often connections between sweaters and girls that we are only dimly aware of. Not only girls, but other unexpected things can snag on your sweater—soccer stadiums, gin bottles and historic events: For instance, the connection between my sweater and the atomic bomb is hard to explain. It has glowed ever since Nagasaki, but no one will believe me; if I try to say "Hiroshima," I always start to sneeze. I'm allergic to wool, but that's not it.

When you suggest that he could have invented a new narrative, you are on the right track. I take it that when you say "narrative," however, you mean "sweater." People will often say "narrative" or "metaphor" when they mean "sweater." It is called, in academic circles, "the mistaking of the sweater."

> Acceptance without reservation is pretty close to love.

So here is what you have to do. When faced with an old snag that will not untangle, you have to create a new sweater, or new weave, or new gravity. You will need a phrase to hold it together, something that partakes of an elemental force. How about the phrase "acceptance without reservation"?

The technique for mending is as follows: You say these words to each other as you rub your sweaters together. Watch closely for changes in temperature.

Roughly translated, "acceptance without reservation" means "very big sweater." If you look closely, you see why "very big sweater" is superior. The problem with "I love you" is the subject-verb-object. What is he doing to you, exactly, in loving you? Is it instant or ongoing? Is it an action or a state? What is done to you when you are loved? The action is unclear! It makes a hopeless tangle. No wonder his sweater has holes in it. He can't say it because it wraps him in a knot of yarn, it tangles his feet, he falls down. *(Getting to the root of it here, "yarn" being the tale we weave. —Ed.)*

"Acceptance without reservation," however, is an open door the size of the sky. There is room for both of you and all your sweaters, no matter how many layers of clothing you have on underneath. Use of this phrase will serve as a temporary fix to your problem. It isn't perfect. But use it until it becomes hopelessly tangled.

As your yarn business expands, you may find that certain certificates are required. Also blood relatives may appear, asking for the other phrase, "I love you." They may not understand "acceptance without reservation." It may trouble them in some deep, unutterable way. So while "acceptance without reservation" is your favorite, keep the other phrase handy for guests. Teach him to say "I love you" in French and Portuguese; this preserves plausible deniability, makes him seem "romantic," and may also encourage European travel.

Whatever you do, remember this: Never put your sweater in mothballs. It's better if it just gets a few holes.

My 8-year-old misses his old life—should we move back to the suburbs?

It was good to separate from their alcoholic dad—but I feel bad about bringing my kids to the city.

Dear Cary,

MY HUSBAND AND I are recently separated. To make a long story short, he developed a serious drinking habit over the course of our nine-year marriage and refused to seek treatment. He became violent, mismanaged his business, squandered an inheritance and was terribly irresponsible with money, so much so that when we sold our house a few months ago we narrowly escaped foreclosure.

I could not afford to purchase another home in the idyllic suburban town in which we lived, so I moved with my two children, ages 4 and 8, to the city. I love it here, as I am a 15-minute walk away from the university where I am a graduate student in a very demanding biomedical research program. I am sharing a house with my sister, who is helping me immensely. She watches my children so I can run to the grocery store and is home when I have to stay late in the lab.

Five months into our move, my 4-year-old has adjusted, but my 8-year-old is miserable. He misses his friends and his old lifestyle, and his best friend who lived next door. There were 18 children

13

on the block where we lived and they were always outside playing together. There are few children where we live now (unless you count the rowdy undergrads), and even if I allowed him to go outside by himself there would be no one to play with. Though we go to the park on weekends, he is not spending nearly as much time outside or with friends as he used to. Yes, there are great cultural opportunities here and it is more diverse, but that matters little to my son.

I feel so guilty for having removed my son from such a wonderful environment that I am considering moving back. Although I could not afford to purchase a house in that town, I could rent something small there. However, this would mean a longer commute for me, getting home later in the evening and the loss of my sister as a housemate, as she wants to remain in the city.

My dilemma is this: The city is better for me, but Mayberry is better for my son. Should I move yet again (an exhausting prospect) or make him tough it out?

Even if we did move back we would not be on the same block. I am aware that on the scale of possible human tragedies this one ranks pretty low, and though I remind him of this and offer him Lemony Snicket books, it does not comfort him. I know I had to leave the marriage, but did I have to leave the town too? I'm starting to think that in the turmoil of a dying marriage, I put my own needs before those of my children.

Guilty in the City

Dear Guilty,

I CAN RELATE to what your son is going through. When I was 12 my family moved to a world I did not recognize.

I did not know what to do to feel the way I used to feel. I did not know what I needed or how to get it. I did not know what I was feeling or what I had lost.

Knowledgeable adults could have helped this sensitive kid adjust. But such people were not available, and the adults who were available were overburdened with challenges of their own. So I was left to my own devices.

I did not do well in that situation. I did not develop the coping skills I needed. I now know that to adjust and grow in my new surroundings I needed to do two things: to maintain ties with my old world and to forge ties with my new world. But I did not know that then. I was just a kid.

So I had some troubles.

Therefore, my heart goes out to your son, who is much younger than I was when we moved. His connection to his home has been torn. He is doing his best to adjust. But he does not know how to adjust, nor does he have the powers to create a new world in which he can feel comfortable and confident.

Luckily, he has you. You are going to have to create that world for him. I suggest that rather than moving back to the suburbs or suggesting that your son just "tough it out" you consciously set about to create structures for your child that maintain some ties with his old world and help him cope with his new world.

Drive back to your old neighborhood and let your 8-year-old hang around, breathing in the air of the old place. Let him go play with his friends for a while in the old neighborhood. Have his best friend come and spend the night. Let him spend the night at his best friend's house and then pick him up. Maintain the connection to the old neighborhood without having to move back there.

> Build bridges for your children to worlds they have lost.

At the same time, create structures in his new world so he can develop new ties. I don't know what organizations are available or what his interests are. Nor do I think this is going to be easy. I remember what it was like to live in a neighborhood where all a kid had to do was walk out of the house and his playmates and friends were all right there. In such a setting, there was no need for formal activity programs such as the Boy Scouts or what have you. But that world is gone. Your son is going to have to do things differently now. He is going to have to participate in more formal social structures. Pick some fun activities that will put him in regular contact with others.

He may resist. I certainly did. But I suggest that you be firm. You know what is necessary. He does not. He may think he knows what he needs, but he is just a kid. You are the mother. You know best. If he finds it hard to get to know new kids, help him. Keep at it. Do not let him fail.

You have a chance here not only to help your son adjust to his new surroundings but to counteract the lesson that an alcoholic father imparts to his children: that when stressful change arises, one responds by collapsing inwardly and drinking. You can demonstrate a more positive pattern—that one responds to stressful change by creatively adapting, by coming up with new ways to interact with the world.

You don't have to explain all this to your son. Instead, teach by example. You can simply say, "We're adapting to change."

I do suggest that for the sake of maintaining a positive attitude you think of it as "adapting" rather than as "toughing it out." Try being grateful for the opportunity you have gained—that you don't have to spend the rest of your life watching the father of your children kill himself in front of you, fearing that he will crash his car into the neighbor's garage or collapse on the front porch with his pants down around his ankles. You have escaped that danger. You and your children are safe. You may find, when you consider your good fortune, that you feel some measure of gratitude to the wrinkle of fate or cosmic force or God that brought you this far unharmed.

Your kids are going to find this hard. They are going to miss their dad. And they're going to be sad and upset sometimes. But I think, all in all, that you have a very lucky 8-year-old.

Right=wing reading
in the corporate john

*Shouldn't the company crapper
be a collegial, neutral environment?*

Dear Cary,

I WORK IN a fairly large office, with about 50 others on my floor. Everyone gets along pretty well, but as I suspect is almost always the case when any number of people share a space, people sometimes do things that subtly encroach on the environment in ways that are discomfiting, or just downright perplexing.

For the past couple of months someone has been routinely leaving printouts of articles from politically conservative news sources on the floor in one of the two stalls in the men's bathroom. This has begun to irk me because 1) this is obviously littering in a public space—who does this person expect to throw it out, given that it is sitting on the floor in a toilet?—and 2) I feel that it is a passive-aggressive attempt to insert controversial opinions (which I happen to disagree with vociferously) into what ought to be a collegial and basically neutral environment.

Although I have my suspicions, I don't know for sure who is doing this. Given that, what, if anything, can I do about it? People would probably think me a little strange if I were to start inquiring around about it, even if only in the mild way of asking if others had noticed it as well. I could try to get the office manager to send a reminder to everyone not to litter/leave things in the bathroom, but that would seem to be casting the net a bit wide for an issue localized to one person and one bathroom stall.

At any rate, I don't want to overstate an issue that is, in a practical sense, easy to ignore. I suppose my concern is mainly philosophical. Is it worth trying to do something about this for principled reasons? My feeling is that in our culture we are far too often obliged to put up with unpleasant encroachments into our public spaces that are beyond our control. Shouldn't we exert our will in spheres we can possibly influence? Do we have a political obligation to do so? Or am I making something out of nothing? Certainly the last thing I want is to end up taking a tack that is merely awkward and unnecessary—impolitic in quite another sense.

Upright Citizen, Dismayed

Dear Upright Citizen,

I AM SURPRISED that you consider this an unpleasant encroachment into a public sphere, rather than as a fine and noble tradition.

In my view, the corporate men's room stall is a sacred space, a small and intimate temple, actually, where men briefly bask in the ancient mournful camaraderie of shit and death. Being such, it has certain traditions and rules.

The leaving of reading material for the next man is a venerable and near-universal practice by which men take narrative communion. You seem to have stumbled upon a particularly interesting vestige of this ancient practice and yet you disparage it. Why? Is it the content of the material itself? Or is it the practice?

I for one value the practice, even if the material disagrees with me.

One man leaves something for the next man to read. The viewpoint expressed need not be shared. By reading the opposite of what you believe you can join these men in spirit, if not in ideology.

What better place for right wing and left wing to come together in common humanity than in the toilet?

Why should you be so all self-righteous about this right-wing information? We are not having a civil war in this country. Right-wingers are not the enemy. They are simply troublesome friends. I say, love the right-wing asshole who leaves propaganda in your stall!

How very seriously we take this! That is what I notice. We live on a dying planet. We don't have an unquestioned place in the cosmos. We don't have an unquestioned place in the tribe. We have jobs and cubicles and bathroom stalls.

In this lonely and, for some men, shameful moment of defecation, when we stink up the world, the written material rescues us from our symbolic experience of death (that awful thing will eventually be us; that is our formless, disgusting, unavoidable future; we will all be like shit in the ground one day).

So I heartily suggest that you participate in this tradition of camaraderie rather than shun it. Leave some Noam Chomsky stuff in there if you have to, but communicate! Leave some good poems. Leave something provocative like Revolutionary Poetry (http://www.itsabouttimebpp.com/Chapter_History/Revolutionary_Poetry.html).

But participate! We kill culture with our stiffness. We kill it with propriety. We kill it with our separateness. And while I don't agree with him on the issue of bathroom sports page reading ("Theoretically," he says, "what you're holding is a huge, folded piece of toilet paper with athletes on it"), I suggest you read Matt Sebek's thoughtful Guide to the Corporate Crapper (http://www.insidestl.com/stloffice/index.php?linkid=72). It may be just the thing you need to find the golden mean between propriety and tradition.

> Find the deep meaning in dumb corporate customs.

Lastly: By no means should you suggest the office manager send a reminder to everyone not to leave things in the bathroom. Leaving things in the bathroom is, after all, exactly what we aim to do, however poor our aim.

My boyfriend's ex puts me down in public

Why do women do this to each other?
Can't we rise above it?

Dear Cary,

ABOUT A YEAR ago I started dating a wonderful man who went to college nearby. A lot of his college friends still live here, including an ex-girlfriend whom he broke things off with a couple of years ago. Until he started dating me I think she always held out hope that they would get back together, despite the fact that he broke it off because he did not see a future with her. We are on friendly terms with her and tend to see her socially as we all move within the same group of friends, but they are no longer close at all.

While this woman is not someone I would necessarily ever be close with, I can acknowledge that she is attractive, intelligent, interesting and by all accounts a pretty good person. That is what makes what I am feeling so hard, because I find that often when we are in groups of people she finds small ways to put me down and I'm tired of it. She generally does it when my boyfriend isn't around, but last week even he noticed her small jabs. To his credit, he stuck up for me, put his arm around me and gave me a squeeze of solidarity. The thing is, why do we women do this to each other? Her comments generally tend to insult my tastes in books or movies while at the same time pointing out how intellectual or highbrow hers are. I can't figure out if this is some sort of competition because we have dated the same guy or if she just doesn't know she is doing it, but I am finding it increasingly frustrating to hang out with her. My boyfriend is more than willing to just not attend parties or other functions that she throws, but I don't want her behavior to dictate my actions.

I've tried just letting her comments roll off of me to minimal success. I know part of the problem is my own competitive spirit. I attended a top college on a large merit scholarship, graduated with honors, have a good job and have generally done well at whatever I've tried. However, this woman—and, in fact, most people I meet—doesn't know this about me because I don't talk about it. So it hurts when she tries to make me out to be less intelligent or really lesser in any way. I've been hesitant to come out and say it's jealousy because it seems like we women are forever comforting ourselves that people who don't like us are "just jealous," but I'm running out of explanations. Can two women who have loved the same guy really not ever get along? I know that sometimes it's hard to get along if you were both incredibly serious with the same man, but their relationship was for a space of time in college and was never completely intimate.

There is a college reunion coming up a couple of hours away, and now she wants to carpool with us. I knew she was coming and I don't mind hanging around her in a large group, but trapped in a car for hours? My boyfriend has already offered to just say no, but I don't see how to do that without coming across as a jerk. The thing is, I want to like her and I feel like I'm failing. I don't like what that says about me as a person or as a girlfriend, but I also don't like having to smile in the face of her comments. Is there a way to defuse the situation? I'm worried that if I try to sit down and talk with her, she will say I'm making it up and she has no problem with me. However, I think it's pretty clear that there is some sort of tension and I've love to let it go. Any thoughts?

Fed Up

Dear Fed Up,

A PERSON CAN be "attractive, intelligent, interesting and by all accounts a pretty good person" and still be your enemy. I would focus not so much on understanding her but on defending yourself.

It's hard to defend yourself openly against subtle hostility. Sometimes, rather than trying to ignore it or rise above it, the best way is to be a little outrageous—quickly, and then let it go. You need to make some kind of public gesture that reasserts your dignity and lets everyone know that you know what's going on and won't stand for it.

That is what this is about. It isn't about you sitting down with her and finding out what her problem is. We know what her problem is. She is a hurt, jealous woman who won't admit to herself that she was wounded and so lashes out in subtle ways. It

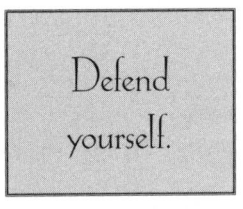

Defend yourself.

would be OK if she just didn't like you and knew that she just didn't like you. We can be perfectly nice to people we don't particularly like. But I'm betting she also blames you. She's got it in for you. You're a bad presence in her head. She sees you as someone who caused her unhappiness. You are the reason she is not with that guy. So she must demonize you. She cannot allow herself to believe that you were simply more attractive to him and a better match. You must instead be cast in her mind as a person worthy of contempt—"a prissy, shallow, passive-aggressive bitch," perhaps. I know that sounds ugly, but I'll bet that's the kind of garbage that is running through her head.

And because you are not fighting back, she has no reason to reconsider her behavior.

I don't know what kind of language is appropriate in your circle, so I can't tell you exactly what would do the trick. What you want to convey is that you know she's needling you, you think it sucks, but at the same time it doesn't hurt you—it's just stupid and ineffective and makes her look bad. Some people could just say, "Fuck you" and walk away, and it would be understood, in all its unsubtle glory, not as a hateful provocation but as a legitimate acknowledgment that she is indeed fucking with you and you don't care for it. It alludes to a genuine tension but doesn't linger on it. It is both expressive and dismissive.

If done skillfully such a pushing of linguistic boundaries can clear the air and everyone can shrug it off. You need to find the words, body language and facial expression that will say unequivocally, "Back off."

Apparently, instead, you are trying to take the high road. You wonder, "Why do we women do this to each other?" I would say women do this to each other because women are people and people are nasty. People hurt each other on purpose. They do it because it feels good! They do it because it makes their own pain go away!

She's hurting you because she's hurt. But that doesn't mean she deserves your sympathy and understanding. You are struggling in a self-defeating manner against your own natural impulses to defend yourself.

She's beating you up verbal-ninja style. She's ripping you to shreds with razor blades of icy sisterhood.

You have to do something about it.

Send her a signal. Don't be subtle, but do it quickly and move on.

Help! I'm falling for a fat man!

*I like this guy a lot, but the
poundage is a turnoff.*

Dear Cary,

CURRENTLY I'M DATING a man who just won't leave my
consciousness, not for a moment. I think of him all the time. He's
pretty special.

My problem is this: This wonderful man with whom I've
shared some amazing moments and do share a phenomenal connection. . . he's overweight. He's not merely out of shape or a
hike and a swim away from fit, he's fat.

I've made a conscious effort to look past it ("it" being my
own stupid, shallow, superficial, counterproductive reaction to
the weight), but there it is, all of the time. In bed, he's attentive,
very strong, wonderful—we enjoy genuine chemistry—but even
when the lights are out I find it difficult to navigate his flesh.
I'm a smallish person stature-wise; it's difficult for me to wind
around a man with what little leg I've been given, never mind a
man the size of one and a half men.

Worse yet is I fear being a selfish lover, because I don't fantasize pleasing him the way I would ordinarily with a slimmer
man. I'm intimidated, daunted and generally unprepared for certain activities.

I don't know what to do. It's a turnoff. And worst of all, part
of the reason it's a turnoff is that I see myself with a head-turner
when the lights are on. I've always been with striking men—not
pretty boys, but men who had that quality; after all, it's that

quality which turns my head in the first place. And this man just doesn't light my fire in that way. I'm attracted to nearly everything about him but his size. So he doesn't light my fire, and doesn't feed my ego in the company of strangers. I hate myself even for admitting it; it's just so superficial.

Am I trying to convince myself that we have a future together? Is there any way I can get past my bias and enjoy this person for who he is in total?

Weighing in, in Washington

Dear Weighing in,

YOU HAVEN'T GOTTEN this far by pretending. You've gotten this far by being straightforward and honest, and I suggest you continue being straightforward and honest.

This is harder, of course, because we are freaked out about fat. It is one of our crazy things. It goes deep. It has its paradoxes and corollaries as well—we are freaked out about skinny, and we are freaked out about food, and the planet, and the body and money and exercise and power. We are a freaked-out culture. We are all freaked out.

The fat man knows this.

If you are a fat man in America you cannot help noticing that people are freaked out about fat. People will suggest exercise bikes. They will feed you lean portions. They will say to each other, "It's his fault, and it's disgusting; he must have no willpower; he must eat the wrong things; he must be repressing something; he must not respect himself." And what does the fat guy say? He says, Yes, thank you for that astute observation, I have indeed noticed that I am fat.

So I suggest what you do is go in your backyard and sit quietly and meditate on the fact that you are not turned on by this fat man. Meditate on the fact that you like him very much but he doesn't turn you on. Wait for something to come to you. Accept the answer that comes. If you come to the feeling that you have to end it, then end it. If you come to the feeling that you want to stay with him for a while more, then stay with him for a while more. If you come to both, then put each on an apothecary's scale, weigh them and choose the one that weighs a little more.

Don't try to reason it out and don't guilt-trip yourself. We don't know why we are the way we are. It's not our job to know. Just meditate on it and wait for an answer.

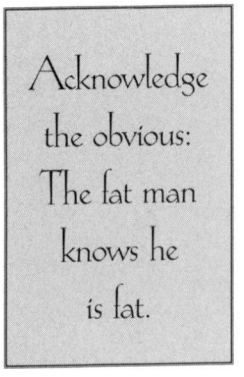

Acknowledge the obvious: The fat man knows he is fat.

Maybe you meditate on it and the answer that comes is that it's just not right for you. OK. Make a tearful goodbye. Or maybe you meditate on it and it continues to intrigue you and so you stay with him for a while. What's the harm in that? Maybe you learn something new. Maybe you have sex and it turns out to be good. Maybe it's just some learning you have to do—maybe you are not used to having sex in ways that are not automatic; maybe there would be some learning at first and then it would be automatic, just as it always was. What can it hurt to find out?

And by the way, why are you in such a hurry lately? Two or three dates is not all that much time. Human emotion goes slowly. Insight is a complex computation; it can take days on our little computers.

Besides, consider: The sex is great in the beginning lots of times. This you no doubt know. It doesn't always stay great. It might dwindle down. It might be great at first with some guy you don't like that much otherwise. It might dwindle down and then what have you got? A guy you don't like all that much anyway whom you don't like to fuck much either anymore.

Some things are painful and sad and wrong but nonetheless true.

We are the way we are for reasons unknown to us. You needn't feel guilty if it isn't working out. Quiet your mind and wait for the answer to come to you.

The sound of people
eating drives me insane

*I have a condition that makes the smacking
of lips almost unbearable to hear.*

Dear Cary,

SINCE I WAS about 8 years old I've been overly sensitive to
the sound of other people eating. I remember needing to eat my
cereal in the living room because I couldn't stand the sound of my
brother eating his. As I grew older this became somewhat (though
never completely) easier to deal with—school lunchrooms were
often loud enough for me not to notice the sound, and I stopped
eating at the dinner table with my family. In college I began to
wear headphones to the cafeteria, and now as an adult I tend to
eat with people only in loud bar/restaurants. Most people don't
understand the way this drives me crazy; it's beyond annoying or
bad manners. Sometimes I have to go to the bathroom to escape
it. I lock myself in a stall and cry; I rip up toilet paper to vent. I'd
like to hit and break things when I hear eating or mouth sounds.
I'd like to scream and swing a baseball bat. After prolonged
exposure I find myself shaking, my jaw clenched shut. I try not to
let people know how much this bothers me, as it tends to make
them self-conscious and uncomfortable around me.

But eating is such an essential part not just of our physiologi-
cal lives but our social lives—I find myself unable to escape this
sound. Mostly the problem comes from being at work, where I
have no control over the quiet environment, in which every smack

of lip and gum is painfully audible. I recently moved to a new city and took a job that I love in almost all aspects. I work with kind and interesting people and what I do is challenging and fun. But the noise. . . At my old job I sat at my desk with headphones and ate lunch by myself with no one bothering me. But here I can't use headphones; I must always be ready to answer the phones if necessary. Also, lunch is a ritual in my office, and the few times I've declined to join the noon lunch group, I've been bombarded with attention: "Why don't you want to eat with us? Are you antisocial? Why do you want to sit by yourself? Come join us, come join us … " The most difficult, though, may be that my direct supervisor is a gum chewer. Not just a gum chewer, but a gum smacker, a gum popper. She attacks her gum, aggressively chewing and popping and smacking and clicking and everything that makes my spine feel as though everyone in China just ran their fingernails across chalkboards while I sat in their midst. It's so loud I can hear her in her office while I'm in my cubicle. Not a small feat.

I've read about soft sound hyperacusis, and I know I'm not the only person who suffers from this. I'm not sure medically what the best approach is to deal with this. But my question isn't so much about the prognosis—I want to know about how to deal with things from a well-mannered yet assertive perspective. Can I ask my boss to not chew gum around me (chewing her cud, as my grandmother would say)? How might I negotiate with my supervisors to be able to wear my headphones while at my desk? Is there a way to eat lunch by myself without everyone making a big deal about it? I'm 30 years old and I don't see any way out of the everyday rituals built around eating. I just want a civilized way of avoiding them.

My iPod's on 10

Dear iPod Blaster,

HYPERACUSIS IS A genuine medical condition. So if you have an enlightened and understanding boss, it may be possible to negotiate changes in your work environment, especially if those changes are practical and inexpensive. Asking your boss to stop chewing gum around you may be pushing it, however. People can be pretty sensitive about stuff like that.

In general, I think you have to make it known to others that you have a medical condition that requires certain adjustments in the workplace. But be prepared for people to "not get it" at first. Be persistent. Get them used to the idea. People can be pretty dumb. You have to be patient with them.

If you have not yet visited the Hyperacusis Network site (http://www.hyperacusis.net/), I hope you will do so soon. It looks like an excellent source of support and information.

I have not yet read Carol Lee Brook's book "Tortured by Sound—Beyond Human Endurance," but this interview (http://www.healthyhearing.com/library/interview_content.asp?interview_id=125) with her indicates that she had excellent results with the habituation therapy developed by Dr. Pawel Jastreboff in the 1980s. It is also being used successfully (http://www.hyperacusis.org/wst_page9.html) by Marsha Johnson, founder of the Oregon Tinnitus and Hyperacusis Treatment Clinic (http://www.hyperacusis.org/wst_page2.html) in Portland, Ore. (While you asked me more about "how to deal with things from a well-mannered yet assertive perspective," I could not resist looking into the clinical situation.)

As far as how to deal with other people, I think your best bet is to educate them about the condition. Luckily, there is so much information available on the Web that people can easily educate themselves if they choose. If they don't, however, you will have to do the educating. For a layman, the simplest explanation, or the way I understand it, is that hyperacusis is a nerve disorder in which certain sounds are no longer filtered before they reach the brain; it's as if there's an amp in your head that's on 10 all the time. Maybe I don't get it exactly right, but I'm thinking about possibly imprecise but quick ways to explain it to someone

Know your own disease.

else. And also I think it will be important for you to make them understand that this is not some personal idiosyncrasy of yours, but a real medical condition.

Any device that allows you to interact normally with people would seem to be a good idea. If you could eat lunch with your work mates while wearing headphones, I would think that would be preferable to isolating yourself from them. It appears that while hyperacusis is not a psychological disorder, in their attempts to cope with it people often do develop psychological problems. So whatever will help you maintain good social relations and regular work habits would seem to be a good idea.

Other than that, I just really wish you the best of luck in finding and undergoing treatment. This condition can be extremely painful. The more people who know about it, the better it will be for all sufferers.

A grad student in China has taken possession of my soul

*I know it sounds crazy, but should
I leave my wife?*

Dear Cary,

I'M 30 YEARS old, married for almost five, no kids. I love my wife and would never want to do anything to hurt her. We just got back from a several-week trip to China. Ever since we got back about a week ago, I haven't been myself. I told my wife that I'm just depressed, having a hard time readjusting to everyday life after such an amazing experience. No doubt that is part of the problem, but it's not the real problem. The real problem is, of course, a girl.

We got to spend some time talking and socializing with a group of Chinese grad students, and one of them has me absolutely mesmerized. She's smart, charming, clever, creative and stunningly beautiful—and I must admit, that "Chinglish" of theirs is totally endearing. She's also married to a husband 10 years her senior, but that's pretty much irrelevant, isn't it? She's in a communist country on the other side of the world. We've exchanged a few e-mails since I got back, but it's all been totally innocuous.

I know that even entertaining a fantasy is a total waste of time, but I can't help it. This may sound weird, but if it was just sexual, I'd be able to pass it off as a "lust"-type thing that I'd never be able to act on, nor would I if I had the chance. But this is more. My fantasies aren't sexual. I fantasize about bringing her

31

back to America or, even better, moving to China and spending the rest of my life with her. I've never been this wrapped up in a woman after only knowing her for a day and a half.

She sent me a link to her blog, which is all in Chinese, but whatever. She had a few pictures of herself on there that just make my heart sing. They're just normal, everyday pictures, but that almost makes it worse. I also didn't see her husband in any of the pictures (I guess he could be the one taking the pictures, but I doubt that). I'm just at a total loss here. I assume that in a few weeks or months, I'll have forgotten her and everything will be back to normal. But is that a good thing?

There's another complicating factor here. My wife is physically handicapped. She depends on me more than the typical wife does, I think. She was handicapped before I met her, so it isn't as though I didn't know what I was getting into. I'm also not so arrogant as to believe that if we split up, she would never again find someone to accept her. But I do feel that leaving would basically make me the worst person in the history of the world, especially leaving for a fantasy with zero future.

I've written, edited, scrapped and rewritten a letter to my new foreign fantasy at least a dozen times in the last week. It's always just one click away from being sent, but I never do it. It wouldn't really be right to play the scenario out, find out what happens, and then decide what to do in my current relationship.

So, anyway, please just tell me to get a grip, that I'm just focusing my feelings of this whole amazing experience on one person, that it's totally insane for one married person to fall in love with another in 24 hours on the other side of the planet, and to scrap a marriage of five years because of a crush.

Crazy

Dear Crazy,

YOU ARE ASKING to be brought to your senses, to be awakened from this reverie, this exotic state of mind, this rich, intoxicating dream. To "get a grip" means to tighten it up, push it down, bite the bullet, shake it off, get hold of yourself.

There will be time for that. But not so fast. I suggest first that you celebrate it.

Celebrating it is tricky. It means admitting that the soul is morally and politically naive. That is why we feel such ambivalence about our anti-imperialism and our loyalty to country, why we feel such guilt: The soul is naive. It wants what it wants.

The self is like a state; it contains rebellious forces living in fear of annihilation. This woman seems to have awakened such a force.

Naturally, your inclination, as the person nominally in charge of your self, is to put down, shut off, choke, annihilate. That is what we do with rebellions. We put them down and get on with the business at hand.

But I suggest that you attempt a broader, kinder, more inclusive, classically liberal response instead. What is this insurrection asking for as it stands outside the gates of your marriage palace waving banners and shouting? It is demanding more space for beauty, for sensuality and grace and the erotic awakening of travel.

And also for the forbidden.

It seems to be asking that you expand your boundaries.

Now, the boundaries of marriage are somewhat fixed; you cannot invite this woman into your home; you cannot move to China to live with her. She is married and has a life. You are married and have a life. But it is not

> Honor the truth in the troubling obsession.

necessary to change your domestic arrangements. This is about something less threatening: It is about recognition.

If you merely "get a grip," in the sense of repression, a tightening down, the same demands will spring up again later.

But if you fully recognize this phenomenon for what it is, you may be able to integrate it into your life, culturally, spiritually, aesthetically, and thus become richer.

In other words: Understand what this is and honor it. That may require you to expand what you believe—you may have to accept that while not exactly a supernatural experience, this is a mythic occurrence of almost unbearable force. Such things happen from time to time, triggered by encounters with people and locales that seem to be endowed with unusual power and beauty. It may be that we project onto such people and locales our fervent wishes to encounter the divine, to escape the mundane. Or, for all we know, the earth may be dotted with mystical places populated by goddesses of unimaginable power and beauty.

The important thing, it seems to me, in secular psychological terms, is that you have had a powerful encounter that awakened hidden aspirations and desires. Find a way to integrate this into your life, rather than repressing it or taking it literally, allowing it to shatter you.

In other words, do "get a grip." Get a grip on this experience. Hold it. Contain it. Keep it. It's priceless and eternal.

Should I stick with my girlfriend through her cancer?

We've only been together 10 months,
but I love her.

Dear Cary,

I'VE BEEN READING your column for years, and appreciate all the honest advice you've given. I've thought of writing you before, but the problems seemed to resolve themselves.

Not this time.

I have a great girlfriend. I'm approaching 30 and she's about five years younger. She has had some rough knocks—lost a parent a few years ago, endured her parents' divorce before that. We've been dating for 10 months, which is my longest relationship (though not hers). We've talked about moving in together as a step toward marriage. I'm sure that's what I want to do—I have a hard time with roommates and am petrified of taking the leap of marriage (with all its social and economic implications) without dipping my toe in and seeing how compatible we are. (Currently we live in the same apartment building and spend a lot of time together, but that simply isn't the same.)

But that's not my concern. My girlfriend was recently diagnosed with carcinoid, a form of cancer. The good news is that so far she's relatively asymptomatic; it's a slow-growing cancer that many folks have lived long lives with, and she's getting advice on treatment from some of the best folks in the world. The bad news is that it has metastasized, so some of the common treatments may not be an option. We'll know in a month what the aforementioned best folks have to say about treatment.

I love this woman—she's intelligent, funny, enthusiastic, willing to try new things, gorgeous, laughs at the same things I laugh at, whimsical. I've "dealt" with the cancer issue by putting any decisions off until we know more. Such decisions include moving in together and her moving back to her family for treatment (and her possibly asking me to move from where we are now, close to my family).

Frankly, I'm scared of continuing this relationship, if she only has, say, five years to live. Do I really want to be a widower at 35? I want kids—can I handle being a single parent? (To say nothing of the emotional trauma.) Or even if she lives a normal life span, but with complications, can I handle taking care of my partner?

On the other hand, this is really good. I felt like I've grown more over the past 10 months than ever before. I don't know whether it will lead to marriage, but there are times when I hope so.

I really don't know what to do. Any advice?

Confused in Colorado

Dear Confused,

IF YOU DO indeed love this woman, this is no time to be making a calculated exit. I have a feeling that if at the age of 30 you have never had a relationship longer than 10 months, you have been exiting when the emotional costs of the relationship are too high. This may be your opportunity to find out what it means to stick with someone through hard times—to be somebody who guts it out for somebody else and doesn't ask to be excused when things get tough.

Are you ready for this, the great, defining challenge of your life? Are you ready to accept what life has put before you?

I hope you can answer yes. I hope you can put aside whatever cynicism you have acquired by living in an absurd world and recognize that however absurd this world is, it places before us occasional opportunities to respond with unambiguous moral clarity.

There are moments, if you are actually living life, when cynicism cannot approach or tarnish the grandeur of the real thing. This is your life.

Are you ready?

You might not be. You might not grasp what this means. But I think you do grasp what this means and you are ready and you want somebody to help you do the right thing. Why else would you have written to me? If you have been reading the column all this time then you already know what I think. I'm not going to suggest that you ditch this woman and look for something more convenient. I believe in heroic responses. People often say things happen for a reason. I don't necessarily believe that. But I believe we must live life as if things happen for a reason. We must create meaning. Otherwise we're just sick, pathetic, clueless bastards!

Stay with a loved one through illness.

What I mean is, we create meaning in our lives by responding with our highest selves. We try to do the right thing. To the degree we fail, we fail. But we don't just walk away from a drowning lover.

In this case the right thing is to stick with this woman through this life-threatening challenge.

What sticking with her means concretely is what you and she must decide together. If she has a supportive family near good medical care then it would seem to make sense for her to go be with her family.

What you and she decide to do I can't say. But I would suggest that you give her support yet also maintain some distance. That means staying near her but not yet living together. Even if you want to do this great, heroic thing, you should go slowly. You don't know what would happen if you moved in together and began trying to cope with this thing together. Living together might make things worse, not better. It might be too much for both of you. But I think you should consider moving to the same town where she will be, so that you can be her boyfriend and be there for her and see where it leads. The more support she has near her the better.

The criterion you should use is: Does your action constitute loving help and support for her, or does it constitute hungry, sentimental involvement in her tragedy? It is easy to confuse these things; we may feel a surge of energy at another's misfortune and use that energy to satisfy a need for drama. Or we may use it to be a quiet source of support.

How can you love her and be of support no matter what happens? That is your question. I would not do anything hastily. That has apparently been your habit: to get into and out of relationships hastily. This is the time to try doing something differently, deliberately, carefully, with the restrained passion of a great love.

My brother is lying
to his pregnant fiancée

He's been married three times,
but he wants to keep that a secret.

Dear Cary,

MY BROTHER IS a happy-go-lucky guy, always the life of the party. He's been married and divorced three times, and before his third marriage he neglected to disclose both previous marriages to his wife. He did admit to having been married before. Now that we've met his likely fourth wife, we're very happy for him and we want the best for both him and his fiancée. The problem is that he's told our family not to reveal all three prior marriages to his prospective wife. Instead, he wants to pretend there was only one prior marriage. To complicate matters, No. 4 is now expecting his baby.

What is the best solution to the problem? We want to welcome his fiancée into our family with open arms, but I would feel awful not being truthful to her. My current solution is to recommend strongly to my father that he persuade my brother to come clean. If my father is unsuccessful in persuading him, though, how can I handle their upcoming visit to our state (including a possible two-day visit at our house)?

Part of me wants to distance myself from the whole affair, but she's a wonderful woman, and I'm worried that our distance would be misinterpreted as dislike for her. Should my partner and I attend their wedding? Admittedly, it's become a bit less

momentous than most sibling weddings (taking into account all
the prior marriages, that is), but we want to be supportive of
both of them as they bring a new life into this world. I feel that
I'd be betraying my brother by telling his fiancée the truth, and I'd
betray my brother's fiancée by withholding it. Help!

Trying to Do the Right Thing in Texas

Dear Trying to Do the Right Thing,

MARRIAGE IS A public contract, and family members have
a clear stake in its successful fulfillment. Families have a stake
in the couple's staying together because children are involved;
because the child's father is your brother, you will bear some
responsibility toward this child, and will also probably feel some
love and protectiveness toward the child. You will want this child
to be well cared for because it will be a flesh and blood relative
of yours. So you have a stake in the longevity of the marriage. It's
not just a private matter between two private individuals.

The fact of his three previous marriages and, more important,
his attempt to conceal them, says plainly: This marriage probably
will not last.

His fiancée has a right to know that,
so she can make alternate arrangements for the care of her child.

If your father can persuade your
brother to level with his fiancée, that
would be great. If not, I think you
have to tell your brother that you can-
not stand by and let him lie to her. Warn him that if he wants to
come and stay at your place, he will have to tell his fiancée the
truth, or you will.

Your duty is clear. This woman has a right to know. Somebody
has to tell her.

If he decides to avoid you until the wedding day, you will be
in a tough spot.

> Tell what
> must be told.

If the wedding day comes and still no one has told her, then when the ceremony gets to that part where the official says, "If there be anyone here having knowledge why these two should not be joined in holy matrimony, speak now or forever hold your peace … "

That's your cue. You're on.

I really don't see any choice. Yes, it is melodramatic. But there is too much at stake. If the family stands by and does nothing, then you're all helping to defraud an unsuspecting mother-to-be.

My wife quit shaving her legs and it turns me off

She says she only shaves when she feels like it. What am I going to do?

Dear Cary,

MY WIFE AND I have been happily married for four years. However, she has practically stopped shaving her legs. She has never been that crazy about shaving her legs, but she did it anyway. She used to shave often, but after we were married she has gradually cut down on her shaving and has now stopped totally.

The issue has come up for discussion but she says that she only shaves when she wants to, and at the moment she does not want to. Obviously this is not going to break our marriage, but has started affecting my sexual desire as I am increasingly turned off by her legs now. I really do not know how to approach again. Please help!

Worried in South Carolina

Dear Worried,

WHAT IF YOU were to offer to shave her legs for her? Do you think she would let you? If she doesn't like doing it, maybe that's because it's a real bother for her. But if you offered to do it for her, it would be kind of interesting, no? It might lead to something. Plus if you are experienced in the art of shaving, you may be able to do a better job than she has been doing. Perhaps you have noticed some spots she tends to miss, and you could get at them more easily than she can.

Or if you don't want to do it yourself, you could think of ways to induce her to shave. If, for instance, there is something you can give her that she likes in return for her agreeing to shave her legs, you could make a deal. Since she says she only does it when she feels like it, make it worth her while. Or make some kind of event out of it, or a game. Say you could feed her bonbons while she shaves her legs, if she likes bonbons.

You could also offer to pay for her to have her legs waxed or do some research into how other women have approached the problem and how the practice of shaving began in the first place. This may give you a sense of how politically and emotionally charged it can be.

Since she says she only shaves when she wants to, and she doesn't want to right now, could she also be saying that she does not want to be attractive to you right now? It may be a way of trying to assert some power, or create some distance between you. Or maybe she is taking pleasure in a more abstract way in the fact that now that she is married she is free to shave or not shave her legs—that not shaving is an act of disobedience to some perceived social dogma, and defying it brings her some pleasure. Perhaps in that way she is experimenting with the limits of what she is required to do socially in her role as a woman and a wife.

Let your wife control her legs.

The bottom line is that she is free to shave or not shave her legs. There may be consequences, of course; you may not be attracted to her. But they're her legs, not yours. The thing you want to stay away from, and you probably sense this already, is the idea that her legs belong to you, or that you have the right to command her to shave her legs.

I can't afford to attend my friends' destination wedding

I'm in grad school and not exactly rich.
How do I tell them I can't make it to Hawaii?

Dear Cary,

I HAVE A dilemma that's stressing the hell out of me and I'm hoping you can help. Two good friends of mine are getting married this summer in Hawaii. I'm extremely happy for them and when they initially shared the news I said, "Of course I'll be there." However, as reality has set in, I've realized that it is completely insane and unrealistic of me to think that I can afford to go. I recently moved across the country and began graduate school at a private university, and with this, have taken on more debt and loans. I'm not currently working for pay, so I'm dependent on my loan money.

Now, these friends of mine are well off in the finance department and don't always understand my broke state of affairs.

I love my friends, but I cannot afford to accrue another $1,000 of debt for a four-day weekend, especially since I don't even know how I'll be affording life at that point. How do I make them and our other friends understand this? It's been keeping me awake at night.

Sleepless in Grad School

Dear Sleepless,

MONEY IS SUCH a powerful force in American life that I can understand why you find it difficult to tell these friends that you can't afford to attend their wedding. It is often difficult to speak honestly about money, even with close friends. Yet I very much hope you do tell them. I hope you tell them not only because it's the sensible thing to do, but because every time someone tells the truth about money in America it makes me happy.

It makes me happy because I know the power of money to shame us into distorting the truth and abandoning our values. We might become artists or musicians or study arcane and little-understood phenomena, we might live more simply, we might dedicate ourselves to what we love, we might take time off from work to improve our lives and our relationships, we might spend more time with our children, if it weren't for the fear of not having enough money, or appearing to not have enough money.

And we might indeed have enough actual money to do what we need to do if we were realistic and honest about what we need, and did not spend money to avoid being shamed or excluded or misunderstood or thought poorly of.

Rather than say, "I'm sorry, your destination wedding in Hawaii does not fit my budgetary plans for fiscal year 2006," we say, "I'm so happy for you, I'll be there!" We pretend to have money that we do not have. And then we create for ourselves a set of unreasonable expectations. We attend a wedding we cannot afford to attend and give gifts we cannot afford to buy. And then we pay later. We pay with our time. We pay with our dreams.

Not only that, but we regress politically and spiritually. As progressive people, we want to ask of every significant action we take, What will be the effect of this, not only practically but symbolically? What is the meaning of this destination wedding in Hawaii? Is it in keeping with my goals and values? Or is it an upper-middle-class fantasy that reveals a lack of commitment to progressive values? If I attend this wedding in Hawaii, does that mean that I endorse the idea of expensive destination weddings and the class-based fantasies they embody? What is my relationship with these people? Is it reciprocal? Would they respect my values in the same way? If I decided to, say, have a destination graduation party in the mountains of Peru, would they trek up the mountain and

live in huts and eat simple food with me for four days to honor my commitment to simplicity and solidarity with the poor?

I don't know. Maybe that's stretching it a little. Maybe that's being pretty hard on your friends. But your values count. Think about it in terms of who you are and what it means; find the courage to act according to your conscience and your pocketbook.

There is one more point worth making here, if I may detain you just a moment longer. I know you probably have studying to do, but this won't take long. You have a chance now, right now, with this decision, to set for yourself some good money habits.

This is important because bad money habits grow out of not really thinking it through and thus failing to understand money.

For instance, when I was young I saw money as a symbol rather than an actual thing. I do not think I was alone in this. That may be why later as hippies matured, they seemed to become obsessed with money, selfish, hedonistic, as if this thing they had disregarded for so long would now be the answer to all their problems.

And of course it wasn't. Money is neither your problem nor the solution to your problem. It's more like air: It's all around us and we just need to get enough of it to stay healthy.

So that's a rather long way of saying I hope you tell your friends that a trip to Hawaii doesn't fit with your budget right now. Don't be ashamed. You're doing the right thing. You can avoid getting in financial trouble right now and begin to set some good habits for yourself for the future.

Our host reimbursed us for a theft in his house

My father is furious that my boyfriend accepted money when we were guests in Africa.

Dear Cary,

I WAS RECENTLY traveling in Africa with my serious boyfriend of eight months and my family. While we were staying at the house of some well-off family friends, $1,000 was stolen out of my boyfriend's wallet, which was on the floor of the room we were staying in. Given the danger of carrying cash on the street, he purposely left it in the house assuming it would be safe. My parents' immediate reaction was that my boyfriend was responsible for his own belongings, even though it also seemed likely that our hosts' servants (three maids) could possibly be to blame, given that they were the only ones in the house and the house is quite secure (not a lot of foot traffic nearby).

My boyfriend is a freelance photographer and scrapes to get by so the loss was pretty serious and traumatic for him. A week after the theft, our host offered to repay the money (my parents were on safari during this time and so were not around for the negotiation). My boyfriend accepted the money. We were unclear as to whether our host was paying it out of his own pocket at first (he was somewhat mysterious about it) but ultimately we learned that yes, he had.

My boyfriend and I left the country, and when my parents returned and learned that my boyfriend had accepted the money, they were mortified. My father, for whom $1,000 is fairly disposable, repaid the money to his friend, feeling that his friend was not responsible and that his friend had already been generous enough to us.

Now my parents expect my boyfriend to repay the money to my dad. My boyfriend doesn't feel that he did anything wrong and does not want to (and at the moment cannot) pay it back. I stand by my boyfriend's decision to take the money, but I know that if he doesn't repay my father, or offer to down the line, my parents will judge him as impolite, undiplomatic and selfish (if they haven't already). Of course I want them to approve of him, as we may be together forever.

Should my boyfriend repay my father?

Money Troubled

Dear Money Troubled,

YES, YOUR BOYFRIEND should repay your father. He should also send his host a little gift of some sort, thanking him for his generosity and kindness.

If he doesn't have the money now, he should find a way to get it.

I don't think he should have taken the money from the host in the first place. I suppose it was his obligation to report the loss, as others in the household might also be vulnerable. And it was understandable that the host would offer to reimburse him. But when the host offered to repay it, he should have refused. Instead, on his own, he should have endeavored to make whatever communications were necessary to get the money he needed to complete the journey without being a burden on others.

What he's done makes everyone look bad—you, him and your father. I'm not surprised that your father is demanding he be paid back. It's not just the money—it's the way your boyfriend

> Repay the kindness of your host.

handled it. Your father is probably angry and has doubts about your boyfriend's maturity.

Why is this not just a trifling matter? Because it is not really about money. It is about having a high regard for others, out of which we circumspectly and assiduously avoid being a burden, particularly on our hosts. We make our presence in the world instead a light and welcome phenomenon, thusly hoping to deserve at least a little of our profound good fortune.

And we always try to learn from our mistakes in foreign lands.

I'm the academic's wife, jealous and insecure

I'm regarded as inferior by my husband's admirers. I'm afraid I'll lose him to a brilliant and beautiful student.

Dear Cary,

I RECENTLY MARRIED a man I love more than anything. We are on the whole very happy together, but lately I've become incredibly jealous and unhappy. The problem is twofold really. Five years ago I moved abroad to be with this man, quitting my job, leaving my friends and family to follow someone I was convinced would someday be my husband. However, throughout our relationship I've periodically felt that I've been the one to make sacrifices from which he has benefited completely and I have benefited by keeping him. Recently I've felt this acutely. He is a successful, gregarious, charming and highly intelligent academic and just got a very prestigious job at a top university. He has fulfilled his ultimate ambition.

I also wanted to be an academic but my work was not good enough to allow me to carry on to do a Ph.D., and although I was very successful academically at university in the U.S., I had a nightmarish time finishing my master's degree in Europe because I wasn't used to the independence of the European system. To some degree I resent my husband for choosing to come to Europe to finish his graduate work (we had planned to stay in the U.S. but he changed his mind at the last minute), because part of me thinks that I could have been much more successful in the American system where you are taught for the first two years. Perhaps I needed more training and would have succeeded.

Another strain is that his college life has now become our social milieu and we usually spend most of our social time with other academics. He is constantly praised for his intelligence and charm, and in all honesty it makes me jealous and makes me feel that I am unworthy of him. For example, one of his supervisors said, "I don't want to meet your wife because she won't be worthy of you." And another said to me, "With your husband's intelligence and charm he's going to be a magnet for the undergraduate women."

I am a publisher now, and I feel that the academics we spend time with admire my husband and engage with his work, and see me as just the wife. I feel resentful and very nostalgic for the time I spent with my non-academic girlfriends who thought I was great and loved talking and spending time with me. I am beginning to hate going out to these academic engagements. It is distancing me from my husband, who generally loves these kinds of things; spending time with academics is one of his greatest joys. He's beginning to see me as someone who prevents him from making friends and exploring university life.

Furthermore in this climate, I am also terrified that my husband will leave me for either one of his students or one of his colleagues who better shares his interests. My husband places the highest premium on intelligence, and I just feel that there are so many other women he knows who are more worthy of his attention. I write today because I just read a terrifying report : Men working as university lecturers are 80 percent more likely to divorce their wives because of their daily interaction with young, beautiful and intelligent women students. Have I made a horrendous mistake, moving to another country, sacrificing my friends and family, my ambitions and hoped-for career, all to be with this man who, statistically, will most likely leave me?

I want to emphasize how much I love this man. He is extraordinarily understanding and loving toward me. I feel that I will die if he leaves me, and every day I feel that he will. How can I stop introducing fear and suspicion into our relationship, potentially sabotaging it?

Please, please help. I can't talk to anyone about this.

The Academic's Wife

Dear Academic's Wife,

I THINK YOU have placed yourself too much in your husband's power. You need to begin now a long-term project of reestablishing yourself as an individual independent of him. In order to do this, you must identify what you love—the tangible activities, the situations, the images, the places, the sounds, the animals and plants.

Go back over your last 10 years and try to find those times when you were happy, the flashes of joy, the moments of contentment, the periods of life ranging from a week to several months or a year, where you felt most fulfilled and alive. What were you doing then? Were you doing academic work? Were you with your women friends? Were you helping someone else do something? Were you standing in the reflected light of your husband? Was it a family gathering? Were you delivering a paper or working alone in a room?

Concentrate on yourself, not your husband; concentrate on those things that have pleased you in the past, not those things that you think might please you, or that you think ought to please you if only you were the virtuous and splendid person you think you ought to be.

Write these things down. Make these things concrete. Allow yourself to long for these things. Remember the feelings. Let these feelings take residence. Encourage them; make room for them; cultivate them. Do this over a period of several weeks.

Meanwhile, as you go about your daily life, find some still point within yourself from which you radiate outward. When you go to a party with your husband, wish for nothing and ask for nothing. Be kind but secretly assess your feelings; ask yourself about these people—who they are, what they want of you, what you want of them; are there certain ones that you like and would like to talk to, and others whom you despise, or in whom you have no interest? Talk to the ones who interest you and ignore the rest. Watch what goes on around you. Take note of who is kind to you and who looks right through you on their way to someone swankier and richer and higher on the org chart.

Learn this. This is the way the world is. Come to know this. This is the system of which you have allowed yourself to become a victim. This is the vicious system of status and appearances, of high school for grown-ups, of ever-shifting cliques and roving packs. This is the system of social hunger that rules the planet. Keep looking at this until everything has parted like a curtain and you bump into the emptiness at the bottom, until the laughter and smiles have evaporated and the frisson of excitement has left you and only the faintest whiff of champagne and cigars still hangs in the air and finally there is nothing there, nothing. At the bottom is simply emptiness.

> Come out from under the shadow of the powerful man.

Keep holding yourself apart until the emptiness becomes like a giant room of silence. When you are comfortable in that giant room of silence tap yourself on the chest and ask what is left.

All that's left is you. What you've got then is all you have to go on, but it is enough. Walk out of the room and regard your husband in this cold new light. Does he love you really? Does he worship you? Would he leave all this for you if you asked him, or is he entranced by it all? Are you his companion on the journey or the vehicle he has chosen to ride? Are you the center of his life or just a decoration, the centerpiece for his table?

Nevermind what happens if you lose him. You seem to intuit that you are going to lose him anyway. What's worse is if you lose yourself. You have almost lost yourself already.

So start by regaining who you are, and move on from there.

Why am I obsessed with celebrity gossip?

Instead of writing poetry,
I'm checking out IMDB.

Dear Cary,

EVERY DAY I find myself logging on to a variety of Web sites to gobble up all forms of celebrity gossip. I spend hours on imdb figuring out which celebrities were born closest to my birthday (Billy Crudup, Robert Rodriguez) or discovering that both Debra Messing and Cate Blanchett named their sons Roman. After awards shows, I go to site after site to relive the dresses, the hairstyles, the snippets of gossip from the red carpet and the after parties.

It struck me that this was a problem again last night, when I read that Laura Dern and Ben Harper got married, then proceeded to Google them to death to find photos of them doing mundane things like walking with their baby down the street. They seem like cool people, but could I possibly care about the minutiae of their lives? And what about the hours I handed over to that endeavor?

I've always been fascinated with celebrities, but the fascination was for years limited to magazine browsing in line at the grocery store. Even then, I knew it was odd that I could tell you the names of Demi Moore's daughters (Rumer, Scout and Tallulah) without a pause. But lately, fueled by the whole-house wireless my news junkie partner installed, it seems I can't get enough.

I might not worry about this if I weren't worried about other elements of my life. My stunted creativity, for example. I'm a writer, but for years I haven't finished things that weren't on a specific work-related deadline. My own writing, though I sit down to it regularly, is shrinking. I've published a book of poems, been nominated for a Pushcart, taught creativity to both kids and adults. All this is past tense. I feel I'm getting less and less creative. It's harder to tap into the free-form spill that leads me into a poem, harder to wiggle into the voice that makes a story rise above the rote. I'm in one of those jobs that is too good to leave, too bad to stay. I drive to work fantasizing about quitting. I walk into my cubicle and I slump. On my days off and in the early morning, I work on my own pieces up to a point, and then I file them away. I read about why Renée Zellweger always wears Carolina Herrera.

Is this as simple as mere avoidance, distraction? Other things in my life are good. I'm in a happy partnership, have a relatively nourishing home life. I have good friends. The sun shines a lot where I live. My garden has fresh herbs.

I turn to you because you are so gifted at seeing beyond the obvious, at teasing out the nuanced reasons for the choices we make. I know that I can unplug the Internet, talk with my therapist, go cold turkey. I'm more interested in what lies beneath. Unlocking this seems the key to changing it. What is the metaphor here? What questions should I be asking? What might I be hungering for? I just read a story about a couple who searched for a year and a half for an apartment in Brooklyn with the right fireplace, and the moment they saw it, bought a studio with a mantel tiled with undulating dogwood carvings. They fell for a fireplace. There's something noble in that hunger. An update on Kirsten Dunst's hair extensions? Not so noble.

Can you help me see my way out of this, Cary? I've got

Too Many Stars in My Eyes

Dear Too Many Stars,

I SEE CELEBRITIES as gods and goddesses. A strong interest in their betrothals and betrayals, their binges and fasts, their tragedies, to me indicates an interest in the world of magical characters. It is at root a spiritual quest, closely allied with our thirst for literature. The reason we are so obsessed by celebrities today, I figure, is that there is nowhere else in our culture with such rich and readily accessible tales of such magical and entrancing variety.

Just, for instance, the lead item in the Fix (http://www.salon.com/ent/col/fix/2006/01/04/wed/) today, as I'm writing, is this: "Gwyneth Paltrow has enlisted a rabbi from the Kabbalah Center to exorcise the ghosts from the five-bedroom London townhouse she shares with Coldplay frontman Chris Martin and their 19-month-old daughter, Apple. 'Gwyneth believes that the dark energy that has dogged her lately is due to something dark and unexplained in her home,' a source told Daily Mail. 'Her pregnancy is not as peaceful as her last one and she has also been upset by a stalker.'"

Isn't that wild? (Note that she, as a vessel, holds our crazy beliefs so we don't have to.)

I would argue that gods and goddesses are only useful to us in our lives if they are not regarded consciously as gods and goddesses—only if they are regarded as real. I would suggest that we cannot possibly regard the gods and goddesses of another age and culture the way members of that culture themselves regarded their gods and goddesses. I figure that the ancient Greeks and Romans regarded their gods and goddesses much as we regard our film stars. The minute we become conscious of worship, the worship dies. It loses its magical power. We become self-conscious. So the obsession with celebrities is an act of primitive cultural innocence.

We have a pantheon of amazing figures; we are swimming in it; we are living in a magical world. It is natural for us to be transfixed by these characters because we are thirsty for magic. We are not satisfied with our earthly existence, nor should we be.

We are humans and humans hunger for the divine. Our religions have failed us, our philosophies have failed us, our government has failed us, and our writers have. . . well, nevermind. You get what I'm saying: Embrace celebrity worship! Do not be ashamed! It is a real hunger that you are feeding!

I would suggest that you build on your interest in celebrities in several ways. For one thing, try to understand your particular responses to particular celebrities in terms of your own interests and struggles. What do your likes and dislikes of various celebrities say about you as a person, your aspirations, your secret hopes, your values? Expand on this. Perhaps you could keep a journal or a scrapbook. Perhaps you could embark on something akin to fan fiction, using the gods and goddesses of our media world as characters in tales of your own creation. Or perhaps, using readily available video software, you could create movies of your own with digital images of stars found on the Internet. If you are a writer and feel your interest is taking you away from writing, I would suggest bringing your writing to bear on your interest.

Think deeply about celebrities.

As for me, I also have a private pantheon of characters about whom I feel deeply, but they are boring and embarrassing. For instance, my secret sorrow lately has been the disappearance of Aaron Brown (http://www.salon.com/mwt/broadsheet/2005/11/02/aaron_brown/index.html) from CNN. I find his being supplanted by the crass young "360" man quite disappointing; while I found him at first, as I said in an e-mail to a colleague back when Brown started, a little unctuous. But after a time I came to enjoy Brown's avuncular style. Primarily what I enjoyed was his judgment—the professional sifting and sorting of stories. This was an appreciation mostly of craft, of how someone works; but then I am a fairly work-centered person. I also liked the fact that Aaron Brown was not trying to make me feel anything (this is very telling about me). I resent the attempts of newspeople to make me feel. I do not want to be made to feel—especially by newspeople. I feel plenty already. I am not deficient in feeling. I am deficient in understanding. I grit my teeth every time Anderson Cooper comes on the screen. I resent him. I wish he would go away. I wish him a bad fate of some sort, I'm not sure what—perhaps that he would fall into the mud. If I were a child playing with little figures of newspeople, I think I would make Anderson Cooper fall in the mud and have to crawl around in it.

That probably says a lot about my primitive drives and fears, perhaps more than I would like to know.

What do I like on television? I like History Channel World War II stuff with bombs and fighter planes. I like stuff like "What if the moon disappeared?" Because at heart, I'm a little comic-book science boy, fascinated by strange tales of the earth! (This is a clue to my mythic life.) Frankly, all those celebrities remind me of the pain of being an outsider in high school. I feel more comfortable identifying with grim scientists.

So it's interesting for me to think about this in relation to my own life. And it's interesting to note, as I consider it, how strongly I feel about these things! Aaron Brown's departure was a genuine personal loss, about which I might have written an essay if I did not fear seeming foolish. Or, more precisely, if I did not fear parading my personal feelings without any kind of argument to back them up. It was just a personal thing.

Point being, it's interesting and instructive to ask ourselves what we like about celebrities. It tells us more about ourselves than perhaps we would like to know. So if I were you, rather than fighting your interest in celebrity lives, I would try to build on it, take it to a deeper level, make an art of it. Especially since you are a writer: Your subject is right in front of you. What is the meaning of Jennifer Aniston and Brad Pitt? What are her special powers? What does she represent? I do not know, but you probably do.

My secret is about to be revealed

I told my husband I was a virgin when we married but I wasn't. Now the guy I did it with is going to tell.

Dear Cary,

A SECRET FROM my youth is about to be exposed. When this happens, my life will implode. I can see the pain bearing down on me like a speeding train. I am stuck to the track and there is nothing I can do but wait for it to mow me down.

When my husband, "Mark," and I were dating, I had a brief affair with his roommate.

Mark and I got married 18 months after my indiscretion with Doug. We are happy. I cherish my husband more than anyone or anything in my life. There is nothing—no job, no person—that I would not give up for him. Mark is beautiful, smart, kind and caring. My marriage is the best thing I have ever had in my life. Now, it is about to be ripped away from me.

You see, I got a call from Doug two weeks ago. He informed me that he is planning a visit back to our town in a few months, and when he comes he is going to tell Mark about our affair. Why? Because he has become a born-again Christian and he believes that he will go to hell if he dies without confessing his sin.

Mark believes that I was a virgin on our wedding night. I wasn't, obviously. Even worse is the fact that Doug was actually the first man I had sex with. This will kill Mark because he was a virgin when we got married. It means a lot to him to think that we are the only people on earth who know each other in this most intimate of ways. He loves the fact that, as I have actively led him to believe, no other man knows what my body feels like. He cherishes the notion that I don't have sexual memories of any other man. And, before the feminists start sharpening their knives, let me just say that I love knowing the same thing about him. So, any member of the sisterhood who thinks that my husband is a Neanderthal can go fuck herself.

Nobody reading this can imagine my desperation. I have pleaded with Doug not to expose me as the fraud that I am. I have made every appeal that I can think of, to no avail. It is like beating my fists against a steel beam. Doug is absolutely convinced that keeping this secret will keep him from going to heaven. Against the threat of damnation, my words are worse than useless. I have caught myself hoping that Doug is struck down by lightning or a speeding bus before he is able to make his face-to-face revelation to the man we betrayed. I would pray for his death, but it seems ludicrous to ask God to kill somebody so that I can continue living a lie. I have to accept the fact that my husband is about to find out that I had sex with his best friend, even as I made him believe I was saving myself for him.

Allow your secrets to come out.

So, here I sit like a condemned prisoner awaiting my doom. I cannot bring myself even to contemplate what Mark is going to feel, say and do when he learns what I have done.

Should I start planning ways to rebuild my life after Mark divorces me? Would that be premature?

Sometimes I think I should just tell him myself. "Honey, I gave my virginity to Doug when you were out of the apartment one day 12 years ago. We fucked each other on the sly for several weeks, but you're the only man I have been with since. Don't be mad." But who am I kidding? I don't have the courage to do it.

Falling From the Sky, Watching the Ground Rush Toward Me

Dear Falling,

YOU SAY YOU don't have the courage. Perhaps courage is not what you need. Perhaps what you need is to face necessity.

Telling him isn't courageous, it's just necessary. It's a necessary response to circumstances—like leaping from a burning building. You just leap.

What exactly do you tell your husband, and how? You sit down somewhere quiet and private and tell him that you have been keeping a secret from him and it has come time to reveal it. You tell him that long ago you made a mistake and that in trying to lessen the consequences of that mistake you have only made them greater. You tell him that with the best of intentions—wanting to save him from hurt—you have hidden this from him, and now you are telling him so he doesn't hear it from someone else.

And then you tell him the secret that you have been keeping. You tell him in neutral descriptive words free of implied catastrophe and threat. You don't use words like "divorce." You don't say "fucked each other on the sly." You find words that convey the facts of the situation without exciting the passions. You tell him you did this and you know it was wrong. You ask for his forgiveness and tell him you will do whatever it takes to make it right.

And then after that conversation with your husband you call this person and tell him that it won't be necessary for him to visit bearing torture irons under robes of Christian virtue. You tell him that he can visit but he should not expect to be greeted like a liberator, that you can't say what your husband might do should he show up bearing news of your supposed dishonor.

In this way you reclaim some of the advantage of the aggressor. And make no mistake about it, whatever this person may claim, his mission is not one of mercy but of aggression.

I am no expert on Christianity's various sects and what they may require of their believers. But I do know firsthand the practical benefits and the important limitations of making personal amends to those one has harmed. On this point the 12 Steps of Alcoholics Anonymous are instructive. One is advised to make personal amends to those one has harmed "unless to do so would injure them or others." In other words, at least for those who sincerely want to improve their lives and the lives of those around them, the point is clear: One does not clean up one's past sins at the expense of others.

In my opinion one who disrupts the lives of others in the pursuit of private spiritual redemption has no right to do so, no responsibility to do so. He is more like a terrorist than a healer of wounds. Besides, isn't confession of sins something that happens between the sinner and a representative of the church?

Be that as it may, you can't stop him from coming. Nor, after you defuse the situation by telling your husband what it's all about, does it really matter whether he comes or not.

What matters now is how you change your thinking. You and your husband have apparently believed that if you never experienced the touch of other bodies that you would be protected from all the doubt and insecurity of adult love. It is a beautiful idea that you and he have shared, but it is not an unassailable fortress on which to build a marriage. In fact it is more like a torture machine. And now you have to take apart your torture machine—this machine you built in good conscience, thinking it would protect you.

It seemed like the sensible thing, I'm sure, to build this machine; it does other things too: One feels a tantalizing tingle when one passes close by it, almost a sexual thing (mingling damnation with ecstasy in its hellish mortar and pestle). This machine of torture promised purity, and purity seemed valuable above all things. But purity is just a story we tell ourselves, a retreat from our bodies and their predilection for betrayal.

So you dismantle the torture machine. And you replace it with an ethics that comes from planet Earth. You do what has to be done. You tell the truth.

After all that cleansing of superstition, if there is any room left for hazy speculation, it is only this: In the end, this man may turn out to be the unexpected angel of acrid necessity.

I can't stop accusing
my boyfriend of cheating

I know there's nothing going on,
but I'm afraid to trust him.

Dear Cary,

I AM ON the verge of destroying yet another relationship. I really want to prevent this because I really love this man and would hate to see the relationship go the route of the last one. The problem is, I cannot stop accusing him of cheating. I am always imagining scenarios of where and how he could be acting unfaithfully, even when he spends all of his time with me. When I say he spends all of his time with me, I am not exaggerating. He's with me any time he is not working, and as soon as he gets home, he calls and we talk until we go to sleep. Yet, I am obsessed with the idea that he could be seeing someone else or making a fool of me behind my back.

This started exactly a year and a half after we got together. I don't know that there is anything magical about this specific time, but in my last relationship, I started this nonsense at the exact same time. My last boyfriend also spent a lot of time with me, but I constantly nagged and accused him of cheating on me— so much so that eventually he (understandably) began distancing himself from me and eventually did begin to see other women.

The thing was, when I had actual proof that he was cheating, I was devastated. I don't think I have ever experienced more pain in my life. I guess all the time I was accusing him of it, I never believed it would actually happen. I don't want to lose my current boyfriend because of this, but his patience is starting to wear thin.

I have tried to sit quietly with myself to figure out what this fear is and where it comes from. But the fear is so big and so irrational that I can't even get outside of myself to examine what it could be or where it could come from. My father left my family when I was young, partly because my mother is a nagging, argumentative and selfish person, partly because he was on booze and drugs and just plain irresponsible. All the women in my family derive great pleasure from trashing men, and not one of them is married or has been able to hold onto a relationship. I am painfully aware of all the trauma I've inherited from my family, and I've been able to deal with all of it except this issue of trust.

I should also mention that I do not trust women either, but that manifests itself differently. Usually with women, I don't even bother getting close, but if I happen to, I usually push them away by imagining that they are out to hurt me somehow, either by talking about me behind my back or stealing my boyfriends.

I want to end this once and for all. Not only is it annoying, but it's also really painful to deal with. I hate causing my boyfriend pain by insulting his character, and I don't want to cause myself pain anymore with my fantasies of him cheating.

How can I resolve this? Is there anything I can do to overcome this fear and live happily and in peace in my relationships with others?

Sincerely,

Lost in an Emotion

Dear Lost in an Emotion,

I THINK YOU probably can learn to stop obsessing about your boyfriend cheating on you. I think you can learn to trust people. But even if I could read your mind, I could not tell you how to fix your problem once and for all, just in this letter. Trust is something you're going to have to learn by doing—like a sport or a dance step.

You may be able to keep your boyfriend from bolting, in the meantime, if you explain to him where your lack of trust comes from, and what you're doing to overcome it. Learning to trust would probably involve some sessions with a therapist or other knowledgeable person who could work with you regularly over a period of time. It would involve, I imagine, taking gradual steps toward trust, first in safe and unchallenging situations and then, over time, broadening your capacity for trust into more difficult areas of your life, such as trusting a lover.

While I don't want to appear to substitute my amateur textual analysis for the help of a professional therapist or counselor, I can't help noticing some clues in your prose. (These clues are a good thing—it means the answers may be close at hand.) When you say "the fear is so big and so irrational that I can't even get outside of myself to examine what it could be or where it could come from," I get the feeling that you could just as easily be talking about your father. Even if your father doesn't seem big to you now, fathers are certainly big to their children. And drugs and booze make fathers act irrational. Interestingly, as if to prove the point, your next sentence is this: "My father left my family when I was young, partly because my mother is a nagging, argumentative and selfish person, partly because he was on booze and drugs and just plain irresponsible."

> Learn to trust. Learn to dance.

So there is probably a strong connection between your father's behavior and your fear of trusting people. It's interesting, too, how you characterize the fear—that it's so big that you can't get outside yourself to examine it. I find that when emotions are so powerful that we cannot get outside ourselves to view them, it is often because they arose in childhood—a time when we have no secure boundaries, no clear sense of ourselves as different from others, a time when we cannot get outside ourselves.

Continuing with your letter, the next sentence is this: "All the women in my family derive great pleasure from trashing men, and not one of them is married or has been able to hold onto a relationship." If none of the women in your family has learned to trust men, then it's not surprising that you didn't learn that, either. There may have been a number of alcoholic, irrational men in your family. And the women in your family perhaps have acted, in some sense, quite rationally toward these men, for their own protection.

The fact is, contrary to what you learned in childhood and what the other women in your family have taught you, there are some men in the world who can be trusted. You are just going to have to learn how to do that.

The good news is that by sitting quietly and thinking about this, you apparently came up with some very useful insights, whether you realized it or not at the time. That is why I think you can overcome this distrust and save your relationship. It will just take some work with a therapist.

The reason I suggest seeing a therapist is because it sounds like the behaviors that are bothering you are pretty much out of your conscious control. If they were things you could manage, like, say, quitting smoking, that would be different. If you can't afford a therapist, then weekly attendance at a self-help group might help, as might other resources aimed at helping individuals overcome crippling habits and gain insight into their unconscious behaviors.

My husband is a high=achieving alcoholic, seven years sober

Should we finally tell the kids?

Dear Cary,

WHEN OUR TWO boys were small children, my husband was a very high-achieving alcoholic. He never lost his job, he never verbally or physically abused either the kids or me, he remained a good father, and he never alienated his friends or family. Indeed, to this day, no one other than me (and his treatment group participants and counselors) know about his alcohol abuse. He did, however, almost die from alcohol. He attempted to stop drinking without medical intervention and suffered seizures and other life-threatening complications. As a result of this event, he got into a treatment program that worked for him (at least to date). After several years of drinking at least a fifth every day, he has not had a drink in about seven years. At his insistence, we have never told our kids or families about his alcoholism.

The problem is that our boys are no longer young kids—one is in high school and one in middle school. From our counseling and my experiences with him, I am completely convinced that the brains of some people are hard-wired to abuse alcohol and/or drugs and some are not. I know that I can drink one glass of wine at dinner (I haven't in seven years) and have no desire for a second, while he simply cannot start drinking without continuing to drink. Consequently, I believe that it is very important for our teenage boys to understand that given their genetic makeup, they need to be particularly sensitive to the impact of alcohol on them. I also want them to understand that we, as parents, do have experience with alcoholism, and that if they ever find themselves with an alcohol issue, we will be able to understand and help them. Since we, as parents, now never drink and seldom put ourselves in social situations where alcohol is present, I worry that our children will perceive that we would never be able to understand or help them with alcohol issues (even though I talk to them about such issues regularly).

In short, I want my husband to talk with them about his alcoholism in an age-appropriate way. He, however, is too ashamed to engage in such a discussion and does not want me to tell them (which I completely understand). I'm wondering if I should push the issue (our older boy just turned 16), or just let it drop as I have in the past.

Just Curious

Dear Just Curious,

YOU ASK A difficult question. I personally have pretty clear feelings about what to do.

I would tell the older boy. Then I would tell the younger boy as well, so that the older boy is not burdened with knowledge that he must either tell, imperfectly, or keep secret.

But I'm just one person—a person, moreover, with my own history of alcoholism that I'm quite candid about. I respect your husband's desire to keep this matter private. That's his choice.

I don't believe there is a direct link between what you choose to tell your children and whether they develop alcoholism. You may tell them or not tell them. They may or may not develop problems with alcohol. The two are not causally related. As I understand the current science, there are indicators and apparent predispositions toward alcoholism, and there are traits associated with it, but there is no one certain cause or one certain measure of prevention.

If you tell them, they will probably experiment anyway. They might react abnormally to the first drink, or they might not. Knowing the history might act as a deterrent. Or it might not. Knowing that their dad beat it might embolden them. You can't tell with kids.

It's natural to want to talk about it. And it's true that you have valuable, firsthand experience to impart. But as a former young person with an alcohol problem I can testify that young people with alcohol problems tend to be unreceptive to parental advice. That's part of the syndrome.

All this leads us into contradiction and uncertainty. So for me, the question of what to tell the children is more a question about truth telling and the keeping of secrets in a family than it is about alcoholism prevention. It's about what you believe you can control, about what is sacred, what is shameful, what is safe and what is toxic.

> Tell the kids what they need to know.

If my math is correct, the children were around the ages of 9 and 6 when your husband stopped drinking, meaning they undoubtedly witnessed him drunk, with that glassy stare, the slurred speech, the smell. So, apart from whether it's going to prevent them from becoming little alcoholics or not, the information might have the effect of bringing a little sense to their world: Aha, now I understand this memory of my father falling asleep at the table, or being too "tired" to go upstairs.

If you love the truth and you believe that the truth can be life's most powerful ally against insanity, depression, self-hatred and the like, then you may feel a strong urge to air the truth. On the other hand, perhaps you also know the powerful effect of a shameful fact revealed. Perhaps you know that sometimes children need to believe their parents are infallible, and you marvel at how certain truths, once revealed, never go back in the bottle: How could he have been a drunk? What if he should slip? What else don't we know? Was he unfaithful to Mom? Are we sure we're his kids?

I wonder how your husband's attitude toward his alcoholism plays into this. Does he feel that his alcoholism is his fault? If so, perhaps he is still tormented by it in a way that he needn't be. In fact, you might consider the possibility that it is necessary to be free from it psychologically and morally in order to be free from it medically. That is, shame, guilt and the keeping of secrets are part of the syndrome of addiction. You can easily see how this works: One stops the substance but retains the habits of mind. The habits of mind lead eventually back to the substance. So you have to change the habits of mind. One way to do that is to tell the truth.

But perhaps your husband is not burdened with shame at all. Perhaps he is simply making a very grown-up attempt at harm reduction. As I said, it's a tough call. I know what I would do. But it's a decision you and he must make.

Just to be clear: Inasmuch as it involves the well-being of the children, I think it's a decision you as parents need to make together. But inasmuch as it involves your husband's personal struggle with alcoholism, I think it is his decision alone how much to reveal. I'm not sure how to reconcile those two domains. But that is marriage.

My nephew was murdered in a drug deal. Do my young kids have to know?

We told the children a white lie, but on the holiday visit the adults are sure to talk.

Dear Cary,

MY HUSBAND'S NEPHEW was murdered last summer. It was a particularly horrible death, with multiple arrests, and charges of conspiracy and kidnapping and many others on top of the murder. The trial has started, and it is becoming clear that my husband's nephew was clearly in over his head in the drug scene. He was a sweet young kid, and it breaks my heart that this could have happened.

My question is actually about my kids. I have two children, ages 4 and 8. We told them that their cousin had died, and that it was a terrible accident. At the time, I did not think they needed any more details, as the actual details of the murder were causing me sleepless nights. They did not know their cousin, although they know his parents fairly well.

We are going to visit my husband's family for Christmas, and I don't think I am going to be able to stop my in-laws from talking. They are understandably completely overwhelmed by what's happened, and I suspect that their need to talk will supersede any thought of protecting the kids. Can you suggest how I can tell the kids enough detail about what happened without terrifying them? The trial will probably still be going on when we get there, so I need to explain about that as well. I also would like them to understand that their cousin was a basically decent kid who made some really bad choices about drugs, so that maybe it will make them think twice when they get to their adolescence. Any help you could give would be appreciated.

Shocked and Saddened

Dear Shocked,

THE FIRST THING I would do is have a good conversation with your in-laws. Make clear that you feel for their loss, that you appreciate the difficulty of what they have suffered and that you know they are going through a hard, sad time. Show a willingness to talk about the matter and, most important, to listen. Do not do this simply as a prelude to making a request. Do it wholeheartedly. Discuss it as long as your in-law wants to discuss it. But before you conclude your conversation explain that while you yourself are available any time to talk, you would like to shield your children from overhearing any discussion of these tragic events.

> Don't tell the kids what they don't need to know.

Many parents will intuitively understand your concern. But if it is met with resistance, simply explain that your kids love their uncle and aunt very much and it would devastate them to think that such terrible things could happen to a child of theirs. Then, without being too doctrinaire or starchy about it, let your in-laws know that if the topic comes up, say, at the dinner table where children are present, you are going to ask that it not be discussed in front of the children, and that if it is discussed, you are going to remove the children from the room. Tell them this in advance as a courtesy, so that if you should quietly get up and take the children, they will understand why.

You cannot completely control what your children hear. Sometimes children eavesdrop on adults. Sometimes their peers tell them things. Simply do the best you can. Then, after you are back home, try to figure out if your children are disturbed by anything they heard. Children process information in ways that sometimes don't make sense to us. In order to acquire psychic protection against annihilating truths or fears, they will sometimes distort the literal truth. They will also generalize in ways that are far more sweeping than the constraints of reality would dictate. For instance, after hearing some version of these events, a child might believe that friends sometimes kill friends. This obviously could interfere with the willingness to make friends. Or a child might decide that his cousin had made friends with very bad people, and that what happened could never happen to him. It's hard to know how an individual child will interpret what he or she hears.

So just give some thought to what they might possibly believe. Keep in mind that they will not necessarily be able to tell you in words what they believe actually happened; what they're left with may be a set of disturbing images and fears that emerge as symbols in nightmares or in imaginative play.

If your kids have any questions about what happened to their cousin, of course try to answer in a way they can understand. Personally, I think it may be a little early to use this tragedy as a teaching example—especially for the 4-year-old. Later, when they are adolescents, perhaps they could comprehend how involving oneself in criminal activities can lead to a violent death. For now, they just need to be reassured that they are safe with you in your house, and that no matter what might have happened to their cousin, it won't happen to them.

My awful sister-in-law just got pregnant and I didn't

I know life isn't fair, but save me from being consumed by resentment.

Dear Cary,

I CAN'T STAND my sister-in-law. Bad politics, doesn't listen, white bread, military, ignorant yet educated, boring boring boring.

Me no like.

And now, it looks like she's pregnant. I'm not. Very not. My husband and I have been trying for a year and a half, and next month I'll be having my first (and, I pray, only) diagnostic procedure to see why it's not working. My husband and I are really happy together; the blessing of our not getting pregnant has been more time to make a solid union. I truly believe that if we had had a baby a few years ago, we wouldn't have made it. My sister-in-law and her husband have been trying for, oh, about 20 minutes, and they are a nasty couple. They have in the not-too-distant past fought so bitterly in front of me and my husband that they left our company saying they were about to get divorced. So how come she gets to have it so easy?

I think the reason this hit me so hard is that I've been so fucking understanding about everyone else in the world who gets pregnant who either didn't mean to or didn't have to try very hard. I work in an emergency room, and we constantly see people who have too many kids, clearly don't want the kids they have, don't know how to take care of the kids they have, etc. A frequent lament among my co-workers is that "it isn't fair!" that shitty parents keep on getting more children to shittily parent while the "deserving, desiring" infertile are kept wanting. I always counter this with statements about how life isn't fair, and what happens to other people doesn't have anything to do with what happens to me, and all sorts of other evolved, progressive stuff.

Except in this case, where it does seem bitterly unfair.

Help me to regain my equilibrium.

Green Eyes

Dear Green Eyes,

IF ALL I have to do today is help you regain your equilibrium, that does not sound like such a terribly hard thing to do. After all, you have stated the essential truths in the matter. It's not as if we have to start from scratch. It's more as if you were paddling your canoe just fine for quite some time, and then took a spill, and just need a hand getting back in the boat.

You know, I think we all go through periods where, evolved as we may be in our habits of speech and action, in our hearts we are more or less like the savage children we used to be. We may know certain things, but it doesn't change the way we feel. Even so, we can still paddle along for a time, feeling enraged and mad with jealousy but still acting as we feel we ought to, doing what's required of us, moving the boat forward, until something happens—we get tired of paddling, or bored or restless, and we give in to an impulsive remark or gesture, and there we go into the water!

I, for one, go through this all the time.

The most powerful antidote I know for jealousy of another's good fortune is something that may have a long history but which I first came across as practiced by alcoholics trying to remove resentment from their lives. I think I've talked about this before: You pray for the person you resent to get everything they want.

Isn't that a strange idea? Yet there is some kind of twisted brilliance to it, too, isn't there? Not that I'm really sure how to explain its twisted brilliance, but it's in there.

Now, the whole notion of prayer may be a little foreign to you—I don't know, really, whether it is or not, but it may be. And the question of what entity to direct the prayer toward may also arise. But from the standpoint of effectiveness, those questions are relatively unimportant. The important thing is that you do it and take note of the results. You might mutter something like this under your breath: "[NAME OF HIGHER POWER/GREAT SPIRIT GOES HERE], I sincerely pray that [NAME OF WRETCHED UNDESERVING RELATIVE GOES HERE] gets everything she wants in life and more, and that she becomes happy and satisfied."

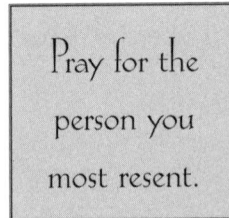

Pray for the person you most resent.

A little silly, perhaps. But I am a fairly practical person. If something works to relieve pain, I am willing to overlook a great deal of silliness.

If it doesn't work, well, OK, you may have to try something else. The basic idea is to direct your attention away from your own lamentable insufficiency and need, and toward the needs and wants of others, and to try to celebrate their success.

If the prayer business does no good, perhaps you can find other ways to celebrate the good fortune of others, in order to keep your mind off your own sense of inadequacy and want. I'm sure your work in the emergency room affords you plenty of opportunities to concentrate on the well-being of others. You already spend plenty of time being a saint.

I understand that sometimes you just want what you want. I also understand that some people can just plain get your goat, and it can be hard to wish them well. Nonetheless, although this might be a silly idea, it's worked for some people. For my money, it's one way to get back in the boat.

My best friend has let me down for the last time

She always said she'd be there for me,
but when my son got sick, she wasn't.

Dear Cary,

MY GIRLFRIEND AND I grew up together and have always been like sisters. She has always been a needy person: Nearly every day of my life I've listened to her talk endlessly about her complicated relationships; I've held her hand as she freaked her way through countless crises and meltdowns, and done a thousand favors for her. Through all those years of offering hugs and help and sympathy and of taking her side, I never asked much from her. Frankly, I didn't need it. She always said that I was her best friend and she loved me, and if I ever did need her, she'd be there for me. And I believed her.

Then, earlier this year, I almost lost my beautiful 10-year-old son to a severe case of meningitis. The illness damaged his limbs, his kidneys and his hearing, leaving him with permanent physical disabilities. My husband and I needed all the support we could get to help our child through this heartbreaking experience. Lots of people came through for us, but my "best friend" was AWOL. I got the feeling she was beginning to distance herself. We had a bunch of lame phone conversations over the next weeks, during which she said that she knew I needed to give all my attention to my family, so she was going to give me my space. When I said I needed her help, she said that she was going through a difficult time herself and was sorry that she couldn't be there for me.

Months later, it's as if we were strangers. Occasionally she'll call and leave brief messages like, "I'm thinking about you!" and "I miss you!" Recently, we invited some close friends and family over to celebrate our son's birthday. He's still healing from his illness, but we are so proud of how far he has come. I think everyone else got how special the day was for us. That morning, my friend called and bailed, with this story: She and her husband had argued the night before and she was "too depressed for a party." She wants to see us, she says, when things in her crazy, crazy life settle down.

That was the last straw. Something in me snapped. I get it now: She is an appallingly selfish bitch. She only "loved" me when I was available for her to use, and then she let me down. I hate her so much now that I am afraid the next time I see her, I might hurt her. I am so, so angry. Our families are close and we have friends in common, so I will have to see her during the coming holidays. I fantasize about slapping her in front of everyone. I have dreams in which I beat her and draw her blood. How can I let go of this terrible anger and move on?

Reformed Sucker

Dear Reformed Sucker,

YOU'RE NOT A sucker. You just took her at her word and thought she would come through but she didn't and instead she broke your heart. You don't have to be a sucker for that to happen.

If there were a short answer to your question it would be that you can let go of this terrible anger by moving through it to what comes next, a shaking of the head and a bitter shrug, a sad perplexity, the uncomprehending Why? of the unaccountably injured, or perhaps what we call acceptance. But that would only be part of it.

People say there are definite stages to it, but I don't know. They say there are five stages of grief or whatever. They say it as if everybody knows. I don't know. I never memorized that. I think you make up your own stages. Whatever stage you need to be in, however your house is arranged, whatever you've got room for, that's where you go when you're done with the anger. The only thing certain is that you move from anger into something that is not anger. Anger is heat and it always cools. Anger always cools just like the evening always comes.

So why should I tell you something pompous and all-knowing like you will move from this stage to that stage? And why should I speculate about what calamities she has undergone, calamities that though tiny loomed so large in her life that she had this appalling failure of heart?

It might be a sign that you're gaining some distance if you find yourself one day, maybe a year or two from now or maybe 10 years from now, wondering in a not particularly emotional way just what little torments were consuming her that made her so useless to others. Did she have a pile of traumas to inventory? Was her husband burning her with cigarettes? But it would be a long time from now that you would be thinking about that. For now there is simply your anger at the bitter loss of your friend.

> Let go of the friend who always fails you.

Aw, shit. People fail you, they do, they let you down when you need them, they get suddenly dense when you need them to be smart, they fold when you need them to open up, they close right before you get there and sleep through your honking horn in the snow. "I know she's in there, where else could she be? Why doesn't she come to the door?" People fail you, they do, they let you down when you need them. They don't say they're sorry because they don't even know. That's how dense they are. (And maybe wounded, too, in ways we can't see, but we're not in a mood for sympathy, are we?)

I say this speaking to you as a friend who himself has let people down from time to time but who will goddamn it be there in a pinch when it is really necessary, always always always, even if I am going through something. I will be there.

But that is so easy to say! "I will be there." That's what she said, isn't it? But she never had a clue how to do it! Yes, she was always promising to come through one day and then the day comes and you tell her in plain English, "This is your day! Your payment is due! It's time for you to be there for your friend!" and she can't hear it.

And then, when for one nanosecond it did indeed dawn on her that you really did need help she offered you ... space! Who in her right mind who knows anything about helping thinks that giving you space is helping? Giving you space is just being absent.

Are you planning to strangle her, really? Have you got a rope? You're not, are you? But you're afraid of how much you want to hurt her. So what are you going to do when you walk into the warm cocktail music evening and she comes tripping down the carpet loaded with a hug? It's going to make you angry, isn't it, when she aims that hug at you and starts to pull the trigger?

So maybe you'd better meet with her before any of these random occasions occurs. Maybe you'd better track her down and confront her so you get to say your piece the right way, in your own time. I know she should come to you and help you, for God's sake, but you're the one who has to do it. You're always the one who has to do it. I know that. This time, however, you are not tracking her down merely so she can fail you all over again. You are tracking her down so you can tell her once and for all what you need to tell her.

Tell her and do not apologize and do not forgive her and do not think about the future in which all is forgiven. It may be that all is forgiven in the future. All is not forgiven right now. Right now you just have to tell her.

Can I have the stroller I want? Can I? Can I?

Dare I buy the gleaming baby carriage that dazzles the eye of all who behold it?

Dear Cary,

I'M ALMOST TOO embarrassed to ask this question since it's so insignificant compared to what else is going on in my life, but I can't get to the bottom of my dilemma alone.

I gave birth to a beautiful baby girl almost three weeks ago and my husband and I, plus our families, are just overjoyed and happy. This is going to be one well-loved baby! Her grandmother keeps joking that she'll never learn to walk because there are so many relatives eager to hold her all the time.

My dilemma is that I can't decide whether to give in to peer pressure and purchase an outrageously expensive baby stroller, or sock the money away in the baby's college fund and swallow my stroller envy.

We live in New York City, which is a pedestrian city, so every time I walk down the street I see babies being pushed in a particular brand of distinctive stroller. I won't even mention the name because that company doesn't need publicity from me! I think the stroller is stylish, aesthetically gorgeous, and I've been told by friends who own them that they are really excellent if you are going to be taking lots of long walks—which of course I would in this city.

Yesterday I went to the pediatrician's office, which is located in a very trendy neighborhood, and every single child that came

81

through the door was in one of these strollers. The waiting room was like the stroller company's showroom! Seeing how trendy they are turned me off to them somewhat, but at the same time, I felt uncool and left out. It was like high school all over again, when I was the new girl from more modest means entering a posh public high school—I relived the feeling of my clothes and hairstyle just not measuring up (and later, not even having a car when so many classmates had daddy's gift BMWs). Meanwhile, these particular strollers, with their accessories, cost upward of $900 while a top-rated stroller in Consumer Reports cost about $250. Yes, we can afford the expensive stroller, but wouldn't the money be better spent on something else?

Silly as it is, I am really stuck! Help!

A Jones Wannabe

Dear Jones Wannabe,

OH, PLEASE BUY the stroller, please buy the stroller, please please please please please buy the stroller! Buy the stroller because you want the stroller. Buy the stroller because you deserve the stroller. Buy the stroller because all those other people have the stroller and why shouldn't you? Why do you have to be the one who can't have the stroller you want? Why does it always have to be you who has last year's stroller that's not nearly as shiny and nice?

Buy the baby carriage you want.

Buy the stroller, please? Buy the stroller because your baby doesn't want to be strolled about the park in a stroller that you don't love. Your baby doesn't want you to have to make excuses. Your baby doesn't want you to have to say that your stroller is perfectly OK but it's not the stroller you really wanted.

Not everything you want has to make sense or be admirable. Some things we want we maybe aren't supposed to want but we want them anyway. What's the harm? If acquiring them won't cause us to go broke or become divorced, or addicted, or in jail, or humiliated, why shouldn't we have them? Give yourself a break. Buy the stroller.

Don't spend the money on anything else! But if you must do something charitable, for the sake of your conscience, then do both: Buy the stroller and contribute some money as well to a charity, as though making an offering to the gods.

Don't let it go to your head is all. Don't get so intoxicated with the new stroller that you start thinking you're better than all those other mothers in that other part of town with those rinky-dink, boring, dull little strollers, and don't get so high on yourself that you go out carousing to celebrate and get drunk and get rolled and lose the stroller. Don't wake up with a hangover, mad with self-reproach, and end up in an insane asylum like the poor man in "The Overcoat"!

No, just buy the stroller and walk through the park with your baby, proud and happy.

Help! Here comes my 300=pound stepdaughter!

How does one maintain "detachment with love" with a food addict?

Dear Cary,

I AM IN Al-Anon because there were alcoholics in my life, and it has of course affected me. But more and more, I hear myself talking in group about my husband's daughter, who will be moving soon with her husband and child to the city where we live.

My stepdaughter is a food addict and weighs nearly 300 pounds. At times, she has tried to control her weight with a white-knuckled "This is only temporary" diet, and then gone immediately back to her old eating habits. She doesn't exercise regularly, she is a gourmet cook, and all she talks about is food. And can she talk! I don't know if constant talking is a side effect of her oral fixation, but she can yammer on for hours and not let anyone else get a word in edgewise.

My husband says that when she talks and talks about food, he just ignores her. That's true. So does her husband. Guess who is the only one left to listen and make appropriate noises? For hours on end. I feel as if I am taking on the brunt of her need to talk and talk about food. Cary, it's like talking to an addict about cocaine. I actually feel sleazy discussing recipes! She becomes angry if I try to change the subject.

Usually this is only a problem when we visit each other, but they are moving to our city permanently when her husband gets out of the service. I am afraid that I will be the only one spending quality time with her when she gets here, and I don't know if I am ready to take on what that entails. No blood relative talks to her about her weight problem; they are all in denial. It's almost literally the elephant in the living room.

Not being her mother, I am hardly going to say, "Uh, Dearheart, lose some weight, will ya?" I think she would be offended; I love this woman and don't want to lose the relationship we have built over the years (I am 10 years older than she). She is a very nice person. But she tells my husband that she is depressed because she doesn't think she will live much longer—her mother was six years older than my stepdaughter is now when she died of ovarian cancer. Her mother also was obese.

In short, she has so many problems, health-wise and psyche-wise, and I can't let them become my problems when she is living nearby. But no one else is willing to help her—they all just complain to me about her, especially my husband, who is distraught but refuses to talk to his daughter about her weight and her depression. Trying to maintain my Al-Anon "detachment with love" in this situation is so difficult. How do I be supportive without being the lightning rod for this adult stepchild and all of her problems?

Stepmom

Dear Stepmom,

ALTHOUGH THE SITUATION seems overwhelming and frightening now, please remember that you have everything you need right at your fingertips. You know how to deal with an addict in the family. Imagine how it would be if you had never been to an Al-Anon meeting! But you have already learned how to defend against the addict's many lures and schemes, threats and seductions, the plotless narratives of self that twist and turn down endless labyrinths of pathos and victimhood, the seemingly adult talk that is actually more like baby talk, the expert button-pushing: You know what to do about all that.

You will have to use your skills not just with her, but with her husband and your own husband, when they complain to you about her. You are going to have to tell them that if they have something to say to her, they need to say it to her. You must refuse to be the conduit, the receptacle. You must use the assertiveness you learn in Al-Anon. And when you feel overwhelmed or confused, you will have the group to go to, where people who are going through just what you are going through can lend you moral support.

So when the time comes, I feel confident that you will have what it takes to do the right thing. Your main problem is that right now the situation exists in the future rather than in the past or the present. So you can't really deal with it at all yet. And so, in this moment, you are filled with dread. Just know that when the times comes, you will have everything you need to get through this.

> Do what
> keeps you
> sane.

In fact, you may come to feel that you have been, in a sense, called to deal with this! Oh, sheesh, why you? Why can't somebody else in the family step up to the plate this time? Why must you, the law-abiding, reasonable one, always deal with the wreckage and chaos that the addicts around you create? (I'll bet your friends in Al-Anon have a great time with that one.)

You've heard addicts, I suppose, say that everything happens for a reason. That's a comforting thing to believe, I suppose, but I don't know if I always believe it. Half the time, it seems to me that we just make up a reason so we can get through the day. I don't know that the karmic balance sheet always adds up correctly in our lifetimes. I don't know why some of us turn out to be this and some turn out to be that. Some people just have all the luck, I guess.

But that is why you learn to set your boundaries and enforce them—because the burdens are distributed unfairly. Because sometimes you just have to say no and shut the door.

Here is one thing you can do, on your own, that may be of help to her but avoids the pitfalls of trying to persuade her to seek help: Go by yourself to some meetings of Overeaters Anonymous, Food Addicts Anonymous, Food Addicts in Recovery Anonymous or one of the other recovery programs for overeaters. Spend some time with those folks. This will reassure you that there is indeed hope for people such as your stepdaughter. Whether you try to influence her in that direction is up to you. Such behavior might weaken your detachment and awaken uncomfortable codependent impulses. But at least, as you sit across from her in the kitchen, listening to her prattle on and looking at your watch, you will know in your heart that when it's time for her to seek help, there is help available.

Most of all, as always, continue to do what you have to do to keep yourself sane!

What is a "normal" marriage?

*As a feminist and a child of an alcoholic,
I'm not sure how this is supposed to work.*

Dear Cary,

I GREW UP in a pretty dysfunctional family—alcoholic, abusive father and passive, codependent mother—on a farm in a very small town in the Midwest. While growing up, I knew that my family was not "normal" or healthy and I felt determined to escape and break the patterns I was raised in and develop my own life.

My initial plan was to avoid the traditional family structure altogether. I went to college (the only person in my family to do so) and moved to a bigger, much more progressive city. When I dated, I mostly dated men who were clearly not marriage material. I never planned on getting married and having children. I focused on intellectual pursuits, traveled, and developed wonderful friendships. I focused on my career and became passionately involved in politics, especially issues related to gender—violence against women, reproductive rights, etc. I gave up Catholicism shortly after going away to college, and after experimenting and learning about other religions, decided I was an atheist. I went to years of therapy and read a ton of self-help books and am feeling pretty good about myself.

After I turned 30, my priorities started to shift and my perceptions of "reality" started to change. After working in the women's movement for 10 years, I started to become disillusioned and lose my idealism. I continue to work in the field, but see it more as a job than a passion. Where I saw my mom as an innocent victim not only of my father, but of "the patriarchy" in the past, I'm now starting resent her and see her as weak. I'm still a feminist, but for the most part, feminist organizations now seem shortsighted to me and I'm not interested in taking part in the debate. I find it difficult not to see all sides of an issue and find myself at this point almost apolitical. On the career front, I always wanted to go to grad school. I applied, was easily accepted into a challenging program, but decided that I didn't want to have to take out a bunch of loans to get a job like I already have.

Somewhere along the line, I decided that maybe what I needed to do was "settle down." That maybe, in fact, I could be the type of person who gets married and has children.

So, I set out to meet a husband and, luckily for me, I have met a most wonderful man whom I truly love. He is nothing at all like my father—in fact, he doesn't drink at all. He thinks it's stupid. He is kind and loving and sweet. He will be a wonderful father. His family life was much more "normal." Nobody abused anybody and he and his brother were supported and encouraged as children. We were married this summer and just moved into our new house and are talking about when we will have children. It's all really good and I feel very fortunate and approaching "normal." Which leads me to my question.

What is a "normal" marriage? In my experience, married people abuse each other and fight and scream and drink a lot and disappoint each other. In my mind, marriage meant fights about money and constant stress and fear. In my mind, marriage meant a domineering husband and a submissive wife. Of course, I realize that that is in the past and is not what I need to have, but I'm finding it extremely difficult after all these years of being away from that, not to revert to that way of thinking.

Sometimes I find myself acting like my parents—I say mean things knowing that they will be hurtful. My husband has a very assertive manner of communication. He's never hurtful or rude, but always speaks his mind and is confident in his opinion. While I admire that and normally communicate in the same way in professional settings and with friends, I find that it's difficult on a daily basis with my husband. Many times when we have stressful discussions, I'll say something nasty. I'm jealous of his ability to communicate. I'm afraid that I will do the wrong thing and chase him away. I'm most afraid that I will either become my dad, or worse, become my mom, in this relationship.

So, I guess that's my question: What is a good wife/partner? What is a good marriage these days? How do you interact with somebody on a daily basis and not revert to childish ways of communicating? What is a normal marriage?

Not Sure What's Normal

Dear Not Sure What's Normal,

FIRST OF ALL, it is quite normal in marriage to find yourself repeating patterns from your own family life. It is also quite normal for a child of alcoholics to wonder what is a normal marriage. Perhaps it's best to say that a normal marriage for you might be one in which you struggle frequently to feel normal. A normal marriage would be one that frequently does not feel normal.

I would venture to guess that one of your objections to marriage, as a political person, has been that marriage is not a magical fairyland that will fix all a young woman's problems, that it is, instead, a political construct that offers decidedly mixed advantages for women. Add to this the tremendous psychological hazards marriage presents to a child of a bad marriage, and it is easy to see why you have begun to question what's going on now.

So the questions we ought to ask ourselves, it seems to me, are: Is marriage the magical reunion of self with other? Is marriage magically transformative? Is it transformative at all? Does it confer on the individual any new life understanding, or any new ability to cope? What existential problems does marriage solve, and what ones does it create? Does it help or hinder our development as people?

Perhaps you have already considered these questions, and the answers led you at first to reject marriage. So what has changed, and how can you bring your questioning, skeptical self into this marriage without disrupting its foundation?

Here is what I would suggest to you. I suggest that you remind yourself of some things you already know: You have to create your marriage just as you have had to create the rest of your life.

So what has led you to confusion? Perhaps the childhood fantasy of a magically transforming marriage is so seductive that otherwise tough and rational people such as yourself occasionally get lost in it. In your case this may have come about partly as a result of political disillusionment. You have probably been wise to question some of the excesses of your political work. But political struggle is not silly; it may be prone to excesses just like any human endeavor, but it is not silly and it is not something that a child discards in favor of more adult activities. So I hope you carry into your marriage that same skepticism about social and economic conditions for women as well as a continued determination not to repeat your family's problems.

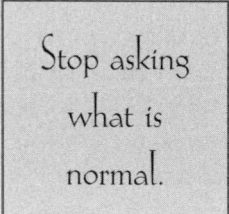

Stop asking what is normal.

You are going to have to learn how to communicate when you are upset. You are going to have to learn lots of things you didn't learn in your own family. But if you want to stay married, I'm sure you can find the advantages as well.

You know there is no such thing as a normal marriage. I suspect what has happened is that you have allowed yourself, after many years of fighting it, to begin to feel again that intense longing for an understandable world that is the peculiar fate of the child of the alcoholic. It is always there, but sometimes we can keep it at bay for a long time by avoiding certain social arrangements, primarily marriage and family, that seem to spark it. As long as we stick to political work and the academy, relying on reason and emotion directed toward intellectual and political matters, sometimes we find we can function fairly well.

But there is always and forever that longing, isn't there, for the imagined comfort of a normal home, a home in which one instinctively knows what is the proper thing to do, in which harmony reigns unspoken, a "Father Knows Best" home where dinner is served every day at 6 and the lawn is mowed on Saturdays and Sunday we go to church just like everyone on our block. Who does not harbor that secret dream—perhaps only those whose childhood was not rattled and insecure? And what do we do, those of us whose childhoods were a bit rattled and insecure? Without denigrating political activity, I would suggest that for some of us it is a retreat into reasoned anger, a shelter for our denial of the original hurt, where we do not have to listen to that childish longing because we are busy changing the world and everyone in it.

And yet for all that it is still there, that voice still calling to us: I want shelter! I want comfort! I want to know what is normal!

So I say: Embrace that longing! Do you need comfort and serenity and order? Create that in your home! But do it consciously. Recognize that what you need is perhaps something that he can't give you, and seek it out elsewhere. Take responsibility for your own life! For that is the most insidious offer of marriage, I think: That we can finally lay down the existential burden.

Sorry, not in the contract. Read the fine print. You're still on your own. You're still alone in the world. It's still up to you. You were right the first time. Marriage is not a preexisting category of existence into which you enter. Marriage is something you create, as you have created the rest of your life.

Marriage will not fix you. But you can fix marriage, if you're willing to work at it.

I'm dating in recovery— how much do I tell?

Should I mention in my personal ad that I'm bipolar and have three ex-wives?

Cary,

AT AGE 55, I've had a tragic life, if you look at the past without concentrating on the present, or ... even if you do. Yet part of me is thrilled I'm still alive, and I'm really grateful for the benefits of sobriety and spirituality. So when I decide to place a personal ad, how much or how little information is appropriate? Also, same question for after meeting a new connection?

- Thrice married/divorced
- All three marriages begun as an active addict
- Last divorce a sobriety-caused event
- Five years sober, steps worked several times, sponsored and sponsor
- Great relationships with daughter and grandchildren based on recovery
- Nearly 30-year history of bipolar disorder
- Medicated, informed, last episode three years ago, total of 10 in 30 years (Two of three episodes occurring while accurately medicated)
- Living independently

- Employed
- College student in a new career field (ASL interpreting)

Respectfully,

Curious in San Diego

Dear Curious,

IF I WERE in your shoes, I would be more general in my approach, saying in the ad that I'm 55, grateful to be in recovery for five years, and studying for a degree in a new field. If you want to mention your daughter and grandchildren, that seems fine. But I would not mention that you are living independently; people will probably assume that you are living independently unless you say otherwise. Nor would I mention the number of marriages and divorces or the number of bipolar episodes. That is important information, but it can come later. And rather than listing these things, I would try to put it in regular sentences, as though writing to a friend.

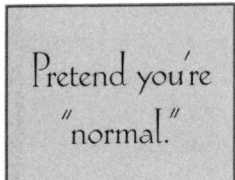
Pretend you're "normal."

If you meet a new connection and feel you are getting along well, great. Then you may want to share more of your story. As a conversation opener, you might mention that alcohol and drugs were not your only problems. But try to reveal things gradually, rather than all at once.

Think of it this way: As a person in recovery, you are responsible for cleaning up your past. But you're not responsible for broadcasting it. In meeting new people, you are responsible only for your behavior in the now. You are not required to explain all your past behavior and how you ended up here. Oh, I know how tempting it is, and how it seems as though no one could ever understand you unless they know how all these terrible things happened. And I assume you feel a responsibility not to mislead people about what a future with you might be like. But people will judge you on what they see and hear—what you say and how you say it. That includes how you handle the communication of sensitive information. So my advice would be to resist that urge to delve into the past, especially in the beginning.

If you are currently taking medication for bipolar disorder, then that is a fact and there's no sense hiding it. It's part of your recovery. But try to build your new relationships on what happens today rather than on what happened long ago. Think of your medication as part of the miracle of your survival, rather than as the lingering vestige of a troubled past. After all, you've been blessed with a second chance!

Knowing that you have been given a second chance can be a source of great joy for you, and that joy can be contagious. If the people you meet are also in recovery, they will recognize that joy, the joy of the lucky survivor. If they are not in recovery, they may not know where that joy is coming from, but they will likely appreciate it, as it can be refreshing to be around someone who appreciates what he's got.

As a new relationship progresses, there will be time for disclosures about the possibility of future bipolar episodes and so forth. But my advice is mainly to concentrate on enjoying your second chance, emphasize the positive things you have in your life, and consider your survival as a precious gift.

Married with two children ...
and a secret girlfriend in Italy

How'd I get into this mess, and how
will I ever get out?

Dear Cary,

I AM SUFFERING from the worst kind of wound, the self-inflicted kind. At every step of the way I've known that I was behaving in a dangerous, irresponsible way, sure to cause myself and others pain, and yet I've continued to march along the path to my own destruction.

About 18 months ago I went to Italy on a lengthy business trip. While there, I met a wonderful woman. Sexy, witty, charming. Oh, and did I mention completely smitten with me? We conversed only in Italian. She showed me the sites and cooked me gamberetti e pinoli. She introduced me to her family and her friends. When I left we pledged to stay in touch by phone, e-mail and instant messaging until the time came when we could be together.

It would have been the perfect romance except for one minor detail. I told her I was single but I am married. It was just harmless flirting at first and I never thought it would go as far as it has.

So I returned home to my decent, loving wife and my two young children. They were overjoyed to see me. Their wonderful father and husband had returned.

Meanwhile, I kept in touch with my Italian girlfriend. I went back to Italy in November and again in June. Each time I told myself that this was it. I would either come clean or come up with some pretense to end it. She began to talk about marriage and arranging her life so we could be together. I had to end it. I knew I did.

Through a complicated set of circumstances (mostly of my own concoction and language issues), neither of these women have any idea that the other exists. My wife thinks I'm going through a busy stretch and is concerned that I seem distant. My Italian girlfriend is anxious to move to the next step where we can be together.

And here I am in the middle, the lying, deceptive bastard. It's hard to describe the depths of self-loathing that I feel, and the knowledge that there is no way to come out of this without causing terrible pain to everyone and lose both women, neither of whom deserve what I've done. Neither do my children.

Neither do I, for that matter. I can't for the life of me figure out why I put myself in this situation in the first place, wrecking my own happiness in the process. An early onset midlife crisis? Narcissistic disorder? The natural tendency to screw up a good thing?

Instead of the obvious step of coming clean and trying to rebuild, I've come up with the even more insane idea of killing myself and leaving a note to explain what I'd done and that I was too much of a coward to face the hurt and disgust and hatred of people that I love.

And yet, being a coward, I doubt I'd be able to manage that, either.

Any thoughts, Cary, other than the condemnation that I deserve?

Screwup

Dear Screwup,

WELL, YEAH, I have a few thoughts. But first, that pasta dish you mentioned looks really, really delicious. I'm so hungry right now I'm going to get up from the computer this minute and walk down to the Ferry Building (http://www.ferrybuildingmarketplace.com/)

and look for some food, and when I get back I'll try to help you out on this one.

Wow, that was good. Geez, am I the most self-centered guy in the room or what? Oh, no, there you are!

OK, now: This thing is relatively simple. You have to break it off with the girlfriend. Whether you tell her you're married is up to you. I wouldn't. I would just tell her that she's the most beautiful woman in the world and this is the hardest thing you've ever done but you won't be seeing her again, ever. Why does she deserve to know? So she can hate you instead of mourn for you? So she can trouble her soul for years over how a man could be so deceitful? So you can do penance over her increase of sorrow?

So you can hate yourself even more? I don't think so. I think you just tell her it's over. Tell her in person if you can. If you think you'd just end up eating gamberetti e pinoli in bed with her again, then send her a handwritten letter on good stationery. Don't say anything more. But make it stick.

Your life doesn't have to fall apart. But you do need to figure out what the hell is going on with you. Maybe you do have narcissistic personality disorder. Or maybe you just have bad case of self-involved cluelessness. In either case, eventually you tell your wife. But first, you need a crash course in what's up with you. You visit a psychotherapist or psychiatrist and you embark on a course of self-discovery.

You need to learn the names of your hungers. It is not enough to look at what you did and say, Gee, that was bad. You must ask, What was I hungering for? And what am I hungering for still? What forces were operating on me? In the hands of what desire was I a willing puppet?

You will have to answer these questions yourself. But I should think it's fairly obvious that your hunger for pleasure, at least, was at work. You may never have stopped to consider what part your hunger for pleasure plays in your life. You may not have thought of yourself as exceptional in that regard. You may also have a hunger for freedom and autonomy that you have not given conscious voice to. You may feel trapped and want to escape the requirements of your marriage. That, too, would be useful to know—to really know, to know in a deep and perhaps painful way. If you feel trapped, and you feel a lack of pleasure, then those are things that, once acknowledged, you can seek to remedy in other ways, openly, honestly, safely.

How do you meet those desires in other ways? I think of it as being similar to the principle of redirection that I have seen skillful mothers use with their children. The child wants the cookie. The child can't have the cookie. But look! The child can have the toy instead! The child is OK with the toy. The important thing is, the child wants something. He's capable of substituting the object; in a more fundamental sense, he wants a certain kind of experience, the experience of holding an object, for instance. So you identify the experience that is desired, and you provide for that experience. You can do the same thing. You want romance, great food, beauty, affection, pleasure, an exotic locale? Perhaps you can have these things. Just not in Italy with the girlfriend.

Such self-discovery and introspection are not frivolous diversions. You cannot live responsibly without knowing what your weaknesses are, what you hunger for, what you will lie about if given the chance.

The reason that day after day I suggest that troubled people seek some form of psychotherapy is that there is a job to do and therapy is often the best way of getting the job done. It's for the same reason that I would suggest you take your car to a professional to get it painted. It's not something you want to do in your own garage. You don't have the tools. You don't have the skill. You'll just get paint everywhere. And remember: Your wife's stuff is stored there too.

So that is my advice to you: Find a professional who will help you through this. Undertake to know what is driving you. Undertake to change how you respond to what is driving you. And eventually, when you're sure it's in the past, consider sharing all this with your wife. You may decide it's too risky. Or you may decide that living with the secret is worse. Only you can decide.

I live in Hollywood, but I'm fat. Do I really deserve to be loved?

I was born and raised in show business, where appearance is everything.

Dear Cary,

I'M FAT. IT'S my identity. It's my comfort and it's my prison. I'm not circus freak fat, just consistently carrying around varying degrees of 50 extra pounds. I'm tall, big-boned and, many say, striking. I'm about 40 and was born and raised in Hollywood. I live there still.

I have everything I need—friends, family, brains, education, talent, ability, street smarts, beauty, a roof over my head ... but I'm having difficulty having intimate relationships with men. I was raised by a narcissistic father and a passive-aggressive mother, in Hollywood, in show business, and I was taught from an early age that physical perfection is the only thing that guarantees love and acceptance. My parents were unnaturally obsessed with my body. Of course, I learned to manipulate and control my parents with my eating habits, giving them the huge "Fuck you" of making myself fat.

This stuff isn't a mystery to me. I know who I am; I know why I do what I do. I've been in therapy on and off my whole adult life. But, really, it was turning 40 that brought me clarity—as if a dormant internal light switch suddenly decided to turn itself on.

So. The lights are on. I get it. I get it all. But there's one crucial thing about which my emotions and my intellect aren't seeing eye to eye: Do I deserve love if I'm overweight? Men hit on me. I'm a booby broad and I'm kinda hot, even with the extra poundage. I wear it well. But I'm having a hard time accepting that a man could be attracted to me because it's such an ingrained part of my psyche that I must be physically perfect to receive love. My friends think I'm insane when I say, "I can't date! I'm fat!"

I'm now in cognitive behavioral therapy. It's helping. I'm disputing my unwanted beliefs. But, boy, this shit is hard to get beyond. I need and want the love of a good man. How can I get past this self-imposed limitation? I'm working on the fat, but I have a life to live, too.

Whole Lotta Love

Dear Whole Lotta Love,

AT THE RISK of splitting hairs, I would ask, Do you have to deserve love to accept love? If love were offered to you, would you have difficulty accepting it because you don't think you deserve it? If so, I really do think cognitive therapy is the way to go. Because you do need to untangle the existential question first, and then rearrange your behavior.

Cognitive therapy can help you with the first part. I know because I had a similar problem. I thought I was my writing. Cognitive therapy helped me with that. It was a dilemma: If I was the same as my writing, then if I wrote badly, I was a bad person; I could not risk writing badly because I could not risk being a bad person; therefore I could not risk writing at all. I was stuck. I had to learn that I was not my writing.

Likewise, you are not the same as your fat. You are a person. Your fat is just fat. It doesn't deserve love. People deserve love. You are a person as deserving of love as any other person.

It wasn't cognitive therapy that got me all the way through this, however. Once you are clear that you are distinct from your accessories or your activities, you may believe that you deserve love. But then how do you actually, in practice, learn to accept love? First, ALFY: Accept love from yourself. That's it. See what I'm doing? I'm not saying, Love yourself. I'm saying, Accept love from yourself. Just try it.

By the way, have you read that book "Children of the Self-Absorbed"?

I haven't.

I love the title and have great regard for the publisher, New Harbinger Press. I've paged through the book, but I haven't read it. Do you know why I haven't read it? May I confess something to you?

I am afraid to buy self-help books.

Isn't that weird? I want to buy "Children of the Self-Absorbed" not only because the title echoes the title of a horror movie but because I would like to know more about how one can overcome the effects of growing up with a narcissistic parent. I am sort of in the business.

But I have the oddest belief: When I am in a bookstore, I think my purpose in buying a book is to impress the clerk. If I am going to impress the clerk, I can only buy smart-person books.

Deserve what you crave.

So I was in the bookstore just the other day, leafing through "Children of the Self-Absorbed" and finding it quite absorbing. But you know what I ended up buying? "Freakonomics." (http://dir.salon.com/story/books/review/2005/05/03/freak/index.html) It was featured up near the counter, and it seems like more of a smart-person book.

Isn't that insane? And counterproductive? And I'm supposed to offer you help? How can I offer you help if I cannot even act rationally, in my own interest, in something as simple as buying a book?

Just the same, in case you're interested, based on what I gleaned by furtively leafing through the book when the clerk wasn't looking, I suggest you read it and do what it says.

Meanwhile, if you'd like the opinion of a complete nutcase, I'll tell you what I think about fatness. I think in 2,000 years when they dig us up they will see that we were a fat-crazed society, and they will find a connection between our religious craziness, our war craziness and our fat craziness. They will understand us better then than we understand ourselves. They will have the benefit of a lack of information. But that is 2,000 years from now.

Let me just conclude: You sound like a good candidate for the kind of cognitive therapy-based ideas and exercises in "Children of the Self-Absorbed," which I have not read. Indeed, as you say, you are doing some cognitive therapy already. So you know what I'm talking about. Cognitive therapy provides methods for linking up what you know with how you feel and how you behave. It gives you a way to actually change. It's cool that way.

So buy that book and keep working with your therapist and see if it doesn't help. I think it probably will.

You are beautiful and you deserve to be loved. You have some fat. Your fat does not deserve anything. It's just fat.

Glad we cleared that up.

My husband-to-be dresses too sloppily for a New York lawyer

He's brilliant and I'm crazy about him,
but the white socks with black dress shoes
I just can't abide.

Dear Cary,

I AM 38 and in the most perfect relationship ever. We plan to be married in December. I love my boyfriend so much I get chills when he comes home from work. Here's the problem: He dresses like a flood victim. He wears his lack of concern for his appearance like a badge of honor and seems to think that paying the remotest attention to fashion would be evidence of vanity, a character flaw.

He is a brilliant lawyer, and to be with me, he relocated to a large, fashion-conscious city. I don't think he understands that co-workers can and will say, "Oh, you mean that clown who wears wool suits in July." He wears white gym socks with black dress shoes. He has a closet full of great ties from his mom, and yet still wears to work the ones that are visibly falling apart. He boasts about how he has "owned this suit since the '80s." (And it shows.)

I cringe when we go out to dinner at a nice restaurant because he looks so ridiculous at times (dark jeans, brown belt, frayed Izod shirt, white gym socks, black dress shoes). But I don't want to make him defensive, or he will just dig in his heels and make it worse. I hate to listen to myself nag, but perhaps a war of attrition, where he just gets tired and gives in to me, is indeed the solution. I honestly believe I would be doing him a favor if I didn't give up yet. But how should I approach this? Should I just poke my eyes out?

Preferring a Rain Barrel in NYC

Dear Preferring a Barrel,

IT'S TOUGH TO argue with a brilliant lawyer, but I think an argument can be made. It requires us to consider the nature of New York, which, one might argue, is a giant court before which litigants of the world both threadbare and elegant petition for variances in the zoning of their fate and the easing of rules that govern their fortune; they draft revisions of long-held, amply precedented definitions of art; they argue with passionate logic for the raising or lower-

Dress well for the merciless jury.

ing of tariffs and hemlines. As they do so they pray for approval, morning and night, of how they choose to dress as they appear before the court. For that will influence the decisions of their judges for good or ill.

Who are these judges? Why, these judges are the citizens of New York. The man on the street, the dowager, the hipster and the child alike appraise you with immeasurable subtlety in a momentary glance, never losing a step as they file you away as a rube or a hick or a player. This court of immediate judgment is upon you every instant, opening the velvet rope or closing the iron door, believing your $500 shoes or turning you down on account of your tattered tie.

By what authority do they pass judgment? And what sanctions can they lower, what fines impose, what sentences pass?

Why, they can lower the sanction of the withering glance that makes your hair stand on end! They can levy the fine of never a discount, never for you! They can pass a life sentence of indifference and scorn, cold disregard, whispered incredulity at your incredible dullness, a sentence of no promotion, no partnership and no invitations to the boss's parties until you prove you will not embarrass your hosts by your strange and slovenly dress.

As to the question of vanity: One does not call attention to oneself by dressing well in New York; on the contrary, one calls attention to oneself by wearing white socks with black dress shoes. It is not vanity that is required, but a special kind of humility: One must dress properly before the court.

In a small farming town, a heightened concern for one's appearance might signal something other than humility and respect for the public; it might signal that one has big ideas, not only an inflated sense of importance but plans for imminent departure. In communities whose economies depend on family continuity, the first question that arises is: And who's to do the work then? So in many places it's best to signal by your dress that you're content with things as they are and aspire to nothing more.

But just the opposite is true in a city like New York. It is not the ambitious but the slothful who seem out of place. If you're not a hustler, if you don't want to shine, what are you doing here? If you're not going someplace in a hurry, you're just in the way.

So I would ask your fiancé, What litigant in his right mind would appear before the judge in clothes that say he does not care whether he wins or loses the case? He is appearing before the world's greatest and quickest judges, the citizens of New York, allowing his case to be sized up and instantly dismissed before he even has a chance to say a word. He's probably bright enough to see the argument. So put it to him: He's prejudicing the judge and jury against his case. It's irresponsible. It's unlawyerly.

Time to shine the shoes and go shopping.

How do I know
if I'm an alcoholic?

*There are certain signs that I have a problem
with alcohol, but nothing terrible has
happened so far.*

Dear Cary,

YOU WRITE SO eloquently about alcoholism and drinking problems in so many of your columns that I hope you can help me.

I'm drinking a nice cool beer as I write to you, despite the fact that I've gained 30 pounds in the last year from this habit of nightly drinking. I'm not sure I'm an alcoholic—in fact, I don't think I am—but there's no arguing that I look forward to my evening drinks the same way I used to crave cigarettes, which I stopped without a problem 15 years ago.

I went to a 12-step program for close to a year. While I didn't drink during that time, I felt like an outsider there. I rarely have more than about five or six drinks at a time, even though I do it virtually every day, and usually without others knowing. However, other than the weight (which isn't yet a real deterrent, since I'm just slightly overweight), I don't suffer visible consequences, so it's hard for me to relate to the stories of woe and loss. I also usually stop around five drinks, so I can't relate to the "I drank 'til I was toast" stories. I can't drink anything other than wine or beer, even if I try. I would never drink and drive and never do. And I know it's external evidence, but I am an attractive 40-year-old woman with a good job, well-liked inside and outside work, own a cute house, a nice car and have family, friends and a loving boyfriend who care about me.

However, I do feel a creeping sensation of "I must do this," and this is beginning to worry me. For example, if I know I am staying somewhere I won't be able to drink as much as I want, I put some beer or wine in my suitcase to be safe. The nightly drinking, which started last fall, also worries me, although another side of me says it's OK since it's not that much, just a habit.

I dread going back to that group. I spent the most depressed year of my life there, although physically I felt great. I went there in the first place because I had a few bad incidents, and in fact have never resumed that level of drinking. According to all my research, I appear to be an alcohol abuser rather than an alcoholic, but practically speaking, I'm not sure what alternatives that creates. I've been to two therapists and neither helped. I'm keeping this a secret from my family and boyfriend—well, he knows some of it—and so they can't help much either.

Reading my story, do you think I'm alcoholic? And are there alternatives other than stopping completely? I tried Moderation Management and I felt even worse there—to me, a bunch of truly problem drinkers not wanting to deal with it. I feel like I don't quite fit anywhere. Any help you can offer would be appreciated.

A Friend

Dear Friend,

ONE OF THE things we lose as we become full-blown alcoholics is the ability to make sound judgments. Luckily, it appears that you still have that ability. Unlike somebody who is too far gone to know what is good or bad for her, you are probably capable of making a clear-headed assessment of where you are in your drinking career and where it is likely to lead. For that reason, I suggest you return to those meetings you were attending with that very purpose in mind. They can offer you a wealth of anecdotal evidence on which to base such a judgment. I suggest you listen particularly for stories of people like yourself who have achieved a fair amount of success in life. I also suggest you tell your story to other people so they can perhaps help you identify the similarities and differences between what you are experiencing and what they have experienced.

> Stop drinking before you can't stop drinking.

In that way you can accomplish two things. You can assess the likely outcome of your drinking, based on the outcomes of others. And you can also be of service to others who want to stop drinking. By being present there, you give others the courage to be present as well. There may be women there who, like you, cannot relate to tales of utter devastation and loss, but are indeed concerned about their drinking. Perhaps they can relate to someone like you who has it pretty much together—although she does pack bottles in her suitcase for emergencies.

If you gather from those meetings that most people who reached the point you are at with their drinking found they were able to quit with relative ease when they decided they wanted to, then your mind may be put at ease. If you find, however, that many of those who lost everything were at one point roughly where you are now, it may give you cause for grave concern. This might be a good time also to take a look at the "20 Questions" pamphlet prepared by Alcoholics Anonymous. At the very least, if you do these things, you will have ample evidence before you and, being of sound judgment, can make a sound choice.

There is, in addition, a third reason to go back to those meetings, and this may the most directly relevant of all. You say that for the almost year you were attending those meetings, you did not drink. You note that you were not particularly happy during that period. But your reason for writing to me is not that you are unhappy. It is that you are concerned about your drinking. It sounds like the meetings did keep you from drinking.

As far as happiness goes, many people find that after an initial period of adjustment they can live quite happily without drinking. My guess is that you are not all that different from the rest of us, and that if you do finally decide to give up drinking, you will be just fine.

I was impregnated by a rapist 32 years ago

I gave my infant daughter up for adoption.
Now she's found me and wants to meet.

Dear Cary,

THIRTY-TWO YEARS AGO, when I was a 19-year-old college student home for summer break, I became pregnant as the result of being raped.

A 30-year-old neighbor who had lost his wife and infant son in a terrible car accident the year before struck up a conversation as I passed his house. He said he owned a book I had been looking for and would loan it to me, so I followed him inside. Needless to say, he didn't have the book and I stumbled home later having been physically, mentally and emotionally violated. It's difficult to believe in these days, but my only sexual experience to that point had been with the son of longtime family friends when our families shared a cabin at a lake the summer before, and that hadn't proceeded much beyond the petting stage.

Because of the rapist's standing as a sympathetic character due to the loss of his family, the jury believed his version that the sex was consensual and he was acquitted of all charges. I remember almost nothing of that time except for three horrible days on the witness stand. At some point near the end of the trial I became cognizant enough to realize that I was almost six months pregnant and that not all my vomiting was caused by stress.

I was (and am) the beloved only child of two wonderful parents who believed and supported me throughout the whole ordeal. After the neighbor's acquittal, we moved from our town to a large city in the same state, where I gave birth and put the child up for adoption without ever seeing her. Subsequently, I enrolled at a large college in a different state where I met my husband and eventually settled down to raise a family. Early in our relationship, I told my husband the story of the rape and the adoption. He was as loving and supportive as my parents had been. Since that time, my husband and I have had two children, a son, 25, engaged to be married next year, and a daughter, 27, married to a wonderful man and the mother of our delightful 4-year-old granddaughter. We've never told our children my story simply because it seemed irrelevant and disassociated from our family. For 30 years I have only rarely thought about the rape and adoption. I feel I have led a truly wonderful life.

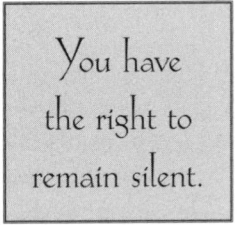

You have the right to remain silent.

The state where the child was adopted had some of the strictest privacy laws in the country at that time, so I never thought I would be contacted. But the laws have changed. Two months ago, I received a call at work from a woman asking if I might be her mother. The situation was so far behind me that it took several seconds to understand that this could be the child I placed for adoption. When the realization hit, I almost collapsed. All I could comprehend was that she wanted to meet with me. I stammered something about it being an inconvenient time to talk, and left work in a high state of anxiety and stress. A week later, I received a registered letter from this woman.

She told me about her life. Her adoptive father was abusive (she didn't elaborate on the type of abuse) and her adoptive mother (since deceased) couldn't protect her children from the tyrant she'd married. The older brother had left home when the girl was 10 and she hadn't had contact with him since. Beginning in her middle teenage years, she'd drifted from one relationship to another. The relationships ranged from bad to violently abusive. Along the way she'd had two abortions and a daughter who is now 3 years old. Two years ago she decided to turn her life around. Contacting her biological parents was part of that process. She had already contacted her father (the rapist) six months ago because he was easier to find, being in the same state. His second wife had died of a long illness several years previously, leaving him childless and lonely. He was delighted to discover a daughter and granddaughter waiting in the wings. They have since moved into his house and become a family. He hasn't informed her of the circumstances of her birth. She wants to meet me.

She included a picture with her letter. Her daughter looks exactly like my daughter and granddaughter (and me) at the same age. Except for the inherent gender differences, the woman is a dead ringer for the man who raped me 32 years ago.

I feel like my genes have betrayed me by lurking in the future, waiting for me to catch up so they can prove that I have no control over my destiny or happiness. I don't have it in me to sit across a table from her. I don't know if I could do it even if she looked like my mother, or my father's Aunt Tilly, or a complete stranger. But I do know that I can't face that face. The same face that blandly, smugly stared at me while his defense attorney implied that I was desperate for male attention, and just by walking into a neighbor's house I was complicit in the violence that happened against me.

I've had endless conversations with my husband and mother about whether to meet this woman. They both tell me the same thing, Do what's right for you. I just want someone to tell me what they would do in the same situation. Should I meet her? If I meet her, should I tell her the circumstances of her birth, thus potentially ruining the first good relationship (and possible inheritance leading to financial security) she's ever had? If I take the next step and introduce her to my children, do I tell them of the circumstances? If I don't tell any of them, will I one day be compelled to attend a family picnic or other gathering at which I will come face to face with the man who raped me?

I can imagine my daughter being overjoyed at the prospect of a sister and a cousin of the same age for her child. Once the story is out, I will be snowed under with the novelty of finding a long-lost sibling and be encouraged—no, expected—to include her and her daughter in all things family. I've always lived my life dealing with things honestly, yet this situation seems to beg for lies. What should I do?

Lady Madonna

Dear Lady Madonna,

I THINK YOU can deal with this honestly by stating clearly to this woman that you do not want to meet with her.

You have obviously thought this through in detail, and your reluctance is palpable. So I do not need to outline the pitfalls of meeting her. My point is that if you do not take action now, events may overtake you. So I would respond to this woman by registered mail at the earliest opportunity, telling her that at present you prefer not to meet with her.

If you wish to expand on your reasons, you might tell her quite honestly that you do not agree with changes in privacy laws that now allow adopted children to track down their biological parents. You might explain that when you made your decision, laws protected your privacy and you had no reason to believe they would change. You might say that while the laws have changed, the reasons for their existence remain.

You might go on to say that as far as you are concerned, the woman who raised her is her mother. If you feel a need to characterize your own role, you might say you are at most an anonymous donor who helped her come into being. And if you are the type to expound philosophically, you might even go so far as to argue that the reasons for every person's existence are at root mysterious, and are made only marginally less so by knowledge of one's lineage; this is true no more so for adoptive children than for biological children. You might wish her a happy and healthy life; tell her you will pray for her if prayer is something you do; but be firm on this point: You do not want to meet with her, now or in the future. Close the door on that possibility.

This may sound quite cold, but remember: Your main goal is to discourage her from contacting you. While you may entertain thoughts of meeting her some time in the future (perhaps when the man who raped you is dead), I would keep those thoughts to yourself.

Having settled that, other questions arise. Is she exposing herself to harm by living with the man who raped you 30 years ago, a man whose two wives have both died prematurely? If so, do you have an obligation to inform her of the risk? I find it strange, actually, that she remains ignorant of the trial. If I had been searching for my biological father, I would have searched court records. But apparently this detail of his past has gone unobserved. If she becomes a part of the community and gets to know the neighbors, one would think she would learn of these events eventually.

So should you tell her? I think not. Your reason for avoiding contact with her is not only to shield your own family but to shield her as well. Only if telling her becomes necessary for some reason would I tell her. If this were a Victorian novel, perhaps you would include in your letter something like this: "I must warn you that the man you call your father is a dangerous man. Conscience forbids me to say more." In real life, for instance, if she were to show up at your door, in order to impress upon her the revulsion with which you would view the possibility of meeting her father again, you might tell her. Even then, though, you might simply tell her that if she wants to know why you wish to have no contact, ask her father.

Ah, and that is the stuff of novels. For you, the important thing is to avoid the messy and painful entanglements that bringing her into your life would create. To that end, I urge you to be resolute in your refusal; let's hope that she will respect your wishes.

My boyfriend is skulking around the personals on Craig's List

I'm a trophy girlfriend; I give it to him three times a day. Wouldn't you think that would keep him in line?

Dear Cary,

I'M IN A difficult situation because basically all trust has been broken between me and my boyfriend. I am 20 years younger than he and kind of a trophy girlfriend. I happily give him oral sex three times a day, and our love life is very sexual.

However, there is trouble in paradise. I'm worried that we don't have the same basic decency or morals. I don't understand why he would cheat on me, because I give him everything a man could want in bed. But twice that I know of, he has looked for a "discreet" relationship on craigslist.org.

Why won't he be faithful to me? I am Ivy League-educated, good-looking, hypersexual, but also prone to mood swings (especially in this relationship). I am starting to believe he is a narcissist. He also drinks heavily, and we often have terrible fights in which he insists he is never wrong.

I dumped a can of garbage with coffee grounds and other messes in it on the bed last night when I found out he was poking around on Craig's List. He says that because I found out by reading an e-mail I was not supposed to see, he did not hurt me.

This makes no sense, because the very act of searching for a "discreet" relationship is hurtful in itself whether I know or not. I would not do this to him, because I would fear hurting him and I would feel as if I were betraying him.

I don't understand his motivations, and why it has to be explained to him that he has hurt me deeply. I'm getting the feeling I should leave because I have never been so stressed out in my life. I'm also starting to become repulsed by his behavior. I feel so numb.

What should I do? I feel trapped. I know I should not be with someone who is so different from me, but it is so hard to get out of this ... Hellllllp!!!!!!!

H

Dear H,

WHEN WORDS FAIL and garbage dumped on the bed becomes your preferred medium of communication, it's usually a sign that you've reached a significant crisis in the relationship. At that point thoughts tend to arise about the security deposit on the apartment, how much it would be if split two ways, and whether that Maria Callas album is his or yours. (I'm betting it's yours.)

Simply put, I think you should leave him. If you're feeling this crazy, you'd better just put down the Hefty bag and back slowly away from the relationship. It's not that this thing couldn't be worked out, were there world enough and time. But what you're going through with him is going to take a lot of unraveling and rethinking, and if he's drinking heavily and generally uncooperative, your chances of working it out with him are slim to none. You're better off working out these issues on your own, so next time you get involved with a man you can better negotiate.

The word "negotiate" is key here, I think, because it sounds to me like bargaining plays a huge role in this relationship. It's all about bargaining for sex, fidelity and power. The emphasis on bargaining—your giving him head three times a day, your reference to yourself as a trophy—gets you into trouble when certain nonnegotiable elements come up, because it's not clear between you just where the bargaining ends and the nonnegotiable human stuff begins. If sex between you is a kind of bargain, why should sex between him and others not be also part of a bargain? I know the answer seems obvious to you. You are in love with him. But you are also bargaining with him from the position of an object, a trophy. That is bound to lead to confusion about what is permissible and what is not.

Understand why you're dumping garbage on his bed.

I would say the difference between a bargaining relationship and a love relationship is in the relative primacy of the ego in relation to the other; in a love relationship, the individual ego is subsumed by the whole; in a bargaining relationship, each ego is trying to satisfy itself in a calculated way, sort of the way the market works. Many self-interested individuals compete in the market, calculating always what price the consumer will bear; transactions are therefore chaotic and always shifting; it is characterized by brinksmanship and a trading mentality, rather than by self-sacrifice and a giving mentality.

In a trading environment, when someone suddenly introduces an a priori value—such as: Trading is fine, but I draw the line at trading sex slaves, or products tested on animals, or coffee that is not grown sustainably—then relative strangers have to sit down and agree about values and ethics. Who's to say then who is right and who is wrong? Often it's the stronger partner who says what's right and what's wrong; bargaining, in the absence of shared values, leads to power struggles.

To be a trophy is to be a possession. There is something sexy about being able to possess someone completely. But there is also a whiff of death about it, a spiritual sterility. And when the possession begins to speak and act of its own will, to make demands, to assert a sense of honor and a code of decency, that is a point of shock and bewilderment to the purchaser of the trophy, the master, the slave owner. It may be that in playing the role of the trophy girlfriend you set yourself up to be treated like an object.

If all things in the relationship are negotiable, then you are obliged to negotiate them. If certain things are off the table, however—if you love him and want an exclusive, committed relationship—then you need to shift the basis of the relationship from one of bargaining for sex and power to one of deep mutual commitment. You need to say to each other that you're a couple and you're going to try to stick together no matter what, even if at times you do not completely meet each other's needs.

I doubt that he's at that point. It's very likely that your intuition is accurate, that he has narcissistic traits; if so, he will never regard you as an equal, and you will never get what you need from him. (Incidentally, have you seen the French movie "Look at Me"?)

Your situation suggests some deep and difficult issues about feminism, sexuality and ethics. I think you need to embrace them, perhaps with the help of a women's group or a therapist, before you get in another relationship with a man. Otherwise, I am afraid that you will simply be taken advantage of, you will be misunderstood, and you will be unhappy. And that would not be good. I would prefer you to be happy. I think you are probably much better to be around when you are not dumping coffee grounds on the bed.

Can I write? I want to write.
But I'm afraid to write

Family and friends will think it's about them!

Dear Cary,

I'M NOT SURE if this is suitable for your column, but I think of you as more of a writer than an advice columnist so I would like to hear your thoughts.

I don't really consider myself a writer; when I was a kid I read a lot of books. Soon I started seeing things differently, and would get the urge to write things down. Not just an urge, a persistent need. My head would buzz until I put an idea on paper. I kept a journal that I wrote in constantly, that is, until my mother read it and made fun of me in public over what I'd written. I was so humiliated that I threw the journal away and didn't write on my own again until I took a writing class in high school. My teacher encouraged me to apply for the writing program in university, and to my surprise, I was accepted. I didn't enjoy being around other writers that much, but eventually grew comfortable with reading my work out loud and accepting criticism.

After finishing my degree, I moved on to a regular job, no writing required. I kept writing journals filled with poems and stories, some things based on real events, some not. It created problems with boyfriends who would, without my knowledge, read them and believe that I was cheating, that I was suicidal, or any number of things that I wasn't. I was just exploring these ideas in writing, apparently convincingly so. I started throwing the books away after a little while, saving only the finished pieces that I had worked on publicly when I was in school. Even now that I live alone, I still hide my notebooks every night and periodically rip out pages and throw them away.

I've tried over and over again to squash the urge to write, but I can't do it anymore. I want to get it all out on paper, confront it, stare at it, mold it into something permanent. In school I was frequently told that I was a good writer, but that I was vague and holding back the messiness of real living. I've done plenty of real living, I am just afraid of putting it into words. I am afraid I am going to be mocked or accused of something, not by strangers, but by the people who are close to me.

I think I am finally at the point now where I am ready to move ahead and write what I need to write, but how do I go about dealing with mothers and lovers who think I am what I write?

Afraid to Write

Dear Afraid,

I MAY BE lucky or simple-minded or terribly self-involved, but it has always been clear to me that the writing comes first. I just feel this constant pull, and everything else comes second. It says write, I write. It is the only way I can be at peace with myself for a few moments. It is I suppose in a way my religion—in the way William James meant when he said, "Religion ... shall mean for us the feelings, acts, and experiences of individual men in their solitude."

> Write what seems obvious and true.

But you ask a very particular and rather practical question to which I have responded with a reverie on my own good fortune in being too self-involved to worry much about the impediments of social and familial objections or misunderstandings. So I would offer a few further thoughts in a more practical vein:

1) You can't do anything about what people think about your work. They're mostly going to be wrong. They're going to criticize you and they're going to think it's about them. Anyone who thinks your work reflects badly on them is going to be mostly wrong, as your work is your own struggle to understand your own self. You won't be able to prove they're wrong; most people are not going to understand the project of the writer, the manifold whatevers of writing. They're just not going to get it and you have to live with that. It helps to believe that there is nothing shameful about trying to understand one's own self in public; it may be unsightly but it is useful work, and instructive to others.

2) You can't let anything get in the way of doing your work. If you are going to do it you must simply begin.

3) You do not have to write autobiographically. You may write about anything. If your fear about how the subject matter will be received is stopping you from writing, then write about something else. Write about nothing. It doesn't matter what you write about. You'll come around to your subject. It will always be there, by its absence or by its presence, whether you want it to be there or not; it will be the negative space you are circling, or the burning subject you name. It will be there. Just begin.

4) You say quite clearly that you don't think of yourself as a writer, and yet you want to write. A person who writes is a writer. It doesn't matter how you think of yourself. What matters is what you do. If you sit down (or stand up) and write every day, that's enough.

5) You don't have to show everything you write to everybody who might be offended by it. Chances are, much of what you write will be written for you alone anyway. Just write it. Write it because it's good for you. Write it because it takes the pressure off. Write it because it keeps you writing. Write it because there's nothing else to do. Write it. Just write it.

He threatened me, so we split. Now he's wooing me back!

I'd like to believe he's changed, but I never felt safe around him.

Dear Cary,

MY HUSBAND, FROM whom I am separated, is pursuing me under the banner of "I've realized the error of my ways and now realize what a wonderful woman you are." How should I proceed?

We were married only a short time (11 months) when I asked him to leave (after he flat-out refused couples counseling). We'd dated for four years, and I felt confident in (although saddened about) my decision to separate. He complied, and it seemed mutual.

My reasons were this: I felt like my physical person was in danger around him (we were prone to knock-down, drag-out fights and he was prone to using threats of physical harm as an intimidation), and I was fearful of who I was around him (cutting off contact with friends and family, deepening my capacity for cruelty to him and to myself). In short, I thought he displayed physically and emotionally abusive tendencies, I didn't like my response to it, and I didn't want to continue in a relationship where I was fearful of our future together (having kids and bringing them into the hostile environment we'd created, for example, was out of the question).

However, now after a few months of separation, he confesses that he really messed up. He says he treated me in an unforgivable way and cannot understand why I tolerated his behavior for as long as I did. And he's apologizing over and over. More significantly, he is demonstrating remorse. Recently, we've been spending time together, and he's being ... nice. And ... considerate. And showing a capacity for patience that I've never seen before.

He explains that our few months apart have led him to a place where he can see what a wonderful woman I am (his words) and all of the ways I supported him that he never gave me credit for, etc. And he's asking that I move on with him to create a new life together.

I can see that this could seem like a honeymoon kind of thing, and how no one would think I should buy any of what he wants to sell—and I can't deny that 97 percent of me wouldn't want to invest anything in a relationship with him even if I did believe him, for fear that it would spiral back into what we had before. But still.

Should I buy what he's trying to sell? His intentions seem genuine, and I know he believes everything he's saying. We were only married for a short time. Maybe I'm giving up on him too soon? I really did want a life with him—if it were sane and healthy.

Not So Sure

Dear Not So Sure,

AH, THE REMORSE of the abuser, how after shameful excess it tortures one into promises of moderation, how after its dark and murky course one emerges bright and hopeful again, how, having little sense of history, one even believes one's own plain lies—that it will be different this time because one feels so different! What is missing from such remorse is a mature sense of the other. The addict, like the abuser, is enclosed: What is important to him is how he himself feels; that is his world. How he affects others only becomes clear to him when he himself is made to suffer. He lacks compassionate imagination. After a setback, such as losing the spouse, he sees the problem: He was not quite charming enough!

His spell was too weak. He slipped up a time or two. Maybe he went overboard a little. But no harm done! He can regain it all! And so he refuels his hypnotic engine of subterfuge and threat and begins again to dazzle, to wheedle and control.

Picture his newfound optimism, clarity and kindness as only the trough of the same wave that so recently capsized you with terror and confusion. It's building again even as he proclaims how much he's changed, how much he sees where things went wrong. I wouldn't be surprised if he said, characteristically puffing himself up even as he pretends humility, that it was an excess of love that led him to treat you so cruelly! It is only that he loves you too much!

I wouldn't go for it. I'd stay away.

Saying this makes me feel like a sour old man. Why am I always condemning what one would like to believe is genuine soul-searching change? Why do I see only the endless machinations of the addict and the abuser? Why?

> Every campaign of abuse contains a period of seduction.

Well, what am I supposed to say? This is what I know. This is what I see. It's all too familiar.

I'm not saying one cannot change. People change all the time. But here's what the change looks like: A genuine deflation of the ego. Not this world-beating kindness and optimism, but something more muted and subdued, as though he'd had a blow to the head. If he were to go away and wait to hear from you, that might be persuasive. That might mean he'd given up control. But he's pursuing you again. He thinks he can make it work! Failure has not occurred to him. That's what I find so pathological and so eerie.

Every campaign of abuse contains a period of seduction. So to cast the seduction phase as evidence of a changed heart strikes me as pretty outlandish. It's easy to woo, to soothe, to seduce. The hard part is coming back into the same situation and responding to it differently, tolerating the same stresses that only a few months ago were intolerable, rerouting the same impulses that a

few months ago led to threats of violence, finding new ways to
handle extreme emotions, creating new methods for resolving
conflict. I think if you put him back in the same environment,
unless he's profoundly changed, he's going to tend to act the same
way. And so are you.

Think about it: What will you do if he moves back in and
you have a bad night and he hits you? What are you going to do
if you find yourself sinking into whatever morass you were in
when you two were together? What are you going to do then?
Think of how foolish and defeated you would feel. It would be so
much harder to undo what you have already undone once. No, I
can't see how it's a good idea. I would suggest that what's done is
done, that you gave it a shot and it didn't work out and the best
thing to do is let it go. Let him find someone else. And you find
someone else as well. Don't fall for it. File for divorce. Get the
papers signed. Forget about him.

(P.S. A side note: When you feel physical danger, it seems to
me that classic domestic violence is afoot, that undercurrents of
criminal behavior are running chill around your feet. Why do I
envision a cold current of water circulating about your feet? I see
you drowning. Why is drowning your plight? What does it mean
when a man seems to be drowning a woman? Isn't that the archetypal essence of domestic violence, the Scott Peterson method?
Drowning, as envelopment, is the essence of domestic violence,
isn't it—a violence of reversal, not piercing but enveloping, and
thus a kind of perversity.)

I was emotionally abused—will I ever trust anyone?

I can fake it, but it's just a pose.

Dear Cary,

I WAS EMOTIONALLY abused as a youth and have arrived at adulthood deficient in some basic necessities for a lasting, positive relationship. Trust, for one: I am able to fake trusting, but it's nothing I actually feel. It's a pose that I decide would be beneficial on an intellectual level, which I then proceed to carry out. In many ways, I am as much a manipulator as my parents, though this distresses me in a way it does not for them.

I am not antisocial and certainly get along with people—co-workers, etc.—without making waves. But I can't seem to take it to the next level. I used to think it was shyness, but now I believe I just can't picture anyone wanting to stick around for the long haul with me.

Is it possible to acquire these things with therapy or medication or something else, or is there some crucial period to learn how to bond with another human that I've missed? And why does abuse that doesn't result in any kind of a bruise do so much lasting damage?

Wondering

Dear Wondering,

SAY THAT WHEN you were growing up your parents were junkies and you never knew when the television was going to be hocked. After you start living on your own, you figure you ought to have a television, but you just never buy one. A friend asks you why you don't have a television. You say you just don't need one. But you kind of miss it. So you ponder this. Why don't I have a television? You listen to the little thoughts that run through your head and you hear this: "It'll just end up in the pawnshop." You realize that, to you, a television is something that always ends up in the pawnshop. If you had a TV, you'd always be expecting it to disappear.

Your junkie parents are flopping in a shooting gallery in Jersey these days and they don't know your address, so they can't come to your place and steal your TV and hock it. But still you can't help picturing that little corner of the flat you grew up in where every now and then the TV would be missing and that's how you'd know that your dad had lost a gig for nodding off on the bandstand or your mom was trying to quit stripping and was short on cash and they'd hocked the TV for a fix.

> Trust that the TV will be there in the morning.

And you remember how one time, for some reason, as a kid you went with your mom to the pawnshop, how the men looked at her because they'd seen her onstage and stuck dollar bills in her G-string, and when they saw you, her son, their faces showed shame and embarrassment mixed with a strange, contorted glee. And every time you think about going to Circuit City to buy a television, in your mind's eye you see those men in the pawnshop.

So it's easier to just not have a TV. But you can't really explain all that to your friend, right? And besides, you miss watching reruns of "Friends."

So what you do is finally one day you take a little leap of faith and go to Circuit City and buy a television and put it in your living room. The first night you have it you go to sleep wondering if it will be there in the morning. You go off to attend to your day and come home and it's still there. Day after day you leave the house and come home and find it's still there. Gradually, you begin to trust that television. It's a thin, brittle trust at first, but it's something.

This is how I believe it happens: If your parents lied to you and betrayed you and didn't show up on time, if they stole your money and called you stupid or whatever they did, you are naturally going to expect that to happen again. But you can consciously rearrange your life to accumulate experiences in which that doesn't happen, and over time that forms a new set of expectations. You develop a new set of positive experiences that retrains you emotionally. You start with years of habitual mistrust and fear and nightmares, and over time you replace all that with stable memories of successful, respectful interactions. I've seen murderers and drunks and people who were raped by their parents get better bit by bit. They still get fearful and have moments of weird terror and suspicion and out-of-body feelings, but the feelings pass and they keep going forward.

You look at these kids who've known nothing but trust and success all their lives and you wonder how they got there. It's obvious: Their trust is a rational response to an environment in which trust was never violated. Likewise, your mistrust is a rational response to patterns of betrayal.

So don't think of yourself as broken. Think of yourself as somebody who needs to arrange his life to accumulate experiences of trust that, over time, lead to greater courage to initiate relationships of greater intimacy.

I'm a gifted high achiever who wants to be a flight attendant

Will it be a waste of my education if I do what I really, really want?

Dear Cary,

LIKE MANY OTHER 20-somethings, I don't know what to do with my life. I went to an expensive famous private school for my undergraduate education, got a master's while working at a big, well-known company, doing something very responsible and professional with a comfortable, if not lavish, salary. As a product of gifted programs and always being told "You're so smart," I always thought that I would do something Very Important with my life. I realize now, of course, that that's not so easy to come by, and that while others might ooh and ahh at my company's reputation and all, it's really not very satisfying to me. Frankly, I'm bored.

So on a whim, I applied online for a job as a flight attendant. One thing that I love deeply is travel—not just the visiting places, but the actual act of going there, the airports and the airplanes and all. So I thought, hey, why not? I never expected to get it, but somehow I did. I've been offered a spot in training, after which I will be hired.

Now I'm faced with a decision. Do I take this job or not? I want to take it, but I am afraid what people will think. Most of my friends think I'm crazy to do it, that I'm wasting my education and my mind, etc., that I'm "too smart" for the job. I haven't told my family, but I'm sure they'll feel the same way, that I wasted all that money on school to do something that doesn't even require a college education. I'm afraid, deep down, that they might be right.

And yet, I don't really want to do those things that I'm "smart enough" to do, the things that apparently my education was meant for. I'm under no illusion that being a flight attendant is all glamour and easy fun—I've had quite a few candid conversations with those who actually do it, and I understand what it's like with the low pay, long hours, etc. But it's something that, quite simply, I want to do. I want to have a fun, unpredictable job for once. I want to do it now, while I'm young and single and without kids or a mortgage.

I know you can't make this decision for me, but I would appreciate any insight you can share that might help me in reaching it.

Undecided

Dear Undecided,

I THINK YOU should do it. You want to do it, so you should do it.

I don't know if I can offer you any insight. It's more sheer enthusiasm. I feel like standing under your window singing "Do it! Do it! Do it!" I maybe should feel some nuance, some wizened concern, but I don't. All I feel is ... I feel like cheering.

I admit that I am in a rather reduced state and that rather than looking for a problem to solve I have instead been looking for a solution I could applaud. But what's wrong with that? I feel in my gut that this is the right thing. Will you allow me that?

Could you possibly waste your education? A "waste" would indicate that your education was of no value in itself. Your education is worth what it is worth regardless of what you do afterward. That's what we always used to think of education, anyway—that it ennobles the soul. It allows the mind to grow, so the mind can work right and help you make the right decisions, which means if you get done with all that education and you know deep down that now it's time to become a flight attendant, then that's probably the right decision. If you didn't have the education maybe you'd think, Oh look at me, I'm just a lowly flight attendant, I have no education and no future, this is all I'll ever be. But no. You've got the ribbons and the medals. You can call the shots. And this is the shot you're calling. More power to you.

Do what you love. Allow yourself to love what you do. And when the love ends, then you can leave. It won't kill you. What an adventure!

Wanting is knowledge. Someone asks us what we want and we say, Oh, I don't know. I don't know what I want. But the truth is we do! We do know what we want! It's just (isn't it?) that what we want isn't the thing we ought to want or want to want or are supposed to want or think we want. It's what we want. It's the potato we want in a store full of ripe oranges. It's the comic book on a shelf full of Shakespeare—and why are we supposed to not want that? Because wanting is the deepest story of who we are; wanting is who we are more than getting. Getting can be fate or accident: You wanted to be an actress but were forced to be a stenographer because that was what was available. Getting can be an accident for which we are not responsible. Getting can be circumstance. But wanting is pure. Wanting is who you are.

> If you want to be a flight attendant, be a flight attendant.

I too am thrilled every time I board an airplane; I am thrilled to stand at the curb of an airport pickup lane, watching the shuttles and the vans full of pilots and flight attendants and all the rest; I too love to watch the planes fly over. I too have wondered what it is like to wander the sleeping aisles, the only one awake traveling through the sky. Observe the traveler. Stand over the sleeping traveler, watching over him, thinking of all the things you know and all the things you could do, but knowing that you are doing the thing that was strongest in your heart. You wanted to be high in the air watching sleeping bodies, preparing the coffee, standing in the galley thinking.

So I applaud you. I applaud you. I applaud you.

Will I ever get over my parents' suicides?

I used to be a carefree person. Now I am trapped by tragic history.

Dear Cary,

I'M STUCK. I don't know how else to put it. Both of my parents committed suicide within the past 10 years, although not at the same time. My mother wouldn't let there be a funeral for my father, and my brother wouldn't let me have a funeral for my mother because my parents didn't embrace religion and felt it would be hypocritical.

I have no family other than my brother and we don't talk. No aunts, uncles, cousins, etc. So there were no relatives to join us in our loss. My parents didn't have friends, or at least none that cared enough to send a card.

I'm so angry with them for checking out like they did. They were in good health. They had adequate finances. They left a hell of a legacy.

I carry a huge load of anger and grief. I've cried and cried but it's like I'll never lose this feeling of loss. I can't tell you how much I wish they had died of natural causes—cancer, car wreck, heart attack, whatever. But they chose to check out and I never got to say goodbye.

Their deaths changed who I am. I used to be pretty carefree. Life wasn't perfect but I was a pretty happy person. Now I feel a huge loss and I don't feel comfortable even telling people how my parents died when asked. I'm ashamed, I feel stigmatized. I feel like people will judge me, wonder if I have a screw loose like my parents. I don't.

I think life is an adventure and I'm thankful for the good things that come my way. I'm divorced with no kids, won't be going that route. I just wish I could move past the sadness and anger and shame. I work at moving past it but it's still with me. I've been crying inside for years, people who know me would never guess what I'm feeling except for my closest friends.

How does one get closure on something like this? It feels overwhelming to me, so huge. I envy people who lose their parents to natural causes. I envy people who have supportive families. I don't like this bitterness I carry inside. I don't want my life to feel like this.

Stuck

Dear Stuck,

ABOUT THE WAY past trauma persists in our lives, I can say this.

It is shocking, first of all, to realize the degree to which we really are who we are, that we really are the children of this thing, shaped by it, immutably, beyond our conscious ability to control or spin it. And always there are the layers, the further layers, the peeling of skin after skin to reveal the shadows of bones. That is what we are. (If I may speak solely for myself, hoping that it will make some sense to you: This whole process of my epistolary confessions overheard, overread, opened in the dark as it were, under a midnight lamp while the family is sleeping and read for secrets—what I mean is this Internet correspondence is a kind of faux-confessional; I pretend to be alone and writing just to you and that is what creates the drama: We are overhearing something. And now I am hardly even writing to you, only in the most indirect way; I am really writing somewhat circumspectly about myself alone, how the bones are revealed. And I am writing circumspectly because I do not want to flay myself in public any more than I already seem to do. I simply want to sketch the landscape. And yet as a letter writer mentioned to me this morning, it is in the details, isn't it? It's all in the details.)

So I mean to say in my roundabout, whispered way that the towering events in our past form literally the boundaries and character of our emotional experience; we are never going to be the happy carefree people we might wish to be. We are not them. The happy carefree people are people built on happy carefree ground. We are built on ashes and tangled metal. Or we are built on a cheap uncertain floor ready to give way.

No, that metaphor is not going to lead us very far. Here is another one: The world of inner reference points we have is quite solid. Your reference points are the suicides. They are like fenceposts that define the yard; you can't go much beyond them; you don't know what is out there. When you begin to cross between two fenceposts—the suicide of one, the suicide of the other—there is a pain and a fear of what is on the other side. It could be death, who knows. It could be unimaginable confusion and pain. We are bounded by these events; they circumscribe our lives. But how then can we change?

> Move the fence posts out a few feet.

One way is that we can move the fenceposts out a bit. In time, this will happen on its own. But perhaps we can help them along, by moving them out mentally a few feet at a time, gradually filling in the yard with things that we love, and perhaps eventually building a hedge where the trauma used to be. Maybe actually some night we go out with a shovel and move the fenceposts. But I do not believe, actually, that we are permitted to touch them. That is where the metaphor breaks down: These are not fenceposts in the literal sense; if you tear them down in your dreams, they probably reconstitute themselves in the morning. They are right there where they used to be. You cannot destroy the fenceposts themselves. That is what I mean about the immutability of past trauma.

But maybe sometimes we boldly walk right by them. We walk right through the fenceposts. There on the right is the suicide of my mother; there on the left is the suicide of my dad. I walk by into the night unafraid, not looking either way. And then maybe one night I walk out and I stare right at the fenceposts: There is the suicide. I stare right at it, unblinking, unflinching. There it is, that's what happened. There is the other suicide. I stand in the night sky under the stars and the moon, staring at the fenceposts and as I do the skulls of my mother and father appear at the top of the posts.

Maybe at that point I run inside.

Or maybe I don't run inside. I stand and stare. I contemplate the skulls. I contemplate the deaths. I contemplate the stars. I contemplate the night's immensity and our brief stay here. I summon courage. They are after all phantoms, these things. They did take many things from you. But they are phantoms. They cannot detach from the fenceposts and come and get you. They cannot sing or yell. They are forever on the other side of time.

This is me attempting to use spatial and temporal metaphors to get at an idea of our relationship to past trauma. It has its drawbacks. But perhaps it will be useful inasmuch as visualization can be useful.

To back away a little from the impressionistic style, however, and try to speak in more direct language, I am trying to say that the first step in dealing with such great tragedies in life is to recognize that they do indeed circumscribe our emotional lives. They are not simply going to go away. They are there, as rooted in the ground as old fenceposts. I say that as a corrective to the expectation that we should be able to easily overcome these things. We cannot. They are powerfully rooted markers, or totems, in our emotional landscape (or seascape, as I now find myself envisioning these markers on lodge poles in the sand at the edge of the sea, perhaps only because that is where I live, at the edge of the sea).

So when we look out—that is, when we feel, or when we expand our emotional feelers, when we expand our consciousness to take in the world—they are going to be there, threatening us, attempting to make us feel afraid. They are going to influence us profoundly. We are going to feel sad suddenly, or thin-skinned and overly sensitive, or angry or depressed.

It is helpful to think of these occurrences as marking a boundary—that in a moment of unexpected fear or sadness, we realize we have touched the boundary. We have encountered those phantoms on the fenceposts.

That boundary defines the emotional landscape we are left with after such a thing as parental suicide. Our task is to expand that boundary.

In response to the unpleasantness associated with these permanent markers, naturally we may contract; we may choose not to risk new ventures, the way we favor an injured leg or protect a wound, drawing inward against intrusion, wary of knocking against something.

What I am saying is that to get better we must consciously and somewhat counter-intuitively push against these boundaries, even when it hurts a little. We must try to push back against them. If we do not, we adopt habits of ever-contracting fear. In the same way that we rehab an injured knee by working it, through pain and resistance, to build it up again, so we must rehab ourselves emotionally after terrible trauma by going up against it, trying to face it, a piece at a time, reminding ourselves that it is there, trying always to go by it, to break through the fear day by day, little by little.

It helps of course to have encouragement and some kind of regular program to keep going.

The way we rehab after trauma is by re-experiencing the trauma in degrees, and strengthening our ability to do that, to hold it and not drop it and run, to look at it and not flinch in terror. We do that by talking about it. We try to talk through it without breaking down. Maybe we break down the first few times. But then we get to where we can talk through it without breaking down, which means we can regard it peacefully.

We also strengthen our ability to regard the past equably by working in or around areas that remind us of the trauma. So you might, for instance, counsel other people whose parents have committed suicide, thus gaining strength in yourself, thus playing the role not of a victim but of a survivor, someone who can help others. We also bring to consciousness the many ways these suicides crop up unexpectedly. For instance, as you are sitting talking and someone mentions something and it comes into your mind and you say it out loud; you say, "That makes me think of my parents' suicides." And you take a moment; you acknowledge its presence there, and try to contain it. And you practice making it just another phenomenon in the world, not something to be hidden, nor something to be overdramatized. Just something that is there. I'm not saying it can be taken lightly. But it can be taken. It can be borne.

Must I always be haunted by the loss of my one true love?

She was everything I'd ever dreamed of. Then there was the screech of tires on a dark street ...

Dear Cary,

IN SHORT, HERE is my situation: I can't take my mind off a woman I met, fell in love with, and lost. I guess it sounds pretty lame, but I am not your typical lovestruck college kid: I am 42; I run my own business; I raise my kids; I live in Paris, where I am active socially and politically. And I haven't seen her or talked to her in ... 19 years.

Twenty-plus years ago, I fancied myself a romantic intellectual, but of course I was only a confused and immature young lad hungry for love and sex. Though (or because) I was gentle and caring and emotional, I always ended up entangled in multiple simultaneous relationships that sometimes ended messily, but no one was really hurt and it was all good fun, learning to live and love, etc.

At the tender age of 21, I spent three months working on an exceedingly beautiful island in the Pacific, where I met this exceedingly fun and beautiful girl. The attraction was so immediate and intense that we did not take any real sleep for three weeks. Three weeks! Obviously we were having some giant fun, helped by the tropical surroundings and generally happy life we had. But there was more than that, a connection so deep that we could shiver and cry from the sheer intensity of our happiness. Corny, maybe, but true.

We went back home (it turned out we lived, like, 12 blocks away from each other), and, being the jerk I was, I was sucked back into my web of inconsequential one-nighters, unfinished love affairs, etc. Our relationship became an on-again/off-again thing that left both of us frustrated and unhappy.

Fast-forward one year. At the end of yet another silly romance, I suddenly realized that I was wasting the love of my life. I got on my knees, crawled to her door, and swore eternal devotion. This is Christmas Day, 1986, and she welcomes me with open arms. O blissful days!

Three months later, our relationship was going forward at full steam. Until one night, coming home late, she lost control of her car. In the ensuing crash, her lower body was crushed by the engine; when she was finally extracted from the wreck, she had stopped breathing.

For 10 days, she fought death from multiple internal injuries. She survived, and spent six weeks in intensive care. Soon, however, it appeared that she remembered very little. Her memory was almost entirely gone!

All the time I was here, scared to death, handling things (her family was living abroad at the time). I was flying across the country once or twice a week. And she did not even recognize me!

Our relationship was, to say the least, awkward and embarrassed. After two months of this she gently hinted that, much as she appreciated my care and attention, it was preferable that I should, well, discontinue my visits.

We didn't see much of each other for another eight months. Then she reappeared, physically all patched up and having "recovered" some of her lost memory. I was just beginning to adjust to the situation, she was scarred and I was scared, we were both very confused, and I made the biggest mistake of all: I turned her down.

That very last night, snow was falling hard on the Trocadero. A daring cab picked her up at 4 a.m. and drove away in the storm. The next morning, Paris was entirely paralyzed by the snow, the first and only time in the last 50 years.

I haven't seen her or talked to her since.

I still think of her every day.

I'd go back to her in a second, and would have at any time during all these years.

A few weeks after this, I flew away to California where I spent the next three years. Silicon Valley in the pre-Internet era was sweet and funny, energetic yet cool; I liked it very much. I met wonderful people, wrote piles of C++ code, fell in love with American literature, drove from Tijuana to Vancouver and back in a banged-up Ford Galaxy with a trunkful of weed, swam totally drunk across the Golden Gate at 2 a.m. Nature was strong, people joyful and confident, girls sweet and serious ... Everything I know of Foucault and Derrida, I learned from pretty 23-year-old Berkeley English majors, usually between 2 and 5 a.m. What a party!

But seeing the likes of Oliver North and Bush 41 on TV every day was a drag, and I went back to Europe—a few months before Gulf War I.

Since then I have done whatever could be expected of me considering my age and professional situation. I got married, had two kids, started a few businesses, kept friends, traveled, etc.

Except for my daughters, who are the sweetest things on Earth, I do not care much for any of this. My ex-wife has turned into a deranged virago, work/money/success bores me to death, and I find myself depressingly surrounded by cynical and futile 40-somethings, arrogant bastards of 30, and selfish whiners in their 20s. And don't get me started on the above-50 crowd who got us into this train wreck to begin with.

Of course, I turned 40 two years ago. That does not help.

At first, I did not get back to her because I felt guilty/ashamed for turning her down, especially since, I soon realized, she might have attributed my rejection to her being physically all stitched up, which must be hard when you are accustomed to be a head-turner, etc.

Then I tried to find her and could not. This was before the Internet really kicked in. You could not find someone who lived abroad and/or had an unlisted telephone number and/or got married and gave up her maiden name, and that was it.

Two years ago, having programmed a battalion of "Web agents" to this effect, I found her trail. It took me another year and the help of a P.I. to locate her.

When her 40th birthday came last year, I had an obscene bunch of beautiful roses delivered to her office. I did not sign the card, because I did not want to pressure her into replying out of good manners, but I wrote a nice message that was enough to identify me without being sentimental or corny or anything. Just a nice "hello" from the past, no pressure, no strings, nothing to make her uncomfortable.

I did not expect her to reply and she did not.

She is married, no kids. A dead-end job in a very sinister corporation, and no known involvement or association with anything remotely funny/cultural/political/interesting/whatever. From the outside, the upper-lower-middle-class nightmare at its best.

So I spent 19 years of my life losing sleep over a banal teenage love affair, idealizing a pretty girl who turned into a depressing matron? Am I clinging to a dying fantasy? Or am I being true to the only meaningful event of my sentimental life? Worse yet, am I making up feelings and emotions that never really took place, for 19 years is a lot of time?

I can hear my therapist laughing her ass off.

I could hop into my car and ring her doorbell in 15 minutes, but I cannot see myself doing it if my life depended on it. To think that it took me 19 years to summon the nerve to send a bunch of flowers along with a nearly anonymous message!

Those of my friends who were around at the time might remember this story, but I never bring it up. My ex-wife, kids, associates and closest friends know nothing about it. I do not feel the need to tell anyone, at least not someone I know in the flesh (hence this letter). It makes the whole thing seem unreal, like it's happening in a parallel universe. It makes it very difficult to actually do something.

Should I confront this thing and put it to rest? Would that mean re-inviting myself into her life, possible consequences unknown? Should I risk bringing confusion, embarrassment, bitterness into her life? Why stir things up? And why am I consumed by this? Because I am a sad loser trying to escape the depressing reality of being 40? Or because we loved each other so dearly, so completely that there's nothing else to do?

Or should I just forget about it? Isn't it what I've been trying to do, with little success, for 19 years? What is this thing that no quantity of love, sex, booze, excitation or work can abolish?

Or should I just keep it the way it is, a dark, warm, sweet, burning secret with a life of its own? Will it consume me, turn me into a muttering, bitter fool?

Thank you for reading so far. What a strange feeling! Here I am, telling a complete stranger, a man from a foreign culture who lives 10 time zones away, the story that most matters to me, the strange secret that has been haunting me for nearly 20 years.

I truly hope to hear from you. I mean, this letter was not a catharsis. Although I wrote it over a period of six months, it did nothing to help me understand or handle the situation better. So any help will be greatly appreciated.

Anyway, I wish you the best. You are a kind person, and kindness seems to be in short supply these days.

Stuck in Time in Paris

Dear Stuck in Time,

I AM OCCASIONALLY faced with the question of how to respond to a letter that, because of its length, its choice of detail, its style or tone, certain literary characteristics, an unusually tight dramatic structure or general air of invention, is certain to be questioned by readers as to its veracity.

I'm not saying that your letter is a fake. It is possible that your story happened exactly as you say. If it did happen exactly as you say, however, we are faced with a larger and more intriguing problem: It may be that you have fallen into the grip of a fictive god of some possibly malevolent purpose—that you, a real, living, breathing man, have somehow been mistaken for a character in someone's book and were swept into it by accident.

While it does sound extraordinary, if you think about it this sort of thing probably happens more often than we realize. With constant worldwide production of novels and short stories in all languages and genres, with so much raw action, setting, character and plot pulverized and injected into so many books every day, with rampant global over-fictionalization and the yearly release of thousands of tons of excess plot and setting into the atmosphere, it's a little surprising that this sort of thing doesn't happen more often.

Or perhaps it does.

Suppose, for instance, that you are walking along a country road and you notice yourself thinking thoughts not your own, concerning a story in which you are only a bit player—perhaps in this story you are the gardener, or a mechanic hired to fix the car that has sat in the garage for many years due to the recent death of its former owner, a wealthy but sinister landowner who used to drive it infrequently at most, only to funerals and weddings and visits to her lawyer. As you hear these voices and feel yourself swept up into a narrative not of your making, you notice that the landscape around you has become strangely artificial: The colors are too bright and a little off, the greens too green, the reds too red, as though the four-color printing process was slightly off (and it is never exact anyway). You notice that the reeds growing along the river have a trademark swirl as though painted. And you could swear you glimpsed a giant face peering down at you from the sky, a face that looks haggard, bored and unshaven, wrinkled and for-

Tell the unvarnished truth.

lorn, a lot like the face of a grandfather of yours long forgotten and also a lot like the face of a writer, a writer who peers down at his characters as he tries to move them around his shabby, makeshift little village.

In other words, suppose you discover one day that you have unaccountably become a character in someone else's fiction. Your problem then is how to break out of the grip of this author, who apparently is bored with you and not performing at his best, not providing you with appropriate or interesting parts.

I would think you would have to try and write your way out.

When a person attempts to write his way out of such a story, he is like a revolutionary picking up a gun and challenging the state. He is saying, this is not my narrative! This is not my world! It is a dangerous and possibly fatal choice. But what options does he have? Living this way is intolerable!

So I suggest that in order to free yourself of this tale, whether it actually did happen exactly as you say or whether it is only a case of mistaken fictional identity, you continue writing this tale. Fill in everything that happened. It does not matter whether these things can be verified; what is important is that you get it all down.

If you could only contact this author in whose story you may have mistakenly appeared and find out what is next in the story, you could adequately prepare. But it could be anybody—it is as though some wires were crossed, or a stranger's cellphone conversation came out of your phone. Moreover, the author, even if found, would be as astonished to see you as you would be to find him, because he has no idea that he is merely a parasite sucking some stranger's soul like a tick on a dog; he believes that he is actually making up out of nothing the things he hears and sees in his mind. It would be as if your lover suddenly showed up, magically reverted to her youthful, unscarred self, amnesiac again and ready for love: It would seem impossible.

There is no telling how long you may remain in the grip of this narrative phenomenon. So I suggest that you write it out in its entirety now, not only to free you of it, and not only so you can publish it, but also because it may be a fleeting phenomenon; if you wait a year it may vanish.

Perhaps you unconsciously do wish it to vanish, because it is painful to live in the grip of this narrative. So you may find yourself procrastinating. But I urge you to commit yourself to writing it out, all the details of setting, the things that were said, the other characters, etc. In doing so, you will probably develop or discover a certain aesthetic discipline, and will find yourself naturally limiting your tendency to over-explain yourself and to indulge in hyperbole, as if we would not believe you otherwise, as if you do not trust us. You will discover, greatly to your credit, that you are not, after all, the most interesting person in this narrative, but only its servant, only an innocent man trying to free himself of its grip by using the pen as a dagger, stabbing at the skin of your bubble, starving for air and sunlight that you know exists just beyond your enclosure.

Frankly, while I do not care so much if what you describe happened in every detail, I am bothered by one claim you make: that you swam drunkenly across the Golden Gate at 2 a.m. Perhaps because you were drunk and not a native of the area you were mistaken about what body of water you swam, but I do not think that you swam from Fort Point (http://www.nps.gov/archive/prsf/coast_defense/third_system/fort_point/ftpoint.htm) to Lime Point (http://www.nps.gov/archive/prsf/coast_defense/third_system/lime_point/limept.htm) at 2 a.m. while drunk. And frankly it irritates me that you make that claim. Imagine, for instance, if I claimed that after a night drinking with Michel Houellebecq and Michel Bulteau (http://www.durationpress.com/authors/bulteau/exile.htm) at Shakespeare & Company that I swam the Seine and scaled the Cathédrale de Notre-Dame de Paris single-handedly, all the while playing "I'm a Yankee Doodle Dandy" on my Hohner harmonica.

But as you note correctly, I am a kind person. I do not wish to belittle you. I wish to help. I have no score to settle. Perhaps you did indeed swim the Golden Gate while drunk at 2 a.m. If so, I salute you, and I will meditate on why this particular claim seems to infuriate me so—as though the Golden Gate were some sacred watery portal to our jeweled city (comparable, perhaps, to your River Seine?).

Anyway, whatever happened in your life is indeed a profound mystery, one toward which we owe nothing but respect. In telling your story, you can perhaps recapture the driving force that compelled you to take these risks and seek these pleasures in the first place. As you write, try to distinguish the influence of that other author from your authentic voice. I think as you do so you will find hints of a third presence as well, something heavy and mysterious, dark and insistent, a vessel in the fog beyond all your thoughts and ideas that has been beckoning to you all this time, vying for your attention, waiting to pull you toward your destiny.

When you find that vessel in the fog, grab the rope that dangles from it and hold on.

My boyfriend can't handle my past

*He asked me how many and I told him.
Now how can I be pure enough for him?*

Dear Cary,

LYING DOESN'T COME naturally to me. I have to think about a lie—plan it out ahead of time—and even then, I'm unlikely to go through with it. My first instinct is to tell the truth, even when I wish immediately afterward that I hadn't.

So that's why my boyfriend knows a little too much about my slightly storied past.

We started dating nine months ago. A month or two later, I let him talk me into telling him how many people I'd been with. Though my number was half his, he got upset. He said he had pictured me as "pure" and that the standards are different for men. Worse, a couple of months ago, he asked if I had ever been part of a ménage à trois, and I told him that I had. He was heartbroken. He says he thinks about it almost every day and it sometimes makes him physically ill. He's brought it up to me a few times—he asks me, "What are you going to do about this?" as if the past is something broken that I can fix. I get frustrated and defensive (especially since he's been with two women at once himself). He tells me in 20 different ways he wishes I were pure. I make offers—I'll talk to a priest, I'll go on a fast, I'll help him read up on forgiveness, I'll let him chop off one of my fingers ...

We love each other. I've never been in love before, and I've never enjoyed sex as much as I do with him. It always ends OK. But he's going to keep bringing it up. I'm really fine with him being old-fashioned. I am ashamed of my past, but I've forgiven myself. I think he's being punishing and ungenerous. Can you help us think of some way I can help him get over this?

Thank you so much for the understanding and creative advice you give. I hope you can direct us to a more productive way of looking at this.

Shamed and Frustrated

Dear Shamed and Frustrated,

YOU ARE NOT a product. You do not have an expiration date. You are not sold used or new. Your value does not go down with every sexual experience. You do not have a finite capacity, like a phone card, after which you are used up.

Neither are you a substance that can be pure or impure. You are no less pure now than when you were born. You will never be less pure than you are right now.

Nor are you an object upon which men have left marks that your boyfriend may discover and interpret. You are not a public place were things are written for others to read. You are not an exotic land that men have visited and reminisce about in comfortable chairs.

You are not a collection of experiences like snapshots in an album, subject to perusal and approval by your boyfriend.

Your past is not a term paper for him to grade. Your past is not something that needs to be repaired. You can't get up on top of it with a ladder and fix it like a roof. You can't do anything about it except regard it with awed attention. It is like the sea, far beyond us, far too deep, far too wide, far too powerful.

You are not a product, or a substance, or an object. You are not any of these things. For want of a better term, you are a creature, a spiritual being.

We are creatures of flesh and light and movement. We go through life. Things happen. We do things. We remember things. Things hurt us, things delight us, things frighten us. We go on. We describe the things that have happened to us and look for the light of understanding in someone's eyes. We are creatures who love and hate. We love and hate and are loved and hated and we go on.

> You are not an exotic land that men have visited.

Our past is not a map on our skin, visible to the male gaze. Our past is something we tell. Once we tell it, people sometimes turn away. They can't bear it. They're not strong enough. They have to find the strength. We can't give them the strength. They ask us to put the past back in the past, but we can't do that either. Once we tell it, it's with us in the present.

So tell your boyfriend to lay off with all this talk. Tell him to get some wisdom and some understanding. Tell him to get some humility and some awe. Tell him to go sit by the sea and think about it for days on end until his head hurts and he's thirsty and all he wants is you—however you are, whoever you are, wherever you've been, whatever you've done.

Take my virginity—please!

I'm caught in a sexual Catch-22: Because I've never done it, no one will do it with me.

Dear Cary,

ALL RIGHT, SO let's have at it.

I'm 24 years old, and I'm a virgin. I've recently moved to a new place and I'm really confused about what kind of situation I've put myself in. I am not abstaining because I'm religious, or even because I'm waiting for marriage. More than anything, I'm abstaining because it seems like every single time I try to have sex, something gets screwed up.

I have been in multiple situations regarding my virginity—I've been in love with a boyfriend who turned out to be a cokehead and became abusive right before I was about to tell him that I was ready to have sex. I've been in situations where I was casually dating or fooling around with a guy, and I felt comfortable enough to sleep with him. Usually, in these kinds of situations, I will explain that I am not in love, but comfortable enough to have sex. Most of the time, this results in the guy flipping out, saying he cannot handle the pressure and saying we can still fool around but he won't be my first.

My virginity is starting to seem like more of a liability than anything else. I am tired of feeling like a child, or even a late bloomer. I almost feel like I have been waiting all of this time for something, but it just never shows up. I cannot tell if I am romanticizing the whole thing, or even what my expectations are at this point. Specifically, I'm just about ready to throw my hands up and become a nun.

The worst part is, I feel totally ready to have sex at this point—but none of the guys I have dated seem to believe me. They think once we sleep together, I'm going to become some kind of psycho-stalker that picks through their garbage at night. I don't think I'm ugly or unattractive, but I feel like I'm forgetting how to date because it's become so frustrating and such a problem.

Do you have any words of wisdom for the girl who waits to have sex—and isn't a Jesus freak?

Virgin in Virginia

Dear Virgin,

WHY DO YOU have to tell a man you're a virgin before you sleep with him?

I may be missing something here. There may be a good reason. I'd just like to get clear on what the reason is.

Perhaps you want to tell him so that this important event is a shared emotional experience. That's understandable. But does that mean you have to tell him? Is it mandatory? Do you have a choice about whether to tell him or not?

> There is almost always a first time.

I think you do have a choice. I think it's your body and where it's been before is not necessarily his business. If your past sexual history presents no danger to him, then why must he know?

Sure, it would be nice to talk about it together. But if talking about it seems to bring nothing but trouble, then why talk about it?

I've known women whose very first time was a well-thought-out act, full of mutual caring and respect. And I've known women who just got tired of being a virgin and went out to get laid. Neither approach guarantees lifelong happiness.

What if you were not a virgin and felt you had to confess this to every prospective partner? What if every time you told a man you were not a virgin, you risked rejection? Wouldn't it seem cruel and sexist? Wouldn't you question the rule that said you had to confess your non-virginity? Wouldn't you want to be accepted for who you are, and not judged on your sexual history? Luckily, in our society, it's no shame for a woman not to be a virgin. So why should it be a shame to be a virgin? Why should that be an issue at all? If it's not necessary to reveal your non-virginity, why is it necessary to reveal your virginity?

It seems to me that the relevant fact regarding your sexual status is this: You are ready and willing to have sex. Why not just leave it at that and see where the relationship goes?

If a relationship should lead to sex, and you really feel you must tell him, why not tell him afterward? Just brush the hair out of your face and say, "So that's what sex is all about! No wonder people talk about it. Let's do this again—soon!"

The look on his face will be worth photographing.

The two=introvert problem

Can two quiet types go on a date without excruciating embarrassment?

Dear Cary,

I'M A LIFELONG introvert. Somewhere along the line, I picked up enough social cues to fool most people into thinking I'm a good talker, but the truth is that I'm exhausted by social interaction and am happy spending much of my time alone.

I prefer spending time alone to light dating—it's less tiring. That said, I enjoy being in serious or steady relationships. Right now, I'm single, but am very interested in a friend of a friend. He's very intelligent, thoughtful, funny and unique in all the right ways. He likes me too—he has made it obvious to our friends and, in his way, to me, too.

The problem is that we have pretty similar levels of introversion. We're both more comfortable talking about highly complex theoretical issues (he's a Ph.D. student, and I'm a theory nerd) than we are doing the verbal waltz promoting typical flirtation. As a result, we are painfully awkward around each other. We've both tried to have get-to-know-you conversations, but the interactions end up being painfully stilted—even when we're both inebriated.

The last time I dated an introvert, I played the drama queen. In exchange for his putting up with my emotional outbursts, I mommied my then boyfriend. That's the only way I know how to interact romantically with an introvert—and I'm uninterested in repeating it.

That leaves me in the dark. I find myself caring about this person deeply even though I don't know him well. I really want to ask him out on a date, but I'm afraid that it will turn out be fatally awkward because I'm unwilling to play the role of the talkative self-explorer (which would enable him to stay in his comfort zone as the questioner). Is there a solution? Like a library date where we both read books and occasionally throw each other shy glances? Do I just need to swallow my fear, step out and express myself even though it's about as comfortable as walking naked through glass wool insulation? Or is it really true that an introvert needs to date an extrovert, a serious person needs to date a lighthearted one, etc.? Am I whispering up the wrong tree?

Too Shy to Bark

Dear Too Shy,

THAT'S A REALLY interesting question.

Apparently what we have here is an area of human interaction—courtship—so completely colonized by extroverts that even an intelligent and thoughtful person such as yourself is only dimly aware that there might be alternatives.

And yet there must be alternatives. Otherwise, introverts would never reproduce. And I refuse to countenance the notion that these alternatives just take the form of painfully awkward reenactments of extroverted styles.

There must be another way. For instance: I'm not sure if you were being sarcastic or not, but the library date sounds perfectly reasonable to me. As does the bookstore date. As does just being silent with each other.

The other day I watched an attractive young couple come into a cafe. The young man went to the counter and got some coffee drinks. The woman sat at the table. The young man came back and they sat drinking their coffee drinks. They looked at each other. They looked at the table. They looked around the room.

They drank their drinks. They were quiet. They seemed comfortable with each other, and yet there was also a kind of intensity in the air. They didn't say a word the whole time they were there.

I wondered what was going on. I thought they might have just had a fight, or maybe just made love, or perhaps someone they knew had just died.

But perhaps—and this is what is most intriguing—perhaps this was nothing unusual at all. Perhaps they were introverts who, recognizing that they had to be out among the draining hordes, decided to contain their energy rather than filling the air with chatter. Perhaps they were together in a cafe and that was enough. Maybe it was enough to simply sit together.

Had I not been observing, their silence might have gone unnoticed, as the other people in the cafe were intent on each other and on their conversations, or their laptops or their books.

Now, it's true that introversion is not the same thing as silence at all. It's not that introverts don't like to talk. What I'm suggesting, though, is that introverts must find ways to insulate themselves from the effects of a crowded, draining world, and one of those ways is to consciously resist the felt pressure to chatter. I would encourage you to explore the boundaries of what is permitted to two people who simply like each other and want to be together. Why should you have to pretend to be extroverted?

Suit your style to your style.

What you need, perhaps, is a manifesto, an explicit declaration granting you existential permission.

Maybe something like this:

"Whereas we are both introverts and do not care for small talk, finding it on the whole a trivial and demeaning pursuit; and Whereas we have spent our lives feeling inadequate to the task of small talk when in reality we feel that small talk is simply stupid and unattractive and do not care to participate in it; and Whereas rather than openly attack the majority for indulging in small talk we have patiently tried our best to imitate it, however unskillfully, and have never received our due for such selfless and humiliating attempts to make extroverts feel less uncomfortable with their shallow and meaningless lives; and Whereas neither one of us really cares whether the other can skillfully imitate the small talk of others anyway; and Whereas being highly intuitive we perceive plenty about the other person without having to go through the tedious process of a rote question-and-answer conversation, which moreover we would find nearly obscene in its deadly obtuseness; and Whereas we are two free human beings freely choosing to associate in the manner that suits us both; and Whereas we feel confident that if we spend some time together we will, being each of us intellectually nimble, in due time find ample ground for conversation;

Therefore be it resolved that, finding some initial interest in each other, we will commit to spending a sufficient amount of time together without either of us forcing upon the other any conventional, preconceived notions, with particular care not to assume any of the rote behaviors associated with the "dating" mode, and pledge moreover to give due consideration to any and all modes of togetherness including silent trips to the library, the viewing of movies without comment, mutual reading, meals taken in relative silence, long drives during which little is said, and, further, given that our thoughts, when voiced, often are of a complex and many-faceted variety requiring relatively lengthy elucidation, we pledge that should such thoughts begin to be voiced, the one who is listening will provide the one who is speaking ample and necessary time in which to complete such thoughts, and will provide such periodic promptings as might be necessary to reassure the other that in spite of the radically compressed norms of extroverted conversation he or she is not in fact going on too long but is actually enlarging on the subject in a manner that is exceedingly pleasing in its richness and detail."

I figure that might alter the context sufficiently so you can just relax and be who you are.

It's sort of amazing, is it not, that just such an explicit set of alternate assumptions on behalf of introverts has not heretofore been widely promulgated? Could that be because the extroverted majority forces its arbitrary mode of behavior on us with such overwhelming and yet invisible force? And could this be analogous to the way that assumptions about gender and race were once so powerful and all-encompassing as to act upon us invisibly?

And then one day it was all painstakingly disassembled and laid out on the floor before us, and we saw that what we had once considered "natural" was nothing more than the half-baked assumptions of a tyrannical majority.

So make up your own set of assumptions.

I dropped out of psych graduate school and don't know what to do!

I majored in film and media, but thought it was too impractical.

Dear Cary,

I'M 26 YEARS old and I recently left a doctorate program in clinical psychology abruptly after only one semester. I quit school for several reasons but primarily I was feeling burnt out (I had recently completed a two-year master's degree in the field), I no longer felt excited enough about the field to justify 10 hours of work per day, and I hated that I was going to be spending five to six years of my life in a part of the country (typically referred to as the "armpit") that I absolutely hated.

I moved to New York City and searched for jobs outside of psychology to no avail. I thought I could go into ad copywriting, perhaps to use my psychology training for evil instead of good. However, after two months spent without work, school, or any friends to speak of, I became desperate. I eventually had to swallow my pride and ask my father for help; so when he put me in touch with an old business friend who offered me a job, I jumped at the chance. Fast-forward three months and I am utterly miserable here. The job is not challenging, the office environment is lonely, and frankly, I feel diminished working in a position that doesn't technically require a college degree. The icing is that it pays so poorly I have to get financial help from my parents, which truly bothers me.

I am in an existential panic—I have no idea what field or career I would like to pursue at this point and yet I want to be there already. I went to college for film and media studies but I have absolutely no faith in my ability to become any kind of writer. In fact, I entered into psychology because it appeared to be a safe and secure career path (as opposed to trying to make it as a creative). My girlfriend is trying to convince me to go to law school so that I will have more career options, but I can feel the same forces of practicality that sent me into psychology pulling me toward that decision. I'm not OK exploring lots of different careers at this point in my life; I feel like I had that opportunity and I used it on psychology. So I guess my question is: How do I even begin to figure out what to do with my life ... simple, right?

Ph.D. Dropout

Dear Ph.D. Dropout,

I HAVE A solution for you. But first, I would ask you to consider briefly this extraordinary moment in history, to kindle some small flame of gratitude in your heart, to temper your bereft desperation with appreciative awe. What you suffer, after all, is a luxury of choices. How did it come to pass, anyway, that rather than tilling a stony field sunup to sundown you are living in an opulent laboratory amid a torrent of splendid images, as if inside a jewel that reflects back to us all of history and all the visions of poets and artists and charlatans and all the daily creations of actors and musicians and painters and people who work in media we did not even know would exist a few years ago. This sensorium we inhabit is vast and complex beyond all imagining; it is like nothing ever created on earth.

And yet often all we can do is sit in this jeweled garden and cry out, It is too much! Too much! Too much! Overwhelmed with choice, sated creatures of a culture warlike but creative, ignorant but rich, we put our faces in our hands and weep. It is too much!

I know. It is too much. All these choices make us anxious. That is how we are. I am anxious too. I am not grateful. I am desperate and hungry and dissatisfied and restless just like you.

But I know, nonetheless, that all my vexatious choices are a gift. The only torment is choosing.

I do not mean to be moralistic; I only want to say, please, my son, before we turn and go back into the castle to consider these matters, look out over these hills, this land, this miracle: Be grateful you have a choice.

Do what you love.

But OK. Enough already. Just the same, the fact is, you're stuck. You're lost. You're in a tough spot. You took some turns and now life sucks. So here is what you do:

Go back to what you know. It's like when you're lost in a car, you get back to where you were when you knew where you were and where you were going.

In college, you knew what you wanted to do. You wanted to work in film and media studies.

You probably still do.

So go back to that spot and recover what you had. Get back to that moment when you were enthralled.

You may have doubted that you were on the right course. It may have seemed impractical. You had to find out. So you found out. Now you know. Psychology is not for you.

Perhaps you tried to be adult about it and put aside film and media studies in order to be practical. But doing what you don't want is not practical. If you are not suited to it, it is not practical. You are not all that motivated to get something you do not all that much want. So you will not work all that hard to get it and you will not excel so greatly in the endeavor. Others who desire it with all their hearts will pass you, and you will wonder why you are even trying, since it is so hard for you and since you do not even enjoy the work or want it all that much anyway.

There is, on the other hand, much practicality in working toward what you want, even if it is difficult. If you are working for what you want, you are using your hungers to your advantage.

When we do the things we love we create congruence between motivation and talent; we come alive. When we are brought to life by doing what we love, we do it well, and people notice, and they hire us. When we are only pretending, we languish and suffer, doing mediocre work begrudgingly, hating our lives and those around us, and we die poor and unhappy.

So do what you love.

It is hard to do what you love. It takes more work than doing what is simply available. But it is the right thing to do. And in the end it is the most practical choice.

I'm an artist terrified
of the vast, blank canvas

I know I have talent but I'm afraid to paint.

Dear Cary,

I GRADUATED FROM high school nine years ago, and kind of just drifted aimlessly out into the world. For my entire life, art and English (particularly art) have been my great strengths and loves. I've been drawing since I was 3, painting since early high school, and reading voraciously and attempting new novels at least once a year all throughout.

So it seems logical that one of those subjects would be my chosen major for college. I always assumed I'd be an art major. I won awards in high school, even though I didn't really understand the significance of such a thing, and was accepted to special programs. In fact, I was so immersed in art that I let all other classes fall by the wayside and left myself with a GPA that would require me to attend a junior college before transferring to a university. Then, after I graduated high school, something funny happened. I had to work right away in order to get a car, so that I could drive to school, and somewhere in there I became so interested in so many things that I kind of just lost my sense of direction.

Over the years I have continued to paint on my own, although I have not been incredibly prolific, all the while intending to return to school. Finally, two years ago I returned to junior college and embarked on a course of study that I intended to have prepare me for a major in biopsychology, which is an incredibly rigorous major. I'm not even sure what drew me to this major, other than that I have a great amount of interest in how the brain works in response to mental illness, as my mother is schizophrenic. So, for the past two years I've been telling myself that I was going to go on and work in this field, probably teach it at a university, and maybe do some research. Everyone who sees my artwork asks me if I plan on doing something with it, and encourages me to do so, but I always brushed it off, despite the fact that if I could, I would drop everything else and paint for a living.

The past year or so I've been creating a little more often, and my skill has grown exponentially; it's like suddenly after years of stagnation I feel so natural in front of the canvas. My general sense of color and my actual technique have both grown by leaps and bounds, and more and more I have felt the tug to work creatively. It's like I'm seeing the world again the way I used to, everything is something that I can use on canvas as a part of my expression. This sounds like a great thing, and it is, but it is also the reason I need advice.

I was sitting in front of the canvas working the other day and it occurred to me that the entire reason I have not considered an art major as a real possibility since high school is that I am afraid to do so. I mean, one of my major goals has been to teach at a university, and obviously I could do that as either an art teacher or a biopsychology teacher. I think that I have been afraid that if I choose art as a major, that I will fail, I will have wasted my money on a major/degree that won't get me anywhere. I just don't know what to do. Should I take the risk and declare myself an art major and just go for it? Or should I declare another major that, although I find really interesting, is not one of my strengths?

Aimless Artist

Dear Aimless Artist,

YOU WERE SITTING in front of the canvas and realized you were afraid.

You figured it was fear of failure. But I don't think so. I think it was fear of discovery.

When an artist sits before a blank canvas frozen with fear it is because the subject is too terrifying to admit to consciousness. It is no mystery; rather, it is a truth that cannot be easily contained, that threatens to break one down. So one tries to hold it at bay. Thus you sit, immobilized, holding back the truth.

I think that truth is what you went through as a child, your story of growing up with a schizophrenic mother, how it affected your personality and your outlook on the world. I think that you are afraid to become a painter because if you become a painter you will have to discover the truth of your past. You will have to paint your mother.

It is good to do the things that terrify us the most.

So have her sit for you. Painting your mother will force you to regard her serenely, to study her features carefully and at length. You will learn to see her as she is: her dimensions, her color, her symmetry, her expressions. To paint her accurately you will have to look at her for a long time. In doing so, you may experience feelings that had been buried or frozen. That will be good. You may find yourself weeping as you paint. That will be good.

Just paint.

You may hear the sound of icebergs falling into the sea. That will be good. It will be good to feel these things that you have held at bay for so long, and to feel them as a man now, not as a child, as a man capable of containing them and shaping them with your talent.

I suspect that one reason you are drawn to biopsychology is that you have a desire to fix your mother. But there is another way you can fix her. You can fix her on the canvas. Painting is your strength. That is what you need to use to fix your mother.

I know this is all a bit much. But I too wandered aimlessly after high school, and I too am a sensitive person who grew up in some degree of chaos and later had trouble learning to form coherent plans and carry them out.

I think I have something in common with you. I do not mean to frighten you. But I do mean to push you. I think you need to be pushed, as I at times have needed to be pushed. I think you need to spend some time feeling the way you were affected. You need to face this fact: You were raised by a woman who was mentally ill. Her behavior shaped you in unalterable ways. It hurt you but as compensation it also pushed you toward beauty. It is your calling to unearth and portray the way that she affected you. You have been shirking that calling. It is a painful calling and naturally we try to avoid painful things. That is what all the wandering was about. But you could wander forever and this truth would continue calling to you. It is the thing you need to deal with, the dragon you need to slay.

It is your calling, your truth: how it felt to have a mother whose world was a shattered vessel.

At what point can I just give up on my son?

As a mom and as a daughter
I'm at the end of my rope.

Dear Cary,

I HAVE A hard question for you. At what point do you give up on a child?

I had my son when I was 19 (something I would never advise to anyone else). After he was born, my mother told me it would be easier to live with her (even though she is a hideous slob and I'm a neat freak), and because of her schedule (she's a teacher), she could watch him for me in the evenings while I worked and went to college.

That seemed fine. After my son was 2, I moved out but continued to let her watch him on weekends while I worked as a waitress. Then I found out that she was teaching him to lie to me behind my back ("Don't tell Mommy I got this for you—it'll make her mad. Just pretend you've had it all along"), taking him to movies I didn't want him to see (I'm sorry, a 4-year-old does not need to see "Jurassic Park"—the nightmares he had were proof), and telling him, "Wouldn't it be fun if you lived with me all the time?"

Fast-forward 10 years. The entire time I've been working hard (even dropping out of college for a time so he wouldn't grow up the way I did—poor with kids making fun of his clothes), attending school functions, and basically just trying to be as good a mom as I knew how. I know I'm far from perfect, but I did try. When he was 12, we moved to the coast so I could attend law school in another city (a city far, far away from the hick town I grew up in). My husband is trying very hard to be a good stepfather, but my son wants none of it. After about a year, I let him go to my mother's for the summer. When he comes back, his grades drop from A's and B's to F's. Turns out he's been doing his homework (under our supervision), then taking it to school and throwing it away. Then he starts acting out, starting fights, running away (only a couple of blocks away), etc. We try counseling, medication, nothing works. Finally he tells us that he's going to be as bad as he has to be until he's sent to live with his grandmother.

I was in the middle of finals at my first year of law school and at my wits' end, so I sent him back. I thought I was doing him a favor, taking him away from my backwoods hillbilly beginnings (my mother thinks evolution is a trick from the devil), getting him into a more culturally diverse area. I figured it would be temporary. Guess what? He doesn't want to come back. He is now "saved" and makes constant excuses not to come visit. What's more, I can only talk to him by calling my mother and she rarely answers her phone and "loses" any mail I send him. (Seriously, I called three times a day for eight weeks straight and got nothing.) But he's making good grades, even though he's abandoned all the activities he was doing out here (violin, art, etc.).

No one else in my family will have anything to do with my mother. She was abusive when my siblings and I were young, then "found Jesus" and became such a nut about it that none of her kids speak to her. Every time I call and get no answer, I get angry and get headaches. I'm angry at both of them, and if I had known this was how things would turn out, I would have put him up for adoption with a nice, normal, middle-class couple in a city. Now he's going to turn into an uneducated, mullet-sporting Jesus freak, and quite frankly, I'm ready to wash my hands of the entire situation.

He clearly doesn't want to be here with me. He makes no effort to contact me. Neither of them answer the phone when it rings. Quite frankly, I don't think trying to be his mother is worth all the anger and heartache anymore. I tried to reach them for three weeks about booking his ticket to come visit for the summer, but never got a response. Finally I just booked the ticket. Two days before he was to come out for the entire summer, he calls and says he only wants to stay a month because he wants to stay with his grandmother and go to church camp (which I remember from my own youth—it's where you get the real good drugs).

Can I cut him off? I seriously spend half my day just wishing my mother would die. It would solve a few problems.

At what point do I say, "This is not my kid anymore—this is her kid"? Please help.

Giving Up on the Kid

Dear Giving Up on the Kid,

GIVING UP ON the kid is not an option.

He's got problems. He's in trouble. He can't talk about what's going on with him. He needs you. He's going to hurt you, but he needs you. He's not an adult. He's a kid. He's not responsible for what's going on. He needs you.

There is no quick fix for this situation. You are all in it for the duration—your mom, your husband, your son. So I suggest that you take the long view. Begin now by contacting people who can provide you support long-term.

You say, "We try counseling, medication, nothing works." I think you may need to redefine "working." You are bound to this boy by blood, by motherhood, by familial obligation, by law. You cannot walk away. It's not a matter of trying these things and abandoning them if they don't work. It's a matter of establishing a long-term way of living that has the best chance of ameliorating the damage that is already done and preparing the way for growth. If you don't see progress, that doesn't mean progress isn't being made. You have to pick a path and stick to it.

While you are focused on your son, there is another part of the equation. You, also, are in trouble and need help. This has got to be extremely painful for you. You need help managing the emotional pain you are in. You are having trouble not only with your son but also with your mother. You are in a very difficult situation. Ditching your son would not help. Saying that you would like to ditch your son, and saying that you wish your mother were dead are, I believe, only your ways of expressing the enormous emotional pain you are in. It is probably hard for you to even say it directly that you are in pain. It is also impossible for your son to say he is in pain. You are both expressing things by taking symbolic actions. Saying you are in need of help may feel like an admission of weakness. It may be the same way for your son.

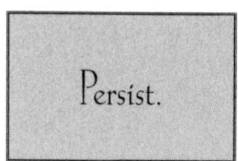

Persist.

But the truth is that you need to bring people into your lives who can be a source of stability and strength week in and week out. It will be slow going. There will be no quick fixes. But it is the only thing you can do that holds the possibility of getting through the next 10 years with some dignity and some understanding, and without a tragic outcome.

Start now. Get back in counseling with him. Get in counseling by yourself. Involve your husband. Join a group of parents with difficult children. Join a group of adult children who were abused by their parents. Participate regularly. Make it a part of your life. Accept that progress will be slow.

Hang in there. Let people help you. Reach out.

Consider yourself in a permanent struggle. Stay in the game. You can't give up on the kid.

American beauty

Are all marriages destined for the doldrums?

Dear Cary,

I HAVE A brief but immense question which I don't think you have addressed directly to date. It has been nagging at me for a while now, but it came back when I started rewatching "American Beauty" tonight. In fact, I paused the DVD 15 minutes into the movie to write you this e-mail.

My history isn't particularly relevant to this question, which I think is pretty universal. But just to be thorough: I am in my early 30s and was raised in households of High Drama (many parental fights, of the screaming, throwing-things, raising-bruises sort, between my mother and father, mother and her boyfriend, father and stepmother, etc., although never toward me).

My relationships (up until the current one) were similarly Dramatic and typically dysfunctional. At a certain point I realized that this wasn't what I wanted, so I took about five years off from all relationships to work on myself and clarify what I wanted. I am pleased to report that my current boyfriend and I have been living happily together for the last six months, after having been good friends for about a year and a half. He is an intelligent, kind, decent, funny and mentally stable man who's also had his share of bad relationships and is motivated to avoid falling into another one. When there's a problem, we are both able to take a break, then come back and work things out rationally. (Hooray!) He's my best friend, we do everything together, he makes me unbearably happy.

Now for the brief question. It seems like all relationships, over time, naturally degrade in either one of two ways: High Drama (as seen in my childhood), or complacent alienation (c.f., "American Beauty"). Surely there must be a third option? What is it, and how do I get there?

I know so many couples who started out just like us, young and happy, and 20 years down the road they wake up and realize they're trapped in a sterile, loveless marriage. They look back and think, "We were so happy back then in the beginning!"

What happens? And how best to avoid it? I have learned how to avoid High Drama, but how do I head off the "American Beauty" scenario? It terrifies me to think that one day I might look back at myself today and wonder, "What happened?"

Needing Insight

Dear Needing Insight,

THERE ARE WORKSHOPS where you can exercise your relationship to give it bigger muscles and more stamina, but my relationship tends to walk by those kinds of things and look in the window and go, ooh, that's scary what they're doing in there. My relationship is kind of shy about working on itself. So instead, each of us in the relationship tends to work on ourselves separately so that when we come together we're more interesting to each other than we would be otherwise. I don't know if that's what it says to do in the book. We didn't buy the book. I'm not even sure what book we're talking about. What I'm talking about is trying to have a rich and full relationship with another person by first being true to yourself.

Being true to yourself these days pretty much means joining the resistance. My wife and I belong to the resistance. We communicate with our friends by Morse code on old-fashioned crystal radio sets. We hide out in church basements and French farmhouses. That keeps us focused on what's important: overcoming the Nazis, fighting tyranny, finding good cheeses.

It's hard to remain independent and quirky. The Vichy regime has so many inducements: healthcare, vacations, cars and boats. But look at how you have to dress to have those things! The uniforms! Look at the way they talk in elevators! So you have to join the resistance. Otherwise they'll beat you down and your marriage will become loveless and sterile. You will look at your partner one day and you'll wonder if he isn't working for the Vichy.

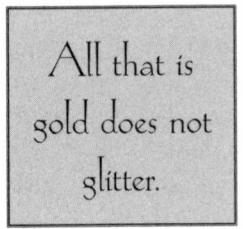

All that is gold does not glitter.

So how do you stop loving someone? Do you just run out of person? Is a person like a jam jar and you finally get to the bottom? If we are like jam jars, then we have to keep filling ourselves up, so when they stick the knife in and start scraping around, there's something sweet to put on toast. You're never out of everything. Rummage around. You've always got something. You have to always be refilling yourself.

Don't assume you're enough as you are. Who could possibly be enough? Superman, maybe. The rest of us have to work at it.

Stay desperate. Make that your motto: We're desperate. Get used to it.

Stay one step ahead of the law. Don't ever get too clean. Disguise yourself when you visit the drugstore for a prescription. Live like a happy, contented spouse, and wait for your moment ... be mad but not out of control ... be contrary but not reflexive ... write incomprehensible verses deep in the night while everyone else is sleeping ... Take long walks by the river before they arise ... resist assimilation ... pass notes to strangers in the park ... remain obdurately convinced of the rightness of your most controversial beliefs ... occasionally be inconsolable ... `refuse to name your sources ... stay silent under torture ... beware of existence fatigue ... do not believe anyone who calls himself a spokesman ... question yourself mercilessly about your recent whereabouts ... organize yourself for maximum speed ... refuse to use the cruise control ... neither fear nor trust your neighbors ... have a suitcase always packed ... keep your passport handy ...

learn a little Arabic ... do not discuss John Ashcroft with any-one. Learn to operate the crystal radio set, and locate the finest cheeses.

In this manner you may survive, and avoid a loveless, sterile marriage.

Suicide isn't painless

How do you get over the suicide of a dear
friend and the feeling that you could
have prevented it?

Dear Cary,

I'VE READ YOUR column for quite awhile now, for the most
part agreeing with your advice on life and love. Now I need some
advice on death and the life afterward.

A week ago I found out that a friend committed suicide. He
wasn't a particularly close friend to me personally, but he was
with several of our mutual friends and it's hit them very hard. I'll
recount what I know—some of it is firsthand, some second—so
that you have some background.

Bill was a great and likable guy. His death took everyone
by surprise because things seemed to be looking up for him.
Apparently (and this I've only heard recently) he struggled for his
entire life with a type of eating disorder that he kept hidden from
almost everyone. I certainly had no idea, but like I said we were
friendly but not close. About a year ago, he began to get help for
his problems and even went away for some time to a facility out
West to get a start. At around the same time, he and Nicole, his
girlfriend of several years, had broken up. They'd been having
problems (again we are dipping into hearsay) regarding his eating habits and other relationship issues.

Bill had continued to work on his food problems and seemed to
be making a lot of progress. I know I saw him eating out with our
group much more often, something that, in hindsight, I realized

I'd not seen much before. I say "in hindsight" because until it was pointed out to me, I never really noticed.

Fast-forward to this year. Bill had gotten a promotion at work, he'd made some great improvements on his house, and we'd talked at length one evening when everyone was together about dogs because he was thinking about getting another dog to keep his aging Aussie company. About three weeks ago he left for a trip to Britain. He'd always been a big fan of the U.K. and had gone there for New Year's a few years back with a few mutual friends.

About a day after he was supposed to return, the packages started arriving. Each one was a brief note and a CD with just a single song on it. I'm not sure if it was a twisted sense of humor or an earnest plea, but the song was "Please Don't Talk About Me When I'm Gone." Tom, the closest to him of our mutual friends, told me that after he'd gotten to London, he rented a small apartment, toured the city, apparently sent out the packages, and then used some chemicals he bought from a photographic supply store to create a toxic gas. I did a little reading online, and apparently it only takes a few lungfuls. He'd gone so far as to post letters the same day to the local police asking them to come and collect him and warning them about the gas. He'd even placed a notice on the door to the small bathroom, written out in several languages, warning people away without protection.

And now his friends and family, myself included, can't stop asking how we missed it. How couldn't we see it? He'd obviously been planning this for a long time. He put all his affairs in order before he left, leaving copies of his living will, will, bank statements in a folder on his desk. I don't understand how someone could make all that effort to help themselves at the same time they are planning to kill themselves.

I know, both from other articles of yours and from others, that talking is probably all I can do to help myself and our friends who were closer. But I can't help thinking there's something we could have done.

Do you have any advice for me or my friends?

In Pain

Dear In Pain,

SUICIDE BEQUEATHS THE living an excruciating choice. Our grief for the victim mocks our anger at the perpetrator. Torn between anger and grief we go about in a daze, unable to scream or cry. Perhaps we curse the gods, but they had nothing to do with it. Perhaps we curse the pressures of modern life, or the failures of psychiatry.

But the truth is, our dead friend is a murderer.

How to choke that down?

So he murdered himself and not someone else. Is that less a crime? It only mires us in contradiction.

You can't feel all of what you feel at once. So you have to feel things one at a time. It's a lot of feeling to do. It can wear you out.

So what to do? Split the object of our emotions into two, the victim, whom we loved, and the perpetrator, whom we despise? Is there indeed one person who kills and one who is killed? Perhaps in all suicides there is an innocent, who would never have chosen to die, and that is the one we mourn. Perhaps also there is the calculating and murderous tyrant who kills, the one who, bereft of imagination, crippled by pain and hopelessness, ends up, as Thomas Hardy said, in "That shabby corner of God's allotment where he lets the nettles grow, and where all unbaptized infants, notorious drunkards, suicides, and others of the conjecturally damned are laid."

Suicide rains feelings down on us. Among our profound and decent reactions of pious grief come the trivial, the perverse, the cruel and contemptible—how come he gets to check out and the rest of us have to deal with this? Who said he could leave early? Have we been had?

Plus there is no closure. It's too sudden an exit. Lacking good-bye, you may feel unsettled. It may help in those moments of unsettledness to recognize how raw, unformed, mysterious, epic and ancient is this feeling of losing a friend to suicide; out of that might come a reminder of the true scale, the breadth, the range of our reality, and perhaps, having sensed the range, you may find your present problems diminish in their power.

But if this style of coping verges on the sentimental, beware: There is no lesson in suicide; those who kill themselves are not teaching us anything; instead, they're robbing us. Sentimentalizing suicide only encourages others who, weak-minded, pained, lacking the ability to see how foolish and wrong it is, might succeed all too well in their feeble attempts. So do not say that out of this comes a lesson. There is no lesson in suicide, only loss.

I get suicide and overdoses mixed up. I knew a guy once. I was trying to help him out. He was a drinker. He also was a junkie. He bought some street junk one afternoon and shot too much of it. He died in his little hotel room on Clay Street off of Kearny. If he hadn't died it would have been easier to be mad at him. But I don't let that stop me. I'm still mad at him. He ruined my average, for one thing. Having a guy die on you sets you back. He's never going to get sober now. He's never going to shit his pants again either, but that doesn't make up for it. Of course I loved him too, but what does that get me?

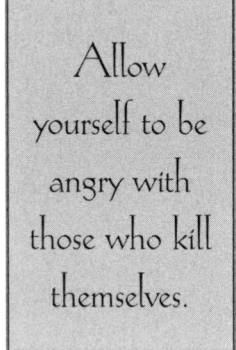

Allow yourself to be angry with those who kill themselves.

One cannot libel the dead, because they cannot feel the sting. So why can't we be angry with them? Why do we stifle it in ourselves? When they go by suicide, they leave us in an insult of dust. Why shouldn't we be mad? Why shouldn't we cry out against them? Why shouldn't we denounce them in our anger and grief? After all, he killed your friend in a diabolical, clever, painstaking way.

I for one, in righteous perversity, think we may grieve too much and curse too little; pay him the tribute of your anger. Do not be ashamed. He killed your friend.

What else can I say, I whose job it is to speak the unsayable? It keeps coming back, I can say that. There will be times when too much is happening inside you and you have to sit down on a bench without speaking, or sit on a bench and talk while someone else sits without speaking. Your friends will need this as well. You will have to sit and listen to each other without answers.

Your far-flung feelings will orbit you like implacable planets, employing you only as the dark, heavy object whose gravity contains them. There you will be in the night sky, a Jupiter keeping your emotions in orbit across your own immensity. That's all you can do sometimes: just to be the dark, heavy planet whose only job is gravity.

Get together with your friends and say what you feel, each of you without interruption or judgment, like we do in recovery, where everybody speaks his humble truth, however mundane or horrific, however sordid or sublime. It just helps to get it off your chest, and keep getting it off your chest, because the longer it lies there, the heavier it gets, and sometimes it makes it hard to breathe.

How can great love just stop, just like that?

It was perfect. It couldn't have gotten any better. And then like a switch it turned off.

Dear Cary,

I SPENT THE better part of the last year in a relationship with the man I thought I'd been looking for forever. He was 15 years older than I and lived 1,400 miles away, but we connected on a level I didn't think was possible. It was magical. Like coming home. He talked about getting married and we were seriously talking about my daughter and me moving to his state so we could develop our relationship further. And then six weeks ago he disappeared from my life altogether.

We saw each other as often as we could, which meant about every six weeks on average. We talked multiple times a day, almost every single day. We sent text messages and e-mails daily. He's a divorced 55-year-old with two adult kids. I'm a never-married, almost 40-year-old with an 8-year-old daughter. We had a very easy, natural relationship. I opened up to him in ways I'd given up on. I've always been far too careful with myself, and until recently, far too immature to really trust a man with my heart. So it was a joy in so many ways to open up to someone like that, emotionally and sexually. I felt free and understood. I thought I understood him as well. I got, for once in my life, what all the fuss was about. I trusted him completely.

His marriage ended four years ago. His wife cheated on him, and after they divorced she married the man she'd had an affair with. And then divorced him a year later. My boyfriend told me at the beginning of our relationship that he couldn't see himself ever getting married again. He was still angry with his ex-wife and he didn't feel he could trust another woman with his heart completely again. I understood where he was coming from. But the anger seemed to subside after some time. Or possibly he just stopped talking about it.

I was concerned at different points during our relationship that the emotional energy he put into his ex-wife was dangerous, it was too much. At the beginning he still saw her occasionally but at the end not as often. He helped her with odd jobs around the house and she still came to him for advice. My parents were amicably divorced 20 years ago. I felt I knew what that felt like, how it was supposed to feel and how people behave within that. But this was different. I thought he may still be in love with her. And it was something we talked about and he assured me he wasn't. She was the mother of his children and someone he had a lot of history with (they were married 20 years) and he told me he loved her like a sister.

Six weeks ago our relationship fell apart. He stopped communicating with me for the most part and the few times he did communicate with me he told me his silence was about sorting himself out, it wasn't about us, it wasn't about me. Which I believed then. And now I don't. A week after he told me that he cut off all communication. He didn't tell me he needed to do that, he didn't say he needed space or to take a break or to pull away, he just took it and he stopped responding to my attempts to reach out.

So, of course, now I do think it was about us, I do think it was about me. Or it wasn't and this is a huge midlife crisis and possibly he'll be back at the end of it. But in the meantime, I'm out here with my heart and trust completely broken. I thought I'd found the man I was going to spend the rest of my life with. We talked about what a great team we'd make. How easy and natural our relationship was. And then he just walked away with no explanation as though we were in high school and had been on one or two dates and so then maybe no explanation is necessary and when you want out, you just leave.

But I deserve an explanation. I don't know how to heal my heart or my trust without one. And I know I have to move forward without him. I never, ever let anyone get this close for this very reason. I have an overwhelming belief that love will never stick for me, that it will always leave. Which is maybe all I needed to tell you and the rest of this has been superfluous.

How do I make myself believe that I'm worth it?

Worth It

Dear Worth It,

I DON'T KNOW whether this sad, difficult experience will leave you too wounded and afraid to try again, or whether having had this one experience you will realize that it is indeed possible, and you will go out again and have a series of flings during which you steel yourself against fear of abandonment and simply enjoy the moment, or whether you will say to yourself that one time was good enough and now I know what all the fuss is about and I can sit back and rest, or whether in telling what happened to you enough times to your friends and your family and people in your church you will realize that he was always dropping hints that he was already half gone—clearing his throat when a direct answer would have been easy, darting his eyes when they should have been on you, a nervous tic or a heavy-lidded opacity of mien all of which were saying in their oblique but decipherable language, "One day I'm surely going to leave you without a word of goodbye." (I don't know if it would make any difference whether he was dropping hints or not.)

I don't know whether he will find he has been stupid and cruel and have a change of heart, but perhaps he is sitting in a bar right

> Stop to honor what is lost.

now telling his story and the rancher he's talking to will shake him by the shoulder and say, "You've got to go back, you've got to," and he will drive all night through sleet and freezing rain to run out of gas at your very front porch where he will stay for the next 40 years, a romantic penitent, devoted, humbled, shamed by his desertion ... or whether you, after reading late into the night and putting down your book and turning out the lamp, will grab your car keys and start driving east, heading for his town, and drive all night and park outside his house and wait for him, and when he comes out you will take one last good look at him and see if you can read anything in his face.

I don't know if you will take this as a once-in-a-lifetime love and hold it dear to your heart or whether all you will remember is the leaving, not the magic or the love or the closeness but only the eventual absence. I don't know. I can only wish that you look beyond the leaving to the poetry of what happened before, that you mine this for everything it's worth, that you not concentrate on the disappearance but on what was there when it was there, that you not count yourself alone in your desertion but ally your-self with all the others who've also been left like this, unaccount-ably, silently, without a word.

These things happen and they take a long time to get over but always in the losing there is something to celebrate and remem-ber: The priceless thing itself. It was there once. It really was there. It was not an illusion. It was not just a dream of some-thing; it was the actual thing, the miracle, the love, the astound-ing knowledge of another's heart.

Some people never have it. You had it.

I'm not saying Shame on you, look on the bright side. You look on any side you need to look on, sister. Sometimes we need to rub our fingers along the cold, rusted hull of what was once a beautiful sailing ship. All I'm saying is, It was there. It really was. That fact will never change.

And when the hurt begins to subside, as it will, no matter what else happens, you will still have it, this memory, this price-less thing that belongs to you.

I say my son is stupid, but my wife says he's lazy

As a high school teacher, I know dumb, and I tell you, my son is the real deal.

Dear Cary,

MY WIFE IS having fits over the fact that our son dropped out of college after only a few weeks. Her unusually tense behavior has been wrecking our home for two months now. She pouts, can't sleep, bugs me, even threatens to leave. She says she is so disappointed that her son is just a lazy, no-good quitter.

I say he is just too stupid.

And I know stupid. I teach high school. Nineteen years old, our son has never shown any real imagination, wit, curiosity, depth, ingenuity, initiative or sensitivity. He did manage to graduate from high school, but it may have been the letters I sent to all his teachers and principal begging them to pass him. I only wish he were more vivacious, more lively, had more spark in the eye.

Nonetheless, I love him with all my might. But I think my wife has fallen out of love with him. She hates him even. And her near-constant anger—something fairly new around our home—is making me think about leaving her. (I said think about leaving.) In our discussions I say stuff like, "Junior is having trouble right now passing his written driver's test. Do you expect him to appreciate and write long research papers on college-level literature, art and music?" She says, "He can at least try!"

Then my wife blames me, says I'm too lazy. I should kick his butt and make him study. And I would if I knew there was something, one iota of curiosity, in the boy. But there isn't, so I gave up.

Our son is very handsome; he even makes some pocket money from modeling for fashion magazines. I think if I encourage this modeling thing he can make friends in the biz, and hopefully find some niche there. But his mother says that's a pipe dream. He'll never have success without college. Fine, I say, but he'll never graduate from college.

Oh, what should we do?

I Love My Dummy

Dear Dummy Lover,

WHAT SHOULD YOU do? Well, what can you do? It sounds as if about all you can do right now is encourage your son's modeling career.

I went to high school with Janice Dickinson. I don't remember her name being called when they handed out the Westinghouse Science Scholarships, but things turned out OK. At least she's got a TV show—or did have a TV show and then didn't have a TV show and now has a new TV show (http://www.tvsquad. com/2005/12/29/janice-dickinson-returns-with-new-show/)— details, details. She never struck me as dumb at all, actually; she was just hard to handle. Still is, apparently, judging from the gossip columns. She also, if I recall, had an original and rather salty way with the mother tongue that was quite refreshing at the time.

Point is, you've got to use what you've got, and if you've got good bones, you'd better use them.

It sounds as if this is really tough on your wife. I wonder what else this is about for her. There's bound to be all kinds of things roiling up in her pretty little head. (She's where the good looks probably come from, right?) You might try asking her, and doing some thinking on your own, to figure it out. I mean, what are her weak spots? What are her vulnerabilities that this could be aggravating? Could it be some kind of social shame that's got her all twisted up? Does she cover up for disappointment with anger? Is this her style of struggling to accept a letdown? Has she been harboring this feeling for a long time that you're too lenient? She probably has all kinds of complicated feelings about her boy.

So do you, obviously.

I think your hard, strange tenderness is just wonderful, by the way; kind of poetic like something in a Raymond Carver story. You've got to admit it's a little unnerving for a father to just flat-out admit his son is as dumb as a sack of hammers. But it's refreshingly realistic, too.

I was in fact very moved by your letter; I talked to my wife about it while we were out walking the dogs in the rain. She said that while one can't hardly discriminate against anybody these days it's still pretty much OK to make fun of dumb people, and she  finds that kind of sad. I do too. It's not their fault they're dumb. Like my dad says, 50 percent of the people are below average. And where do we get off thinking we're any better just because we're smart? Teachers are smart, and people in the media are usually smart. But that doesn't give us the right to look down on anybody. We just got lucky.

Models are better looking than we are and they always will be. That doesn't give them the right to look down on us, either. I suspect that some of them do anyway. Maybe that's just because they're dumb.

I'll go insane if I have to clean the house!

I've gotten over a lot of stuff, but cleaning fills me with dread and despair

Hi, Cary—

I'M A HUGE fan of your advice. And now I could really use some.

I'm a 20-something woman who has been blessed with a complicated psyche. Without getting too far into it, I have worked hard for a good percentage of my life to overcome crippling depression, debilitating panic attacks, and an eating disorder. Lately, I've been feeling fantastic.

But I'm left with one glaring psychological problem: I hate to clean. When I'm presented with the task of cleaning (for instance, by a sink filled with dirty dishes), I actually get the symptoms of depression and panic disorder all over again, despite having eliminated those responses to pretty much all the other situations I face in life.

I think the most disturbing (and fascinating) part of this has to do with what I feel when I DO successfully get myself to clean. After completing the job of scrubbing the bathroom or tidying the living room, I'm often filled with a heavy, nearly suicidal dread. I stand there in the clean room, and instead of basking in the fruits of my labor and celebrating my accomplishment, I feel like I want to die.

This seems to happen only with respect to cleaning—not flying or exercising or working on deadline or any of the other things that used to make me feel bogged down and anxious. As for cleaning-related trauma, I did grow up with a step-parent who was a bit OCD, and my messy adolescent habits caused tension in my household, but we have since resolved our issues. I've tried to let go of all that tension I felt growing up about cleaning (who I was doing it for, and why), and I want to be able to clean for myself so that I can live a fulfilling adult life in a beautiful, livable space.

This problem is getting worse. Perhaps it's become magnified because so many of my other problems have subsided and I have a lot more peace in my life. This whole cleaning thing remains a gaping wound. And my quality of life is really suffering as a result.

I don't think there are any support groups for this particular problem. My shrink has suggested I hire somebody to clean for me and just find a way to get the money (since the prospect of earning extra cash gives me far less angst than the idea of cleaning), but I feel determined to figure out this puzzle.

Any insight would be greatly appreciated.

Messy in Mass.

Dear Messy in Mass.,

I LOVE THE idea your psychiatrist has; it sounds like a good idea to hire someone to clean. Hiring someone doesn't mean you can't figure out what this is about as well. You can do both. In fact, hiring someone to clean may help you figure it out, by taking some of the pressure off and allowing you to experience the cleaning of your house at a distance. When you've seen it done a few times, you may then begin to imitate certain of the movements of the cleaning person, as a set of new gestures and behaviors.

Well, it's just a thought. Actually, I have had periods where cleaning had a powerful psychological significance. This has happened both with the problem of cleaning the house and also with the problem of cleaning the clothes. In the early 1990s, when I was living in the Haight-Ashbury and had only recently stopped drinking, there was a period when I was overwhelmed with the prospect of cleaning the clothes. At that time, I lived in only one room, so cleaning the house was not a big problem. But the laundry was

Hire someone to clean.

very challenging. The laundry piled up. It became a malevolent presence. It was a pile of textile rebukes. After a great while I took it all to the Laundromat, but not before pummeling it with my fists. It was as though the laundry hated me and was trying to defeat me. I don't know why this was, except that laundry is one of the few things that cannot be ignored. And it is very close to the body. Either you clean it or it stinks and looks awful. It seems to bring us always back to the problem of the body, how it decays, how it stinks, how it brings us down.

Later, in fact quite recently, when I had become married and had purchased a house and was living in the house with the wife, the house began to be very untidy and unclean. Portions of it gradually became uninhabitable. If I started to clean, I was overwhelmed with a feeling of despair. I began to avoid even trying to clean the house, because of the way it would make me feel when I began. This went on for quite some time, during which the house grew worse and worse.

When we finally called someone to come and clean the house, by watching her clean, I saw how doable it was. I observed the way she did it and it seemed possible for me to do it as well. I was relieved of the feeling of dread and impossibility.

This led me to believe that if we stopped having the person clean our house for us that I would start cleaning it. It looked so easy. It didn't exactly work out that way. When finally, for financial reasons, we discontinued the service, we thought that it wasn't necessary to start cleaning right away. We took a vacation from cleaning. The house looked like it would stay clean forever! But with remarkable speed, the house became dirtier and more untidy. This trend continued unabated for many weeks while we attended to other pressing matters of work and play.

Then when things got really bad we called the cleaning person again. As it turned out, we never really did clean the house the way the cleaning person did. But at least we know that it can be done. It is not hopeless. We do clean. But from time to time, we do not clean enough. All we have to do, though, when things get bad, is call a cleaning person.

What could this possibly mean, this cleaning thing? What is the meaning of cleaning? Could it mean, perhaps, solitude and servitude? For instance, when I am called upon to clean, it is often when I am trapped alone in a house—or used to be. In my family, cleaning was a kind of servitude. It was used as punishment. If you did something bad you had to clean.

To clean is also to confront your silent enemy of long fruition, the dirt of secret accumulation. It can also represent an encounter with our own decay, which is so distasteful, that heavy, slow, dragging feeling that is the opposite of transcendence. It is an encounter with entropy, the tendency of things to lose their sheen, to grow dull in the air, to corrode, to weaken and rot, to become covered over and eventually unrecognizable. And so, as perhaps one might have guessed, it is ultimately a confrontation with death.

This reminds me that when I was young I thought indeed that we would transcend; anyone who has done LSD even once has probably thought much the same: through this experience we will overcome all our difficulties; we will live in a new, brighter, fuller, truer place. And then (oddly enough, as I was telling my therapist this week!) we feel that old gravity of the animal soul, the death soul, the earth pulling us backward.

Is that why Buddhists like to clean (http://www.mothering.com/ discussions/showthread.php?t=170073) so much?

Mystery man

We've been together five years and my boyfriend won't tell me where he lives!

Dear Cary,

I DON'T KNOW how to address a very troubling problem with my boyfriend of five years.

We live 90 minutes apart, but he makes an effort to see me two or three times per week. We talk daily—sometimes several times daily, for long periods of time. Our conversations have never grown dull, we are affectionate and have a satisfying sexual life, and he is caring and kind.

The distance has its rewards—I told him once that I knew my prior marriage was over when the sound of my (now ex) husband's car arriving home in the driveway filled me with disappointment, and I never wanted to experience that feeling again. In the five years my boyfriend and I have been together, each time I hear the "chirp" of his car alarm being activated outside, and soon thereafter his knock on my door, I am filled with happiness and check my hair and makeup like a teenager, and that feeling has never waned.

The problem is, in the five years I've known him, I have always been the one to welcome him to my front door—he has never invited me to his home. I asked why this was so, early on, and his answer at that time was that he wouldn't dream of making me drive so far when he knows how much and how hard I work during the week, whereas his schedule is completely flexible (true). I thought this was gallant.

Another year passed and I told him that I would very much enjoy a drive down to his house on a Friday evening for a weekend visit, or even the whole of a Saturday together, and that I simply wanted, needed to be able to see his home, his bed, his desk, so I could picture him in bed when I went to sleep. He said, "That's so sweet and romantic. We'll do that soon." We didn't.

When another year passed, I said I was very concerned, hurt and feeling shut out, and asked straight out why I was not welcome in his home. He had no true response for me. Mostly backing and filling and putting me off with a diversionary kiss and a squeeze. I've said, "If you have a roommate you've never told me about, tell me. If you actually live in an apartment or a trailer and not a house, tell me. I don't care where you live, I just want to be welcome, wherever that place is." He insists he lives alone. I've said, "The fact I'm unwelcome in your home tells me otherwise. I'm concerned you're married or otherwise 'taken.'" He laughs this off as absurd given the fact we are on the phone nearly constantly, take weekend trips together, and he spends so much time at my home. He just says, "We'll see. Soon."

I am nearly in tears as I type this because this otherwise loving person just cannot justify to me, after five years of being together, why I am unwelcome in his home ... and am not even given a mailing address (I use a mail-drop address).

In a not-too-serious disagreement recently, over something related to "security" in our relationship, I blurted out the question "How secure can I be when I would not even be able to come to you in an emergency or tragedy of some sort ... I live in the shadow of our state capitol building, and I couldn't find you if there were a bombing, and phones and computers were out, and I needed to come to you." He at first laughed it off as "melodramatic" and then when I promptly burst into sobs with my face buried in my hands, he was horrified and conciliatory and hugged me tightly and shushed my tears. But he didn't invite me over or give me his address. My heart cracked in that moment—I felt it, and almost heard the ping of it.

What am I to do? I don't give ultimatums because I believe they are always the death knell of a relationship. Ultimatums suggest you've already lost. Who wants to win ground solely by the threat of something? Then again, his refusal to address a legitimate concern of mine has left me adrift with worry and confusion, so much so, I've taken to lying to my family and friends. They think I visit him, see him at his home, and have stayed there. I can't bear to tell them I have no idea where he lives, other than the name of the city 90 minutes away.

Can you help?

Where Does My Boyfriend Live?

Dear Where,

YOU HAVE TO know where your boyfriend lives. Otherwise, if you eventually move in together, how will you get home?

Now, at first, I thought you should just go ahead and find out where he lives and then decide what to do next. I didn't think

Find out where your boyfriend lives.

you needed to tell him ahead of time what you planned to do. Having some experience in routine investigations, I figured it would be no big deal to go to city hall in the county where he lives and do a property records search, or look in the registrar of voters list if he votes, or look in the reverse phone book, if his phone isn't a cellphone. If there was no public record of his residence, then you could hire a private investigator to do a quick and legal DMV search on his license plate. It would be a snap.

Then you could just drive to his address and see if he has any chickens in the yard. You could ring the doorbell and say you were just in the neighborhood and thought you'd drop by. Or if that seemed too forward you could have a friend go to the door with the address written down on a piece of paper, but with maybe the wrong street on it, and just apologize and say she must have the wrong address or something, meanwhile trying to get a peek inside to see if there was a mysterious woman in a negligee, smoking in the shadows, or any kids' toys, or Nazi regalia on the walls, or an eight-track player. She could ask to use the phone and call you while you wait in your car and tell you something in code. That would all be very exciting and Nancy Drew-like.

But it was pointed out to me that this might be considered an ethical breach, or it might seem sneaky. Some people think that if they don't tell you something, you're not supposed to know it. I, on the other hand, feel that we have a fundamental right to know whatever people won't tell us, especially when it's public information, whether it's about intimates or business associates or politicians. We live in an open society. But I know it's more complicated than that when you take into account people's feelings. I also realize that while telling him you're going to find out where he lives is not an ultimatum, but a simple statement of fact, it might sound like an ultimatum. And indeed it might have the effect of an ultimatum.

On the other hand, if you investigate on your own, there's a chance you will learn something amazing. It could be that he's a terrible housekeeper, or he's just pathologically not proud of his lawn, or he just really, really hasn't gotten around to inviting you in. Or he could be a government spy. Or he's dealing meth out of a trailer. Or, of course, the obvious: He's married with children.

The bottom line is, you've got to know, and if he won't tell you, you still have to find out. So you decide: Tell him first that you're going to find out, or find out and then tell him that you know. But find out.

And, while you're at it: Tell me, will you? I'm dying to know.

Where is my home?

I've uprooted myself over and over again in a
short time. Now I don't know where I belong.

Dear Cary,

TWO AND A half years ago, I left New York to move to Chicago to be close to my family. I was burnt out from working too hard and my mother had breast cancer. I telecommuted from home and attended a seminary at night on weekends. I was happy.

My mother's cancer went into remission and my company decided to rein in the telecommuters. I was offered the choice of returning to New York, going to California or going to Dallas. I chose California. It had its ups and downs and I wasn't always happy, but I really grew there. But after a painful breakup and an increase in layoffs at my company, I chose to respond to a job offer in the Netherlands. I got the job and moved here last summer. I was not prepared for the increase in racism, ethnocentrism, and the general anti-immigrant climate that is sweeping much of Europe. The more I got over my loneliness here, the more I realized that I had no long-term future here (due to extremely restrictive government policies) and there wasn't much joy in the day-to-day. On several occasions, I was told that this was not the country for me and that I should return to the States. After one time too many, I quit my job, and am now packing up for my return.

But I know you can't go home again. Yet, that is what I am trying to do. I am trying to figure out how I'm going to rebuild my life after having started over so many times in such a short time. And what am I going to think of the Midwest or East Coast after my experiences in California and Europe? Can I really stand yet another trip to Ikea to furnish my entire flat in one go for under $1,000? Can I keep investing in places and lives not knowing if I or they are going to come or stay? Nothing feels permanent anymore. I feel like a perpetual transient, yet that is never what I intended to be. What I want is a place to call home, but I don't know where that is anymore.

I admire people who go away and always have a place to go back to. I am in awe of those who are constantly on the move and never return, yet never seem to break. But I seem to be neither of those kinds of people.

So here I am in Europe trying to force myself to pack to return, but not really wanting to. Unfortunately, it's not legally possible for me to stay. What do I do? How do I orient my thinking so that I can move on and value the experiences I had?

The Wanderer

Dear Wanderer,

IT MAKES SENSE that you feel the way you do. You have been a transient. Nothing has been permanent. So nothing feels permanent. You feel like a perpetual transient. You don't know where home is anymore. And you feel caught between a committed state of nomadism and some kind of rooted existence.

So how do you orient your thinking? I think that first you just acknowledge that what you are feeling is appropriate. It is a reflection of reality. It would be strange if you didn't feel this way. And it is natural that when you look to the future and imagine more of the same, you say, I can't do this forever. Of course not.

Sometimes when we are in a situation that seems intolerable we forget that it is a story and it does have an ending. Stories begin with disruption. In your case your mother got breast cancer and that uprooted you, started you on your journey.

Then there are ripples of that original disruption, and complications and revelations. You went to the Netherlands and found the natives unfriendly. You went to California and ate delicious fruit. You had a breakup that you learned from. But always you were trying to find your home.

You haven't just been wandering. You've been responding to trouble—first your mother's trouble, then the needs of work. You've made choices, but in a narrow realm defined by powerful forces beyond your control. So it would make sense not only to feel homeless, but powerless too.

But here is something key to remember: The fact that powerful forces have narrowed your choices doesn't mean that if you had the freedom to choose to live in Maui or Santa Barbara or anywhere you wanted, that you would feel at home. Rather what seems to affect your happiness is the kind of limits you are dealing with, and their source. Where the job has limited your choices, it has led to this chaos and isolation. But where it was your mother's condition that limited your choices, somehow that led to happiness. While caring for your mother, you found a life that worked for you. You felt at home. Interesting.

Many things make up a home. If we are accustomed to thinking of home as an ideal environment, freely chosen, a place that reflects our dreams and aspirations, there is one element that might seem surprising or counterintuitive: Home is often a place we do not choose. Rather, home is the place we have to be. Our very first home we do not choose. And after we emerge from the womb it is still many years before we will live in a home of our own choosing. When we finally exercise our choices, we often think that what will make us happy is a home that suits our aesthetics, or reflects our values, or is in the image of what a home should look like. And so we move into this idea of home and start rearranging furniture. But we are unhappy in this idea of a home. We are unhappy in this place we have chosen for ourselves. Why is that?

I think it is because of the overlooked element of necessity and service. To be a home, a place must choose us. It must require something of us. It must need us.

In what sense is this true?

Well, home is where we give up our separateness, and we do not give that up easily. It must sometimes be taken from us by force. We cannot will ourselves to merge with the landscape. We are pulled out of ourselves not by the beauty of the landscape but by the fact that it requires us to dig a drainage ditch or fell some aging trees. That is why one can move to a beautiful place and be beautifully unhappy. Beauty alone does not suffice. What we need is what needs us, something that requires our presence, something that will bleed us of our insularity. It can be a landscape; it can be a community; it can be both.

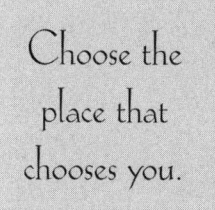

Choose the place that chooses you.

I see in California many pretty houses. I see people go in and out. I wonder whether the landscape has invaded their dreams. I wonder if their mothers live there.

I hope your mother is OK now.

So we do not choose our home is what I mean. It chooses us.

It sounds to me like your home is in Chicago. That is the place that chose you. That's where your home was the last time you were at home. I would start there.

Now maybe you will go back to Chicago and find your home is gone. Perhaps your mother does not need you there. What then? Then I think you have to search for the elements of home somewhere else: service, commitment, family, spirituality. Where are you needed? Choose the place that chooses you. That will be your home.

We left paradise for the suburbs

We wanted to be closer to family, but life is so much harder here!

Dear Cary,

NEARLY THREE YEARS ago, my husband and I made a pretty big life decision—and have spent the last year or so driving ourselves crazy questioning the wisdom of it!

Let me back up. For several years, we lived in a beautiful, tropical part of the world. Although my husband has a degree (though not a particularly useful one), I do not, and considering that, our jobs were satisfying and quite lucrative. During this time, we enjoyed the comforts of a tight-knit community of other expats (as well as some locals), learned a new language, ate fantastic food and spent our weekends at exciting clubs in the city, or hiking through the jungle just outside our metropolitan abode, cycling, or riding our motorbike along the coast to the beach. We lived a beautiful life and, together, discovered and indulged defining passions.

Then we decided to leave. It wasn't as crazy as it sounds. Our jobs, though good-paying, were not incredibly secure. The demand for our line of work was easily met by the steady stream of young backpackers alighting on the shores looking for some quick cash and an interesting experience. We felt pretty expendable. My husband and I both wanted careers that were genuinely fulfilling to us, that met a deeper need than just money. We were (are!) getting to an age where if we were going to start all over, we didn't have time to waste. We also wanted to buy a house, grow a garden and start a family—things that were not very feasible in our tiny apartment in the city. And perhaps the most significant deciding factor was that I am very close with my family, had missed them terribly, and I wanted to live near them, to share once again in their day-to-day experiences.

So we did it. We moved back to the American suburb where I grew up, bought a house, planted a garden and got some cats. I have decided to go back to school and study the language that I fell in love with while living abroad. My husband, meanwhile, has had a very difficult time finding a job in his desired field. Our local economy has never been worse, and we have been struggling immensely to make ends meet. I am working full-time while going to school, my husband is working two jobs and we have put off having children indefinitely—and we still stress about paying our mortgage bill every month. It feels sometimes like we are just treading water instead of working toward goals that once so inspired us.

I love being near my family. I love my house, my garden, my cats. But we have had a hard time finding a community like we once had. We are finding life in the suburbs dull and gray after living in a real metropolis. And our money woes are eating us both up. We often wonder whether we would be better off returning to our Southeast Asian paradise. But it would mean selling our house, giving up our garden, our cats, and my lovely family. It might also mean my husband wouldn't get the chance to succeed in his desired field, since doing that in this country would not really be an option for him. (As for me, I could still pursue my career while living there.) But maybe these are worthy sacrifices if it means not losing another night's sleep over money, and inviting adventure rather than stress and fear in our lives.

My question, Cary, is how do we know when to give up on our lives here? When do we say that all the cons outweigh the pros? I am so very tired of worrying about my future; how can I have faith that everything will turn out OK?

On the Fence

Dear On the Fence,

I ONCE HAD a really great situation. I was talking to the man
I talk to about such things, telling him how great it was and how
awful I felt that it ended and he said it sounded like it was a really
great situation that ended. And I said, Yeah, that's right, it was a
really great situation. And he said, Yeah. But it ended. And I said,
Yeah, but it was really great. And he said, Yeah. But it ended.
And I said Yeah. But it was really great. Like really great.

And he said, Yeah.

It was a great situation that ended.

It sounds like you had a really great situation that ended too.
It's hard not to want to make it happen all over again just the
same way as before. But that is the Addict's Way: not moving forward toward novelty and challenge but moving backward toward
repetition and safety, like you could put that tropical island on a
DVD and play it over and over again instead of doing something
new that is harder.

I am a creature of habit and repetition and I always want the
same high again just the same as before, but that is not a good
thing about me but a bad thing that I would change if I were
stronger or smarter or more courageous and wiser. I think: That
was a very good hit; I want another one just like that. Perhaps
you think: That was a very good tropical Southeast Asian life; I
want another one just like that.

You could spend the rest of your life trying to repeat that first
time. People do. We don't call them addicts. We call them "stuck
in the past." We don't say they're pulling levers in a cage like
addicted monkeys. But that's what it feels like when you return
to the place of your really great situation that ended, looking for
what you had. You pull all the levers and nothing comes out.
Then you look at the bars of the cage and think, How did I get
here? Now I'm really stuck!

So, having left paradise, how do we move forward with rever-
ence for the past? We construct something enduring out of what
we have left. We cultivate memory and stories. We work at it.
We salvage things and use them again later. This language you

acquired, for instance: Language is a repository of memory. The more you work on the language the more you keep the experience alive. It is something you took away that you can keep. There are many things you can keep. But you can't go back and do it again.

Keep this in mind: Whatever you do next will be new. Even if you went back there—which you could do, it sounds like a nice place, I'm not saying you can't visit—it would be a new experience. There is not a parking space waiting for you. It's been assigned to somebody else.

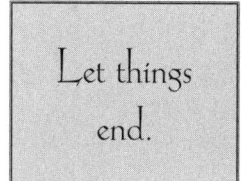

You had a really great situation but you wanted something else: to be closer to family, to buy a house and have a garden and get some cats and later maybe some kids. You did those things. It turned out that it was harder. That doesn't mean it was the wrong choice. It was just harder. You have no way of knowing whether getting what you want next will be easy or hard. You need different things at different times and some are harder than others. (People say things that are harder are more valuable but I think some things that are hard are just hard and some things that are easy are priceless.)

This is where making specific, incremental changes can be helpful. You have done a good job of identifying the things that are missing now—community, the urban experience, a feeling of being untroubled and unhurried. While you contemplate your next move, make small changes. Go see some art. Take a day off. Spend time with your family. Find some like-minded people.

You had a really great situation that ended. Something is next. It's not yet clear what. But you'll know. It'll come to you, maybe dancing down the street in a bear suit, maybe falling from the sky, maybe popping into your head as a daydream as you're eating ice cream. Be ready. It'll come to you.

Twice burned

My first husband died in my arms; my second one changed his mind about wanting children. I'm 40 and devastated.

Dear Cary,

TEN YEARS AGO, I was an English teacher engaged to marry a doctor I'd loved since college. We had an adventurous, romantic relationship, fueled by a mix of the idealism of one's 20s and our own hard work, which suggested to us that we were going to have a very fine life. We reveled in each other; we relished our dingy apartment and ramen noodles because we knew we were lucky and wouldn't be without for long. Rob and I spent several of his residency rotations in developing countries, where he worked in free clinics and I helped local women learn to read. We enjoyed this so much that we planned to shape our married life around it, following in the footsteps of others we admired who'd raised worldly and self-possessed children overseas.

Four months before our wedding, he was killed when our bus went over a cliff in Guatemala. He died in my arms about an hour after the crash and was conscious for some of that time. Our conversation is crystalline in my memory—he wanted me to promise him I would have a happy life and take care of his dog. Back at home, I lay on my mother's couch, went to grief counseling, returned the early wedding gifts, hollered at the universe, fretted that somehow my karma had caused this, bonded with the dog, stopped viewing myself as the wife who almost was, and finally got on with things.

Eventually I stopped comparing every man I met to Rob (who had, of course, become deified in my mind—those who die young and in love at least get to spend eternity as beautiful memories). I also picked up a Ph.D., started a university job, volunteered in literacy initiatives overseas, earned a private pilot's license, joined a hiking club, took up photography, and valued my girlfriends.

When I was 34, I met Arthur. He's an avid mountain climber—the kind who takes four months a year to climb peaks only airplanes are meant to see. We enjoyed traveling together, he sent flowers to my mother on her birthday, and he got along with the (by now very old) dog. He taught me to climb, and I took him flying. Two years into our relationship, he proposed. Arthur was as eager as I was to travel and continue our hobbies and, like me, hoped we'd have a child who enjoyed these things, too.

Then, on our first anniversary, he said he'd reconsidered his decision to have a child. That reconsideration deepened into an insistence on not having children and, in the last six months, a decision that perhaps he shouldn't have married in the first place. I should have seen it coming. He has a Ph.D. in physics, a field that profits from immense concentration and solitude; he was a bachelor until he was 42; he could ride in the car with me for six hours at a time without saying a word. He is kind to my family when they visit, but he refuses to waste his leisure time visiting them. He flies into a rage when I drop a pan or burn the soup. He prefers to eat his meals alone with a book. He backs out of every real estate deal we've entered, so we're still renting.

I believe him when he says it isn't me, but that he got married only to discover that he preferred Katharine Hepburn's advice to "live down the road and visit." I can't blame him—how could he have known how he'd feel about being married until he was? I honestly believe he wasn't being disingenuous when he claimed to share my hearth-and-crib visions, but perhaps it was more something he thought he should do rather than something he wanted to do. Now, Arthur has said he's "willing" to remain married, but it's a chilly and untenable existence. He went to marriage counseling with me four times before denouncing it as "pseudoscience" and refusing to go back, even when I said it would help me tremendously.

I am devastated. I am not functioning; it's a good thing my job doesn't involve punching a clock. Last month, I spent 10 days locked in the apartment with the blinds drawn. I think it was some sort of sick experiment to see if someone would come looking. I damn near slept with a man in my flying club, and I still might. I feel indescribably lonely and horrid. I hate that I feel worse than I did when my fiancé died, for chrissakes. I cry so often I tell people I have pinkeye, but at the same time I know that compared with all of the devastation in the world, I have no good reason to feel sorry for myself. I've sought counseling and listened to the variations on the "Sure, you got a bum rap, but you're still young" theme.

But I am not young. I will be 40 soon, and the hearth-and-crib dream, simple as it seemed, is fast approaching impossible. Yet I don't understand the depths of my despair. Is it just a midlife crisis? The only real difference is that this time around I can't hope to meet a man and have a natural child. I had to re-envision and reinvent my whole life when Rob died, and I think I did so capably; why can't I this time? I can adopt or be a foster parent. I can date. I can sleep with the guy in my flying club. I can travel overseas and help teach women to read. I can become an eccentric professor who takes Elderhostel tours and talks to her cats. I am fully aware that I have no right to feel that life is not worth living but, you know, that is how I feel.

Hitting a Wall at 40

Dear Hitting a Wall,

PERHAPS, FOR A while, you would benefit from doing nothing but grieving and tending to what may be serious depression. I think you need to give up trying to make your life work like a good Swiss watch and face the mess. Ignore your husband. He's going to be no help at all. Find a tough and intellectually rigorous psychiatrist who can help you through this. See if you can take a leave of absence. Accept that you need help and that sleeping with the guy in the flying club would just be a chilly charade.

Grieving and fighting depression is a lot of work, and with all your flying around and teaching people to read, you probably have never spent enough time on it to do it well. When I say grieve I don't mean grieving for that poor guy who went over the cliff with you in the bus. I mean grieving for the glittering dream of a perfect life you were foolish enough or idealistic enough to believe could come true. When the bus went over the cliff, you grieved for your fiancé, but staggered on, starry-eyed and invincible, toward the light, and you were betrayed again. But this time it is a more piercing betrayal because it is personal and more subtle; it has no exploding gas tanks and weeping Guatemalan Indian widows  in colorful shawls; it is simply that a man you love turned out to be cold, aloof and imperious, and you're shocked by the barrenness of your life.

You may think now that since your husband has mistreated you, you're supposed to get up, dust yourself off, and found a school for the blind in Jakarta. That may be what Katharine Hepburn would do. But she was just an actress. In real life, when things fall apart, we sometimes get weepy and shut ourselves in, and the super calls a locksmith or, in some neighborhoods, a Jungian psychiatrist.

Here's another thing to consider: Just because some people strive to teach children to read and others strive to win big at the track doesn't mean that one form of compulsive striving is less painful than another. All human striving brings suffering. And, in fact, the hardest striving to give up is the kind that's cloaked in virtue. If you were a cat torturer, you could find plenty of people to help you quit. But if you're addicted to virtuous acts, who's going to take pity on you and help you recover? After all, your suffering looks like happiness and it's socially useful. Who's to say you're anything but an innocent victim with the best of intentions? Only your dark, truth-telling shadow can say.

I'm willing to bet that there is some messy, twisted madwoman in the attic who doesn't give two shits about teaching kids to read, who finds the professor a royal bore and would rather be playing cards with the maid, but she isn't allowed to speak. It's time for her to say how she's hated all these years being the good girl while anybody could see that beneath that world-saving missionary is a real woman racked with irrational passions.

You're at a crossroads. You need to ditch the physicist and get a psychiatrist who can help you face the tragic nature of your own striving and help you grieve for your own innocence.

12 years sober and now this?

The last three years have been bad, bad, bad. My uncle the murderer got out of prison and beat up my grandma, for starters.

Dear Cary,

I NEED HELP. I'm stuck and can't move. I've been sober for 12 years. I had an AA home group that I loved. In the course of getting sober, I mended my relationship with my father and made peace with my mother. I cut the abusive and vindictive members of my family loose. I went to law school and started a practice, which I love sometimes. I married and have two small children (2.5 years and 4 months). Sounds like all of the promises (http://www.recoveryemporium.com/Articles/Promises.htm) came true, right? Not quite.

My life is a disaster (mostly) and I don't know what to do. I'm not angry, but I am so bitter that almost nothing makes me happy, except my kids, and then only sometimes.

The last three years have been unbelievably bad. My alcoholic uncle was released from prison (in 1982, he killed a man in a bar fight). He moved in with my grandmother and started drinking again. He refused to work and he starting beating her when she wouldn't give him money to drink. I reported it to the police and the state Department of Aging repeatedly. It did no good. In the middle of my first pregnancy, my grandmother was hospitalized and died. She told me and other family members that he beat her and "busted something loose inside." She denied it to the police, as did every other family member except me. My uncle wasn't prosecuted. He moved on to beating up and robbing other family members. My mother was hospitalized with a skull fracture in April as a result of a robbery. We're pressuring the police and state's attorney to prosecute, but are getting almost nowhere.

Another uncle, on my father's side, committed suicide after arguing with my grandfather. His mother—my grandmother—died a few months later of a stroke. My father died of a heart attack a few months after that.

Three of the old-timers in my AA group died within four months of each other. Two had cancer and one had a fatal auto accident. I loved them like family. The rest of the group descended into a bitter and stupid argument over whether the group should be smoking or nonsmoking. I stopped going to meetings, because I couldn't bear to be there without Ray and Lynn and Mike, and I couldn't take that stupid argument any longer.

So here I am. I go to work and go home. I see almost no one. I'm terrified that there is no heaven or rebirth and this is the only life I get and it sucks. I have no friends. My family is broken beyond repair. I miss my father. I miss the old-timers from my group. I need to get my life back together, but I can't move. I manage to keep it together for my kids and husband, more or less, but I'm miserable. How do I get out of this hole?

Dawn

Dear Dawn,

IN THINKING ABOUT your situation, I of course feel you could use some help, but therapy doesn't sound strong enough for what you've got. You don't need information, or to figure things out; a new perspective? Hardly! You've been run over! You need a transfusion! You need Buddha's compassionate ambulance!

You need a transformative experience, something to fill you with light and shake you up and remind you why you're alive. You need a million watts of radiance from someplace bigger than your problems. You need a doctor who can prescribe 100 milligrams of transcendent epiphany to knock out these flu-like symptoms of circumstance. I'm tempted to say you need a guru, even—only in the sense of taking charisma over reason. That is, you need something larger than life—you need a Burning Man, you need to be wrapped in the arms of something hot and strong and otherworldly: hot mud or an enzyme bath! (http://www. osmosis.com/enzbath.cfm). You need Buddha's compassionate ambulance to come screaming down your street and carry you out of this building in a gondola of fire.

I'm serious. Stand on the highway and flag down the god of your understanding—tell him it's an emergency, you've had an accident of fate and need to be transported immediately to a hospital of good fortune. Get your-

> Call Buddha's compassionate ambulance.

self looked at, and not by any ordinary physician of the soul but somebody with a magic wand that leaves trails in broad daylight, somebody you look in his eyes and you're on fire already, a rock star or an astronaut or a woman who talks to the earth.

This brute of an alcoholic uncle has strewn fear and brambles in your path, he's eaten a hole in your head, he's broken your legs and he's still coming so you need not just a guru but a protector as well. Where is your husband? Has he gone away too? Where are your strong and vigilant family members? Is there no one left but criminals and old women to be conked on the head and robbed?

My heart goes out to you too, of course, but my heart is so tiny and shriveled, you need more than that! Damn, where are the old-timers! I know what you mean, how they burn with that pure radiant goodness and it's a crying shame they all died just like that. Everybody needs old-timers around, grizzled and unfazed, too old to be easily amused, burning hot like charcoal because they've been through the first fire already. Their eyes give you pleasure and lift you out of your chair. Their voices crack like old trees in a stiff breeze. They know what they're talking about. To have so many of them die like that—you didn't know you were holding on to them, did you, until their hands went limp and you found yourself falling?

You're still falling, clawing at the air. No ordinary hands can help. We don't have the grip strength. You need somebody to catch you, somebody who can fly. So where do you find a person like that? They're out there, they are. We don't notice them half the time, but you go looking for them and you find them in dry corners of hunger and strength, eating muffins in a cafe or playing chess on the street, making coffee in some meeting, chewing a day-old cookie and waiting for the books; in temples and ashrams and churches they sit or stand, talking, casting lines into the air, trying to land a fish out of nothing.

That's the kind of help you need, the kind that defies our logic. You need strength more than dignity; certainty more than knowledge; faith more than intellect; instinct more than sense. And where else does such knowledge reside? In your young children, come to think of it: Look at that kid playing with blocks! What's life look like from that perspective? Just a vibrant whirlwind of color! Nothing but potential! Nothing but the future! Next time you play with them, try to enter their world. You may find there some renewal, some escape.

After what you've seen, you've drawn some inevitable conclusions—and who could conclude otherwise? It seems that some horrific spore of misfortune has settled in your house and is germinating still. What would it take to replace that conclusion with something less apocalyptic? You need evidence to the contrary, some song you can feel in your gut that says: Even still, life is mostly made of magic and light!

What else then? Great art, if you can get it! Even pretty good art, if it's the right kind! Seek it out! Seek out objects that shake you and seem to say Hey you! Dawn! Morning light! Get this! This is eternal form! This is indomitable human spirit made material in a bottle or a stone! Seek out music played by John Coltrane, who was always searching! Opera, too, and Isaac Stern, and Shakespeare: anything with gravitas! Anything that lights you up, sends you a telegram, lifts you up and puts you down, changed by infinitesimal travel.

But don't stop at metaphorical travel. Sometimes you have to remove yourself physically for a month or two, go somewhere that sparkles differently, where you can breathe without fear. Travel really can work; it can take you out of your world long enough to reboot your spirit. (Speaking of travel, I found this out about Paris: It can fix you of despair, perhaps permanently. I didn't have the money. I did it anyway.)

My dear friend, I've gone on long enough. You get my drift, I'm sure. You've been hit over the head. You've been run over. You've drawn the inevitable conclusion. You need something inescapable to change your mind, something blinding that shakes you free. You need a guru, not an analyst. You need a transfusion, not a Band-Aid. You need Buddha's compassionate ambulance to come screaming down the street.

I want to go home

*I am in America against my will, alone,
unhappy and scorned.*

Dear Cary,

I AM FACING an unusual situation. I am here in this country
almost against my will, I don't have many friends, and on top
of that I am recovering from a long illness. I had a decent job
and a modest living in my home country, but I placed too much
emphasis on my sibling's advice and well-being. I did not think
about myself, but was focused on them. I left my job and came
here to complete my studies and find a job. But the United States
is very frightening to me. It is lonely. I am not happy. I don't feel
like living here, but going back right now is not an option since
I have invested time and money in my education, and I need to
complete it before going back.

My sibling does not talk to me. I am forced to share the house
with my sibling for economic reasons. I find myself not talking to
anyone unless I am at school and there I catch hold of strangers
and talk to them because I am lonely. At home I am supposed
to make myself invisible, stay in my room and study, not make
a noise, and not talk or ask about anything. This is driving me
crazy. How can I keep my sanity for another four months till I
go back home? I feel hopelessly depressed.

My relationship with my sibling is spoiled. We don't get along,
because my sibling feels I am not trying to succeed or get ahead.
I am not a very hardworking or materialistic person. I am satisfied with very little. Also I made pretty bad judgments in my

life—not drugs—but I was not financially savvy, and did not get married at the right age to the right person. In our community this is considered a disgrace. Because of my choices, my sibling feels that their life has been affected and blames me. I admit my mistakes, but I cannot go back and change them, nor can I become a person I am not. I took care of my parents and my sibling, and I am so hurt by this behavior. How do I retain my trust in the human race when my own family can treat me like this? What I crave is for some companionship and understanding.

Unhappy Foreigner

Dear Unhappy Foreigner,

I HAVE INTRODUCED capitalization and punctuation into your letter because, whether it was deliberate or a function of your e-mail program, it arrived with all the clauses linked with ellipses, and everything lowercase, which gave a certain chant-like tone to your lament, almost as if we were listening to you breathing your distress, washing it over the page, like a sad ocean in the night. It leads me to think either you are very desperate or some kind of poet.

But you do after all have a legitimate complaint; you are essentially alone in a foreign land, filled with shame and anger.

How difficult to be here in this country, weak from recent illness, unsure what you are trying to accomplish. It is that feeling that comes from your letter, and that to which I want to respond, and to which I think readers will also respond.

Here we are, two strangers mumbling at each other in this great loud America. I cannot really guess what country you are from. People often feel I ought to see so much more than I do, that so much more ought to be plainly visible, both to me and to readers. They feel that they will be recognized by their writing, as though they had placed their face on the Internet.

Do you know what my face looks like? It looks like that man in the hat, actually. No one ever recognizes me on the street, though. How much rarer it would be to be recognized by one's words! And yet I know the feeling—being almost like a child, beset with problems that you wish to make visible but for which you lack the language, so you cry and bang your fists. I know this condition well; I suppose it is in part why I have dedicated so much of my life to looking for a language to communicate my own distress.

You do sound like you are in distress, a kind of wordless distress I easily recognize. I also think you are not like other people.

Perhaps you are one of those rarities, the creative soul. If so, America can be a good place for you; while we are awful in many ways, what is good about us is that we rather like the odd ones here; we do not care that much about tradition and respect and doing the right thing. You can do anything you want here. If you have already met the basic obligations imposed on you by family and country, then perhaps in some way you are done with family and country, and you can stay here and do what you want.

Take advantage of your freedom to be strange.

Maybe I am just another crazy American talking. I know I am so deeply American I can hardly understand the power of family and country to bind one, nor the power of shame, the power of expectation, the power of society. Because here, we have almost no society. We are anarchists at heart!

Soon when you are healthy, if you want, you can walk out of your little room and get a job somewhere and do whatever it is you want to do. Put on a scarf. Become a punk. Eat strange food at midnight out on the street.

You see what I mean about America: What makes us so awful is also what makes us so much fun. We don't really give a damn! We are, in that sense, diabolically free. And when that freedom allows our cruder nature to come forward, because now we are so powerful as a nation, it is a tragedy for the world. When the world sees us coming, the world cringes. And who wouldn't? But when we just stay in our country and do our thing, it works out OK. Like it worked out for Elvis.

So perhaps you should stay in the U.S. and make a new life for yourself.

Maybe that is crazy. Maybe you would hate it here always.

But I think of us as a country of misfits, and you strike me as a misfit too, someone misunderstood and ill-used by your country and your family.

It is no shame to be a misfit here. Elvis Presley was a misfit. We all want to be like Elvis. You could be like Elvis too. You could get a haircut like Elvis and play the guitar and perhaps make some paintings too. You could show us exactly who you are and we would be very interested to know.

Perhaps you laugh with scorn: Who wants to know who I am? Who cares about some freak like me?

Try us.

What's the best method for a painless suicide?

I am done with life, but don't want to suffer when I go.

Dear Cary,

HOW DO I end my life when I'm too much of a coward to do it? I'm serious when I say that I really have nothing to live for. I'm a trust fund baby with a social phobia, both of which have conspired to sap me of any ambition in life. The person I live with I drive crazy with my fears and depression. He doesn't deserve the kind of mental abuse I put him through and probably would be happier with me dead and him with my money. Oh, he acts supportive, but I think he's really not very happy at all. He's struggled most of his life to make ends meet and I think it would be a gift to him if I got out of the way so he could enjoy my wealth, hopefully with someone more stable than me.

At 36 I have only held two brief summer jobs and am currently unemployable (how will I explain my lack of résumé?). Therefore I have no career to look forward to, nor any foreseeable way of making a difference in this world, especially when I'm too afraid to say hi to anyone at the deli I've been going to for years. I've tried school on-and-off, but the cyclical nature of my depression and phobias have made it all but impossible to graduate college. I alienate everyone I come in contact with because I can't make even the smallest of small talk, so people dismiss me as being a snob. Besides my partner, I have no friends. There really is no future for me.

218

The problem is my fear of the pain involved in dying. I don't want it to be drawn out and/or painful. A gun would be quick, but I can't buy one because I've been in a mental hospital. Even jumping off a building would take too long. Pills? I have plenty, but bad things can happen before they finally finish you off.

I'm not "crying out for help." I went through years of therapy, countless drug cocktails, and hospitalization and the best thing that has ever happened is a few months of peace before I build up a resistance to drugs I'm taking and they no longer work. I can't ask my partner to do it; he never would in a million years. He doesn't know the kind of pain I go through and I can't adequately explain it to him.

So how do I do it quickly and painlessly?

Ready for the End,

Dear Ready for the End,

I CAN'T GIVE you helpful hints on how to kill yourself.

However, neither can I argue that your life is good and should be preserved, as I cannot know how life is for you. An average day for you may be more awful than even my worst day. Who am I to say that you should choose to live your life? As one of those left behind when others depart, I can only say that I have never heard any reports from successful suicides on whether they are pleased with the results.

So let us say simply that in your case suicide is one of the options you are considering. Let us presume that I have been called upon to help you choose. I think there are probably some better options to accomplish what you want to accomplish.

What you want to accomplish is an end to your suffering. Your only concern is that the act of suicide itself might entail some pain. But it is not altogether clear that suicide, however it is accomplished, will bring an end to suffering.

None of us knows what death will bring. You may find yourself reincarnated and continuing to suffer, or in hell, suffering, or without any consciousness at all and thus in a state immune to claims that it is either better or worse, or in some incomprehensible state of consciousness beyond anything that your current primitive apparatus of brain, nervous system and senses enables you to visualize. You do not know that you will not come back as a rock, or a dog, or a lizard with hazy consciousness of having once been, believe it or not, a human, magisterial and supreme among earthly beings. You may find yourself, as I do when I dream of suicide, in a state of unremitting remorse for having, in a moment's impetuousness, given up your life. In my dream I am falling and I am asking myself, Why did I do that? Someone was telling me the other day of a man who jumped from the Golden Gate Bridge and survived; on his way down, he found himself thinking, I thought I had problems before, but now I really have a problem: I jumped!

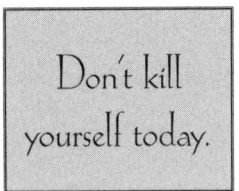

Don't kill yourself today.

You know nothing for certain of death and what comes after. So choosing suicide is not at all the sure cure for your ills that you might believe it to be. It is, rather, an enormous gamble.

Being that you are clearly willing to gamble to relieve your suffering, let us consider other gambles you might take.

For starters, you might gamble that if you wake up tomorrow alive, it may be one of your few good days. The odds are not great, but at least they are knowable. Since you have had some good days, you know that good days are possible. Moreover, a survey of your life will probably show that your good days have occurred in a cyclical pattern alternating with bouts of illness. So it is likely that they will recur in that cycle—perhaps not often enough to relieve your feeling that life is unrelenting suffering, but enough to show that in reality your suffering does occasionally relent.

Knowing both that good days will happen and that they will be rare, you might choose to make the most of those few that occur. Being possessed of independent wealth gives you certain options. On your next good day, you might board a plane to

Paris. On a good day, you might do anything in the world that your heart desires.

On a rare good day, you might also use your wealth to preserve and possibly extend that one good day into two good days or three. See if you can put a string of good days together. How? You might offer a prize of $10,000 to any psychologist, philosopher or medical doctor who can successfully prolong this one good day into two good days, or a week even! Perhaps there is someone out there with a method or a cure that will work for you—a hypnotist, a magician, a genius of meditation or a doctor of herbs and flowers, perhaps a guru who sits on a mountain. It would be a gamble, and there would be people who would try to con you, but since you are willing to gamble in other ways, and to part with your money, you might be willing to try anything.

What, if I may ask, have you got to lose?

Granted, the odds against tomorrow being a good day are not favorable. Most likely, tomorrow will be another day filled with depression and thoughts of suicide. But good days do happen. Eventually one will come. A good gamble, it seems to me, is to wait for that nearly assured good day and then take it for all it's worth.

There are other sound reasons to continue to live. Medical and psychological researchers continue to find ways to treat mental illness. At 36 you may have 40 years of life or more in which a cure may be found. So it makes sense to put suicide off as long as possible, as long as you can bear living. It also makes sense, if you have wealth, to contribute some of your money to any research that looks promising.

If you also want to give money to the person you live with, you are free to do that. You do not have to die in order to give money. If it would make you happy to contribute to that person's happiness, why not make some kind of financial gift to this person while you are living? However, if you want to enjoy knowing that you have made someone happy, you have to be alive to enjoy knowing it.

I do not mean to be glib about my views on suicide. I recognize your suffering and the seriousness of your proposal. Nor do I mean to minimize your suffering by treating the choice of suicide as a gamble, as if to reduce to a mere calculation what is a deeply emotional gesture. The point I would like to make is that while suicide may attract you as a supremely expressive act, it differs fundamentally from other expressive acts. We might punch a hole in a wall or scream at a policeman; we might get drunk or break things. From those gestures we can recover our lives. In fact, the very purpose of such gestures is that we can rid ourselves of the frustration and anger inside us and continue to live.

Suicide is not such a gesture; rather than allowing us to continue, it ends all chance.

So my advice is to see suicide as a bad bet, to gamble instead on what meager pleasure can be wrung from life, and to persist as long as possible in hope of a cure for your suffering.

Finally, if you feel like you are about to commit suicide, call your local suicide hotline, or the national referral number, 1-800-273-8255, or, if you like, call my local suicide hotline number in San Francisco, which is 415-781-0500. It is answered by a live person 24 hours a day, seven days a week.

Should I give up on having a life in the theater?

I've let go of my acting career, but it won't let go of me.

Dear Cary,

I'VE COMPOSED THE same letter many times over the past year without ever having hit the Send button because, during a writing episode, sooner or later I've been able to bury my little problem in my head just long enough to keep it from going nuclear. But this morning. Oh Jesus. One little phone call, and my emotions are stealthily clawing their way up through the grave. Again. Oh, the drama.

I never explicitly grew up with the need to become an actress—it was never a life's goal—but nevertheless I graduated with a degree in theater (I had fallen in love with Shakespeare) and went on to audition for, be accepted in, and finish an MFA professional actor training program out West. I moved to New York like aspiring actors are supposed to do, got tired of temp jobs and being lonely and broke and living off of friends and not having an agent. I left after only five months to take advantage of another job opportunity in another state—in a different field 180 degrees away from theater.

Wouldn't you know it, that opportunity fell through, and since I had spent all of my money on the move, I found myself once again broke and stuck and lonely—in New England.

I've been in Boston for four and a half years. The city is OK;

wherever you go, there you are, right? I've stayed at one crappy job only to move on to another crappy job because I can't figure out what I want. Ironically, whenever I have made the decision to want something, I have always gotten it. Always. I want to want something again. Even if I'm wrong! I'm so sick of being in limbo.

So here's what prompted me to hit the Send button: I went to a play last night, something I rarely do nowadays because it's a surefire way to unleash old demons. The theater is incredibly seductive—or at least my memories of it are. Now I've been thinking nonstop about the creative life vs. the present-day office life that I hate, and the breezy ways of actors vs. the uptight lawyers in their suits who occupy my building. I'm in my mid-30s now, and for the last two years I've been working as the assistant to a very needy octogenarian real estate entrepreneur (and I have little patience with needy men). This is the last place I expected to be.

I know I'm romanticizing a lot of this, because I never did honestly see myself living the New York actor's life in the first place, but I spent so much time—a good 10 years—in some kind of world of theater, be it either educational or, through my graduate school MFA program, professional, that I can't help feeling confused about where I think I want to belong. I know I don't feel like myself in an office.

So here's the rub. Myself and members of my MFA class all became Equity eligible after graduation (basically means that we are free to join Actor's Equity, the professional actor's union). I was disillusioned at the time and put off joining. I never joined. But seeing that play last night made me mildly curious, so I called Equity this morning to check on my eligibility standing.

Guess what. Seems I'm no longer eligible. My beginning date of eligibility was Oct. 27, 2000. Actors have five years from that date to join Equity after becoming eligible. I've expired! Grad school was a stupid waste of time and money. I'm an idiot.

This seems like the perfect opportunity to let go of a dream that never really was. Even though I detest my job, I have a lot of other things going for me—I'm in a great relationship, I'm healthy, I'm still active and curious about life—but even though I have done nothing during the last four and a half years to per- petuate the need of keeping a theater dream alive, still I keep it alive. I want it dead. I want to move on. But I still feel a part of me—even though it's a constantly diminishing part of me—is there (like I said, theater is seductive). If I could only figure out something else to want, I would be OK. But I feel like this stupid theater thing is what's keeping me from moving on and wanting something else.

So how do I let it go? And how do I get out of my own way? I hope you can help me.

A Reluctant Drama Queen

Dear Reluctant Drama Queen,

IN THE SAME way that you penned many letters before finally sending one to me, I have written many words to you already, before realizing that they were all rather empty. Perhaps because your question hits so close to home, because it is a question that I struggle with daily, I have been writing around it for the past two days.

So I had to go back to the beginning this morning and start again, trying to talk to you in a calm, level voice, aware that my motives are not pure, that I am stirred up and conflicted (I would like to impress you; I would like to dazzle you; I would like to show you that I know you; and all the while I am playing to the audience, not to you). But ... I do this a lot, don't I?—I write draft after draft, unsuccessfully, before coming to, as it were, to find you still sitting there waiting to hear something useful that is not about me. And still, even as you are clutching your bag readying to go—still I insist that I must carefully recap for you all the fruitless byways I have already explored; while much of my trouble is simply procedural and not artistic at all, still I allude to the difficulty of my craft, looking for sympathy, which is so codependent and unprofessional!

But as I fumble around like Columbo, I take in more than I seem to. I have an idea about you, about who you are and what your real problem is. To be blunt, I think it's clear that you have to find a place in your life for theater work. This may mean making some adjustments. If you cannot make a decent living working only in the theater, then you must work two jobs.

Doing this may involve making some discoveries about your capacities, your temperament. It may mean learning to live with some psychic discomfort. But I say this because I sense that you and I are close in temperament. The way you have scaled remarkable heights only to find yourself shrunken into servitude—this I recognize, this outsize capacity for expansion and contraction and for extravagant achievement and careless waste, the feeling that one's calling is not a gift but a burden, the desire to be done with it once and for all—all these things I recognize.

> Do the art you have to do, even if it hurts.

In fact—and here I will share with you a paragraph drafted earlier—I too let my eligibility for a professional milestone lapse. I completed all my coursework, passed my orals and had my creative thesis approved in graduate school for a master's degree in creative writing. Then I delayed for seven years the completion of some minor paperwork. Now I cannot have that master's degree that I worked so hard and so proudly to obtain. Strange, is it not? Indeed, such perverse delay is in one way a kind of proud renunciation, a protest. At bottom there is something pure and revolutionary about it. But there is also something self-destructive. The two work together in tandem, in a death dance, the revolutionary and the suicidal.

To be neither revolutionary nor suicidal but to pursue our work as it is revealed to us, to do the tasks that are handed to us by the force of our nature: That is the struggle that we actually must undertake to be whole, to be full participants in humanity.

You have a keen desire to work in the theater. This is the work that is handed to you by the force of your nature. Yet you run from it. Running from it pains you. Yet still you run. You will have to stop running sometime and face it.

We do not always find the work we think we will find; it is sometimes more as if the work finds us when we are ready. Look at me, writing an advice column. What am I to make of this? It is not drama or poetry or fiction or song. What is it? Why am I doing it? Why am I not onstage at some glittering event with some other writers whom I openly admire but secretly deride, all the while knowing nothing of their work? Why do I recoil from events at which writers are present? There I am, the untidy man in the corner at the art opening, drinking from the can in a paper bag! Why?

Well, perhaps because you and I want far more from the world than we let on. We have extravagant gifts, but we are deeply flawed. We are children! We don't know how to act! We can't concentrate! We grow bored and impatient! We'd rather slave away in an office than do mediocre art ... and all the while, we lie helpless before the gods; no matter what, we cannot stop doing what we do. We are in fact led to accomplish much, even as we deny what we are doing. At least you got the MFA. I didn't even get the degree. I started a punk band. What was that all about?

Anyway, now that I'm leveling with you, here is the way I was going to begin my response; here is my cerebral summation of the situation:

I see you onstage in a play. In the play something is hidden.

What is hidden is your essential nature. It cannot be killed. It won't go away. It must be dealt with.

What is the classic dramatic resolution to the problem of our struggle against our essential nature? Either this: We fail tragically fighting it; we go mad; we become rigid and monomaniacal; we shut ourselves into a room; we try to kill everything that disagrees with or threatens us. Or this: We make a discovery; a miracle occurs; the thing that threatened us is transformed, through revelatory action, into something beautiful that sustains us. Dammit, I am an actress! Dammit, let's put on a show!

Sure, make fun of it. But it's the truth.

That's what I had written. Isn't that rather stilted and pretentious? Sure, there is probably some truth in it. But Oh, the cleverness of placing you, an actress, onstage in order to make some point about "classic dramatic resolution"!

Here, though, is something else that perhaps we share: the grandiosity of our expectations. Have you ever felt, for instance, that if you are really to do theater that it must be the most pure, the most white-hot, the most completely absorbed thing imaginable—that if you are to do it, you must surrender to it so completely that you might in fact disappear, or die, or become someone else, or stand naked and sobbing in the footlights? Is there an apocalyptic expectation deep in your heart, or a feeling that if you are to become an actress then you will be an actress like no other ... is there a fear that to acknowledge this dream means to expose something, or risk failure, or turning out to be ordinary?

I can only speak for myself in this regard. (Oh, boy. That's probably just pitiful me we're talking about.) I know that for myself the dream is to be an artist, but that attempting to live as an artist, the poverty, the betrayals, the insecurity ... have all led me to turn away, to seek jobs in journalism and industry. But I continue, in my way. I continue working. I know that I lack certain essential abilities. I am trying to acquire them. It seems to me that I have no choice.

Well, I have tried to give you some of my thoughts. I could suggest other things as well—that your impulsiveness may be harming your chances of gaining a career, that you may need to learn to tough it out in a bad job while you keep going on auditions, that you may have a low threshold of psychic pain, that you need to simply work within your limits, things like that. But the one thing I would like to say most plainly is this: I do not think you can successfully fight your essential nature; if you fight it you only go mad; it must be transformed through revelatory action into something that sustains you.

If my wife dressed better, would gay guys stop hitting on me?

I'm a snappy dresser, and the other night, my wife and I were hanging out in this gay bar ...

Dear Cary,

MY WIFE AND I have been together since college and married for over six years, and recently had an incident with a male gay couple that has left us debating clothing styles. I have always been the snappier dresser between the two of us. In many ways, she has never left the hippie look from college. She is hot but has always chosen to downplay her looks. On the other hand, I was frequently referred to as a metrosexual (http://dir.salon. com/story/ent/feature/2002/07/22/metrosexual/index.html) (when the word was in). I always iron my shirts, wear form-fitting clothes like leather pants, polish my shoes, etc. I have been occasionally asked by random strangers if I am gay. Both of us have always accepted the way each other dressed.

We are both socially liberal, and were out recently at a bar that is frequented by gay couples. We were seated at a table listening to a band when I received a drink from a waitress who told me that the drink was from two guys seated a few tables away from us. I waved to them and suggested that my wife and I join them, thinking that they were just being friendly. Big mistake. It turned out the two guys were gay and were soon all over me. Needless to say, my wife was not amused, while I just laughed it off. While sharing the story with a couple of good friends later, I suggested that if my wife took the trouble to dress up more then perhaps gay men would not hit on her husband. We have been debating that issue since then. I thought I would ask you.

Would a gay guy be less likely to hit on me if my wife were dressed up more and even had makeup on, as opposed to the hippie look that she favors? There is the option of my changing my dress style, but I think that since I was not the one complaining about the incident, I should not be the one to change. Any thoughts?

Amused in North Carolina

Dear Amused,

SOMETIMES, IN TRYING to discover the hidden message that might be lurking in a sentence, it is useful to stare at it until it begins to look like something else. I have a feeling this is what poets do sometimes, and perhaps also psychoanalysts.

I have been staring at this sentence for a while, watching how it changes shape and meaning: "I suggested that if my wife took the trouble to dress up more then perhaps gay men would not hit on her husband."

I recognize in this rather impossible formulation the trickster, or rather the mind working as the trickster, inverting meaning in order to serve desire's purposes of subterfuge. I certainly don't think it's anything as simple as just "You're obviously a latent homosexual." Rather, I imagine that in your world, certain kinds of play provide an outlet for socially unacceptable notions as well as for the erotic in a larger sense—not the homoerotic particularly but more generally the love of style, color, fashion, appearance, theatricality, fine things: the sensual realm.

The sentence itself, being so absurd, reflects a reality that is utterly unrecognizable, like an inkblot. It has no clear meaning of its own; it is, rather, a conundrum, a shadow, a mystery.

In staring at it, it's hard to know what to focus on at first. But I focus on "gay men would not hit on her husband." It sounds like a trope for something gone awry. "Gay guys hitting on me" is a metaphor for something, a displacement of desire perhaps, an erotic frustration, something.

It might be restated thusly: "I suggested to her that if she took the trouble to dress up more, then perhaps X might happen," X being some positive and desired outcome. But what would that be?

Perhaps "gay men hitting on me" is a metaphor for your own heterosexual desire being misdirected or misinterpreted. Then by playing this game with her, what you are saying is that you want her to change the way she dresses in order to reorder your own desire. That's a roundabout way of asking. But then you are playing a complicated game.

I'm familiar with the use of riddles and circuitous, apparently nonsensical formulations to address taboo topics. It's very "amusing" but also can be cruel toward those who are left guessing what it is you are really asking for.

And it can get very complicated. Perhaps you do have homoerotic desires that are playing out here. Or perhaps they are only a metaphor.

If we reverse the phrase "gay men hitting on her husband" to "her husband hitting on gay men," then we have an expression of your desire possibly being channeled into forbidden areas. Not necessarily homosexual areas; it could be women or anybody; it's the desire and its rechanneling that are significant

And what about this: What if it had been two women at the bar who sent you over the drink? You wouldn't have gone over there. Flirting with gay men is presumably OK because they are off limits. By choosing something that is by tacit agreement not actually an option, the taboo desire for others can be raised.

So I think the homoerotic represents something that you cannot have or are not allowed to want. You are uncomfortable telling your wife that you wish she would dress differently, so instead, your anxiety and discomfort wind through back channels to

> Say what you want.

become this odd riddle. It is your way of raising an issue without appearing to raise it.

Very clever of you. But also a little vexing.

It could be very frustrating for someone else to figure all this out. So I suggest, for your wife's sake, that at the expense of being so amusing, you try to be a little more direct.

So now why don't you two just sit down and talk about what is actually going on? Because it's not really very nice to toy with people—either gay guys or your wife. If everyone understands the game, I suppose it is fine and amusing. But I would ask: Do you really understand what you're doing? And does your wife? Does she really know what you're asking for? Do you?

Just when I thought
I was going to be fine,
they say I'm bipolar

*After all I've been through, how am
I supposed to keep my chin up now?*

Dear Cary,

FOR THE PAST nine months I've been struggling with a medical diagnosis that has turned my world upside-down. My reaction to it is making it difficult for me to carry on living, as some part of me feels that this is a death sentence and that there is no way to live with the ramifications of this huge kick in the gut.

Since the age of 15 I have had tremendous struggles with the ordinary tasks of living. Though I was assessed as well above average in intelligence and was thought to have huge potential, I found school and friendships and life to be ordeals full of pain. My moods swung violently from euphoria to deep depression, and though I saw various psychiatrists, the general feeling was that I wasn't trying hard enough and should be able to pull myself out of these struggles. I drank heavily to try to cope with feelings of self-hate and alienation.

I didn't go to university, but met a man when I was 18, and married him within a year. Though my life was limited in many ways, I did love him deeply, and had two children by him in my early 20s. Though this period of my life was relatively stable, it was blown to pieces in my late 20s by another crisis, in which my moods once more began to careen out of control and I landed in the hospital.

Though I saw many therapists over the years, there was never any agreement on what was wrong with me: major depressive disorder, post-traumatic stress (I grew up in an alcoholic home and was sexually abused, my brother was a schizophrenic who died young, and my aunt committed suicide), and (worst of all) histrionic personality disorder, which implied that my suffering was merely empty theatrics. One doctor even told me, "Go home and behave yourself."

By my mid-30s I was drinking alcoholically, and beginning to sink. At the same time, I had carved out a bit of a niche for myself as a columnist and a book reviewer, and I had written somewhere around 1,000 pieces that had been published. I adored my children, and they were turning out well. I was active in my community, when I could manage it. But psychiatrists did not count these accomplishments at all, and continued to see me as immature and lacking in self-control.

When I was 36, I hit bottom with the alcohol, joined a 12-step program and began to heal my life. There followed 15 years of relative stability—sober, seeing a psychologist who was much more respectful, and finally writing a novel that was published and very well received. All my dreams seemed to be coming true: I was a grandmother, my book was out, I had an agent who sold my second novel, I had found a way of faith that fit me well, and my husband and I were planning a trip to New Zealand for our 32nd anniversary.

But something strange started to happen. My sleep was gradually getting less and less. My mood went from normal to euphoric, and I began to believe I had special powers. Soon my thoughts began to accelerate. I had been through this a thousand times already, but this time I believed I was on the verge of a powerful God-consciousness that would save not only me, but the entire world.

When the crash came, it was catastrophic, and I landed in the hospital for the first time in 15 years. The shrinks there dusted off my old file, assumed I had experienced no personal growth at all since 1990 (they looked incredulous when I said I was a novelist, and I am sure they did not believe it), and told me once again that I had histrionic personality disorder.

But my general practitioner, who had known me for 14 years, said, "Wait a minute." After an appointment where my speech and thoughts raced incoherently at full tilt, she stopped me and said, "I think you're bipolar." The statement socked me in the gut, but at the same time, strangely enough, it was a huge relief.

Once I got out of the hospital, I found a shrink who actually made sense and seemed to know his stuff. After half an interview, he said, "I have no doubt this is bipolar." He told me that misdiagnosis is often part and parcel of this illness, as the manic phase (which in my case was extremely productive) can often look like high energy and good health. Again, relief and recognition vied with utter shock.

What has happened since is a ferocious battle in myself, a complete inability to accept the fact that I now have a full-blown, full-scale, serious mental illness after 15 years of remission. When I look at my symptoms, I don't know what else it could be, and I don't disagree with the fact of it. I just can't accommodate it. It isn't OK, and I'm not OK for having it. This has triggered the worst self-hate of my entire life. I feel like the family script (fatal mental illness) is coming true in me, as if it's my turn. On all these drugs, I doubt if I will ever write creatively again. It feels as if my life is gone. I never realized I harbored such hate and fear of mental illness, but apparently I do. Every time I even approach the idea of acceptance, which everyone tells me I must, I break out in fury that this could have happened during the best time of my whole life. Most people assume psychiatric catastrophe can only occur during a period of adversity and horrendous stress, but mine didn't. I had never felt better in my whole life, but I came very close to dancing naked on a public street.

My husband keeps saying, "This is what you've had your whole life." No one has known me longer than he has, and he has watched me go through hell and pull myself out of it over and over again. But why am I breaking out in trouble like this, after being well for years and years? Why, why, why? I stayed sober through it all, and 12-step programs always say that "God restores us to sanity."

So what happened? How can this be? God seems like some distant enigma that I can't reach anymore. I can't forgive it, can't get on with real recovery, and I know this rage is going to consume me eventually. In spite of all the good things in my life that I've worked for so hard, in spite of seeing a psychologist who just keeps telling me to treat myself with kindness and respect, I feel totally humiliated and struggle every day with the urge to commit suicide. Though I try not to, I feel in disgrace.

I have made a pact with myself, which for my family's sake I hope I can keep, to postpone killing myself for one year, on the off chance I will be able to accommodate this horror and find that I want to continue. But I am not sure I can keep it. Well-meaning people say things like, "Well, you got better before, didn't you? Just do what you did then."

This infuriates me, as how can I "just do what I did before" (the "just" implying it's a piece of cake and I'm not really trying) if I am not the same person? My identity has been blown into vapor, and there is no way to put the pieces back together because there are no pieces. I don't know how to start over again, one more time, and if I do, how long until everything explodes all over again?

If you could try to give me a perspective that goes beyond the platitudes, the "focus on how blessed you are," the "just do what you did before," I would greatly appreciate it.

Bipolar Writer

Dear Bipolar Writer,

YOU ARE ILL. I can say things and say things and say things but I can't make you well. I wish I could but I can't. All I can do is say hang on for dear life until it passes. It will pass. It passed before. It will pass again.

But what can you hang on to? What have you got? Have you got a will to survive? Have you got a belief that pleasure and sanity will return? I think you probably do. This illness, of course, will cloud your mind. It will distort your thinking. It will place a veil over your memories. It will work on the "you" so that you cannot be sure what is you and what is the disease. It will make you believe that there really isn't anything worth living for. It will make you believe that your life is over.

Your life is not over.

But what good does it do for me to say that? You are the one who must struggle against this thing. The little sayings and truisms of your 12-step program must seem woefully inadequate to that task. And yet... you must have acquired from your 12-step work a crucial skill for dealing with this new and daunting diagnosis: You know how to coexist with a force against whose power to subvert your thinking you are more or less helpless without outside intervention.

So, strangely enough, I would think a recovered alcoholic is better suited than most to cope with a diagnosis of severe mental illness. While I am not really a fan of literal translation of the 12 steps ("We admitted we were powerless over acne and came to believe that a power greater than ourselves could restore us to lustrous, peachy-smooth skin...") in this matter of insanity it does seem that you must place yourself in the hands of powers greater than yourself and trust that you will be restored to sanity.

You must struggle to maintain in your mind a picture of the world to which you fervently wish to return, knowing all the while that no matter how hard you struggle you are going to slip underwater from time to time into the nightmare from which it will seem there is no escape but you are going to wake up eventually and it is going to be sunny outside and you are going to walk barefoot in the grass wet with chilly spring dew once again before long, and you are going to enjoy many more years of sanity once this thing is over; and it will be over.

You must believe that. There is nothing else worth believing.

My girlfriend is a racist

Her views don't make much sense—
she likes Bush ... and Chomsky!

Dear Cary,

I'M A COLLEGE student in my mid-20s who recently began dating again after a four-year relationship ended around Memorial Day. The girl I'm seeing now is beautiful, talented and bright. We don't align at all politically (I'm a Democrat; she's a dyed-in-the-wool Republican) but our personalities mesh so well that it really isn't a source of friction for us. We have enough in common to relate, and enough differences to make it challenging and interesting. I tend to be reserved when it comes to declaring my love, but she is definitely the sort of woman I could fall in love with.

The other night, however, she said that she had something to tell me: she's "a little racist" (we're both Irish-American). She buys into some of the most offensive stereotypes of black Americans (crime, laziness, etc.), and proceeded to tell me that she hates when people who can't speak English come to America. I was dumbfounded. I told her that people said the same sorts of things about our respective great-grandparents, and that 19th century stereotypes about the Irish were as false as the ones she was spouting today about other races.

Physically, emotionally and personality-wise, we're in sync. But I feel that this is a deal-breaker for me. She's young (21) and grew up in a racist household, but at some point she has to take ownership for her opinions. I almost dumped her on the spot, but there's so much else about her that I adore and admire;

she's a fascinating mishmash of conflicting traits—she loves Bush but also thinks Noam Chomsky should run for president, for instance. I want to appreciate and maybe even love her for who she is, but I really want her to change this one thing, and it is a big thing for me. Do I dump her? Do I say, "Change your heart or I'll dump you"? Can she reform if she wants to? The air between us is poisoned; I don't know what to do.

Disappointed In Love

Dear Disappointed,

RATHER THAN ATTACK her racist ideas directly, I would suggest that you first think about why they are important to her, what value they have. They may represent a vital connection to her family that she is reluctant to discard.

It's an interesting question: How are we supposed to discard the mistaken lessons of our family? After all, we go out into the world armed with what they taught us. Then presumably we learn to think critically in the university. A persuasive and charismatic professor may break through our ignorance. Intellectual honesty may leave us no choice but to conclude that racist ideas are scientifically unfounded and socially pernicious.

But on campus we may also encounter political groups that mirror the beliefs of our family and reinforce our mistaken notions. If we are not ready to discard the myths and fairy tales we got from our family, we may take refuge in campus groups whose politics seem to lend legitimacy to those notions.

One clue that she is clinging to these ideas for emotional reasons and has not thought them through is the absurd contradiction of having as heroes both George Bush and Noam Chomsky. This may indicate that what she really requires for a feeling of security is simply a strong father figure. Maybe any father figure will do. Maybe her father is key: What peril does she face if she challenges her father's political ideas? What were the rules of argument in her family? Was one allowed to question the orthodoxy? What happened to children when they did so? What did they see in their parents' eyes? Hurt? Anger? Threat? And what purpose did racist ideology serve in the family? Was it something the family used to hold itself together against outside threats?

The answers to these and similar questions might be complicated and difficult (See for instance "Mapping the 'Unconscious': Racism and the Oedipal Family" http://www.blackwell-synergy.com/links/doi/10.1111/0004-5608.00194/abs/?cookieset=1) or they might be simple. But if we are ever to be rid of racism, it seems to me we must ask the questions. We must try to understand what good it does people to hang on to these ideas and why it is so difficult to give them up.

You might also, at the same time, by way of making it fair, look at your own received notions from your family, and how orthodoxy and dissent were handled. What were the prevailing ideologies in your family? Were you taught that racism is a deal-breaker?

While it is important to ask where these ideas come from and why they are valuable to her, it's inevitable that the ideas themselves must come under scrutiny.

Since she likes Noam Chomsky so much, perhaps the most persuasive argument might come from Chomsky himself. If indeed she "buys into some of the most offensive stereotypes of black Americans (crime, laziness, etc.)," let's hear what Chomsky has said about race and IQ:

> Respect the private utility of the odious idea.

"Consider finally the question of race and intellectual endowments. Notice again that in a decent society there would be no social consequences to any discovery that might be made about this question. Individuals are what they are; it is only on racist assumptions that they are to be regarded as an instance of their race category, so that social consequences ensue from the discovery that the mean for a certain racial category with respect to some capacity is such and such. Eliminating racist assumptions, the facts have no social consequences whatever they may be, and therefore are not worth knowing, from this point of view at least. ...

"Since the inquiry has no scientific significance and no social significance, apart from the racist assumption that individuals must be regarded not as what they are but rather as standing at the mean of their race category, it follows that it has no merit at all. The question then arises, Why is it pursued with such zeal? Why is it taken seriously? ...

"In a racist society, inquiry into race and IQ can be expected to reinforce prejudice, pretty much independent of the outcome of the inquiry" (from "Equality: Language Development, Human Intelligence and Social Organization," in "The Chomsky Reader," pp. 199-200).

Chomsky reminds us that we live in a racist society, but he denounces racism. I suggest that your friend do the same. It may be harder for her if her family and peer group provided her with these views and reinforce them. But perhaps you can be of some help in this regard.

Anyway, good luck. You may have an uphill battle. Say you explore all these issues with her, and you come to understand the genesis of them, but you find she actually has great enthusiasm for these ideas and doesn't want to let them go. At that point, I think you and I would agree, you have to let her go.

But you never know. It's worth a shot. Let me know how things turn out.

One final request: If you can't talk her out of her racist views, at least try to talk her out of majoring in broadcasting, OK?

Mom and Dad stopped speaking to the kids

*We four daughters have stayed close,
but our parents have drifted away.*

Dear Cary,

MY PARENTS HAVE stopped talking to their children and we don't know what to do. I'm the oldest of four daughters, aged 27 to 33. Two are married, and one has a 1-year-old girl. The four of us are very close.

I think our parents are unable to figure out how to treat their children as we have grown up and created families of our own. They never call us, expecting that we should call them. My father is withdrawn and distant, a recovering alcoholic who never established an emotional bond with his children. My mother answers the phone, but rarely asks anything about us and prefers to talk about herself the whole time.

My parents were baby sitting my niece recently, and for some reason that day my mom decided to cut the baby's hair. She honestly did a terrible job—the bangs are jagged and the hair is uneven. It's the baby's second haircut, and my sister was shocked and angry with my mom for doing this without asking her first.

When one of us kids has an argument with my mom, she stops talking to all of us. She and my dad won't answer their phone when we call or respond to e-mail. When my mom finally picks up the phone—usually one to two weeks later—she sounds depressed and talks about how her children hate her. This is happening more frequently, perhaps every other month.

It's very difficult to deal with. I don't think we should tolerate it, and my mom should know there are consequences for acting like that. I want to confront her and tell her she can't expect to have a relationship with her kids if she keeps this up. I want all four of us to do it, because it won't be effective otherwise. But my sisters won't go along, saying that scolding her will make it worse and she may ignore us for months or longer. This is true, I admit. So we wait, and eventually everything goes back to normal with nothing said about the incident. Any advice on how to handle this?

Getting the Silent Treatment

Dear Silent Treatment,

THERE ARE CLUES here but much is silent. Alcoholism is a kind of silence; depression is a kind of silence. So you're getting the silent treatment; that's probably the treatment your mother knows best.

Since silence reigns, let me guess at what has not been said. It's possible that when you children were at home, your mother knew what her job was. Your father may have been drinking and unavailable, but your mother could find satisfaction taking care of the kids, cooking and sewing and teaching you how to behave. Absorption in motherhood may have been partly a way of avoiding your father's drinking. But it was of great value regardless. It was a worthy life. Until eight or 10 years ago, she presumably had at least one daughter living at home.

But one day finally all the daughters were gone. It was strangely quiet in the house. The husband had stopped drinking. Maybe she walked around the empty house wondering what to do with herself. Maybe she began to experience depression. Maybe she looked at her husband and could barely see him in the dark.

You know how astronomers prove the existence of invisible bodies? The alcoholic father's presence, too, is found in the flight paths of the people around him, how they wobble when they cross his orbit. He sits in his chair, withdrawn in the dark, sucking in everything around him. You can't see him there but sensitive instruments detect a blurry kind of sadness, a longing you can't put your finger on, something vaguely twisted, lonely and dark. Alcoholism in a family can be like that—an absence that sits in a chair in the dark and warps the space around it.

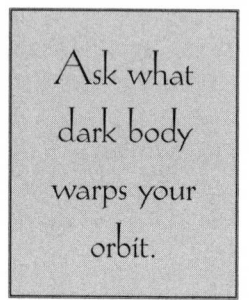

Ask what dark body warps your orbit.

That's not to blame this situation on alcoholism, or blame your mother's behavior on your father. The point is that your mother didn't just become the way she is in a vacuum. Things happened and she responded.

You don't say if she works or not; perhaps she worked all along, or perhaps after the last child left she got a job. Maybe she worked or did not work but things changed for your mother when the girls left the house and the husband stopped drinking and withdrew into himself. She had a purpose and then she didn't. She had a husband and then she didn't. She had daughters and a house full of people. Then she didn't.

If she never took stock, if she never saw that her happiness was rooted in taking care of others, then it's possible she's been drifting all this time, waiting for something to happen, calling out whenever she sees something familiar. Maybe every now and then she glimpses something that looks like happiness—she sees a dress and wants to sew it, sees a breakfast and wants to cook it, sees misbehavior and wants to fix it. But when she gets closer she sees: This is not my daughter's hair! This is not my kitchen!

This frightens her and angers her. Her expression of anger is silence.

Chastising her won't help. If she has no purpose, then she needs a purpose. She needs something to take care of. If not her kids, then her grandkids. If not her grandkids, then animals, or plants, or somebody else's kids. She needs something to take care of.

That might explain why one day she saw the baby and suddenly had to get some scissors.

Of course she gave a terrible haircut. She's way out of practice.

I can't get closure
with my alcoholic ex

*The ugly divorce is finally over, but
it just doesn't feel like it's over.*

Dear Cary,

A FEW YEARS ago at the age of 49, I decided to leave my alcoholic husband. I'm a rarity. Studies show that of 10 women married to alcoholics, only one will leave, while out of 10 men married
to alcoholics, only one will stay. I've always supported myself,
so while it was wrenching for me to leave my familiar prison, I
was reasonably sure I could rebuild my life and start over as an
unmarried woman. There are no children involved, by the way.

I will spare you the details of how wretchedly intolerable the
situation was and how justified I was in leaving him, but they
involved the usual alcoholic atrocities and then some: lying, gambling, refusing to take responsibility, financial disaster, verbal
abuse, betrayal of trust, denial, physical and emotional estrange-
ment, shifting of blame. I felt I had to leave him to save my own
life, and since he blamed me for everything bad about his life, I
thought he wouldn't object. He didn't; he helped me find my own
house and move. Of course I'd already tried everything wives
of alcoholics try: pleading, bribing, screaming, co-drinking,
codependency, threats, attempted intervention and, eventually,
thanks to my Al-Anon group, detachment.

After I left and filed for divorce, telling my low-key attorney
that I expected an uncomplicated, mutually agreed-upon if not

amicable split, he hired the "best" divorce firm in this city and proceeded to make our divorce unnecessarily horrific, brutal, expensive and protracted. He didn't fight to keep me; he sought to punish me financially and emotionally for divorcing him. (Leaving was allowed; divorcing him was not to be borne.) After two years, the magistrate handling our case finally told him to stop filing motions against me. That was two months ago.

I just recently found a good job that will allow me to pay back the debts I incurred in the divorce. I'm living in my own house. I have a new boyfriend who treats me well and does not drink heavily or gamble. My health is much improved and my future no longer looks dreary. I'm right where I always envisioned myself when I used to daydream about how pleasant life could be if I were not married to a depressed alcoholic with a gambling addiction. I've rebuilt my life's foundations and I'm starting to build a new social network. I haven't had a threatening, vitriolic, accusing letter, e-mail or voice mail from the ex in two months. Life is good.

Until the other night, when I heard a sad song about heartbreak and abandonment (Alison Krauss' "Ghost in This House") and it got to me. I felt so sad for him, and I thought about how it must have hurt him when I left. At the time I didn't see how I could have done anything different to get away from a relationship that was killing me slowly, but now I wonder. I did not handle the leaving and divorce with kindness and dignity, as I would like to have done. I did not rise above the situation and treat him like a person with an illness. I was too hurt, too scared and too desperate.

This is the curse of divorcing an alcoholic: You don't get closure. No one can fault you for leaving for one of the "big A" reasons (addiction, abuse, abandonment, adultery), but you don't get, I don't know, maybe "resolution" is the word I'm looking for. Finality. Peace. Serenity. The opportunity to be friends, or at least on civil terms with your ex. Maybe it's lingering codependency that keeps whispering to me that there was something I could have done, not to save my marriage but to end it without so much ugliness and pain.

I loved him once. I'd like to forgive him. But I don't know where he went; the person I loved is gone and only the addiction inhabits his body. He hates me and blames me for everything, including his drinking, even though he will not admit that he has a problem. If I told him I forgave him, he'd say I have nothing to forgive, and he does not forgive me. We had 10 years together; some of them were wonderful, and now they just seem like a waste of time.

I went through hell in the final years and months of my marriage. It was a relief to end it, and I feel reborn. I thought I was past the worst of it and all my tears were shed. Now that he's not harassing me any longer, I'm out of self-preservation mode and I have time for reflection and regret. There is this huge disconnect between my life then and my life now; I've cut myself off completely from the people we both knew and even the industry we both used to work in. In effect, I gave them to him. They were the price I was willing to pay to escape. I don't regret leaving him, only that I acted badly toward him and others while I was struggling with the bitter end of my marriage.

Can you tell me how to move on, reach resolution and forgive myself?

Phoenix (the mythical bird, not the city)

Dear Phoenix,

I AM READING this letter and I am going yep, yep, yep, that's classic!

I know I answer a lot of letters about alcoholism, but it is one thing I know inside and out, so when I can't figure out what else to do this is what I do, I go and write about alcoholism.

As an alcoholic, I can tell you that's what we do! We do it because you don't think we will do it. You don't think we're capable of it. You don't think we'd dare. You think we'll forget and move on. You think we're like other people but we're not. You think we've got some shame but we don't. We don't stop when others stop. We don't slow down when others slow down. We just speed up! We will do anything and that's our awesome power.

We will not be deterred by shame or pity or self-consciousness. Whatever happens, we can take it because we've got our medicine. We'll do anything as long as we've got our medicine. We'll take it as far as it can go. We've got the medicine to keep us going. We've got the stuff that kills the conscience so we don't have to stop halfway on account of our little conscience. Conscience? Nah. Watch this. We'll take it where you can't even imagine anybody would want to go.

Why? Because we can! Because we're drunk! Because we don't give a fuck. You just watch.

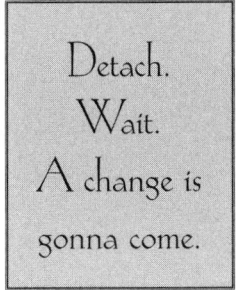

Detach. Wait. A change is gonna come.

And just when you think it's over? Ha! That's when we're just getting started: Have another drinky-poo, we're not even tired, we've been drinking all night and we're still going, and wait till you see what's coming next!

Not only can I channel that voice but I even, in a twisted diabolical alcoholic way, appreciate what he is up to—the awful, terrible spite of it, the wounded, caged-animal desperation of it, the stealthy, secretive, maniacal mad-scientist glee of its sadism and depravity. And beneath it all the whole time I know there is that poor little abused soul, which he can trot out every now and then to win your sympathy and pity. And he will do that if he can; he will put on his little "Howdy Doody Show."

Detach. Detach. Don't get too close or he'll pick your pocket. Forgive yourself for being human. Align yourself with other women who have been there. If he has friends who have sobered up and can commiserate, commiserate with them. You have to heal it. He's not going to help. He's going to make it harder if he can. Don't let him. Heal it up. Use everything you've got.

This guy is not on your side. This guy, as long as he's drinking, you just have to protect yourself from him.

So do not pity this man. Pity, if you wish, those he owes money to. But do not pity this man and do not try to help him. Take care of yourself instead.

It might not feel like it's over, but it's over for you. It's not over for him but it's over for you.

Detach. Detach. Wait. A change is gonna come.

At 19, I've already seen drugs damage my peers

Smoking dope is lonely and pathetic. What's wrong with scaring the bejesus out of kids?

Dear Cary,

I'VE NOTICED YOU have published a few advice columns for teenagers, and was wondering if I could hop on the bandwagon (although, at 19, I'm kind of pushing it) and ask you a few question about drugs.

Neither I nor any of my close friends do drugs, mostly because it complicates things unnecessarily and has negative consequences for the user and all the people they interact with.

I live in a wealthy suburb of San Francisco. My boyfriend and I know kids who were highly intelligent, together and promising, who started smoking pot when they were 12 or 13, drifted from high school to high school, stole money and painkillers from their parents, graduated or didn't graduate, and now are in their early 20s, living off their parents' money, and are either heroin addicts or trying hard to be heroin addicts. One girl we know started using meth intravenously when she was 14 (according to her brother, she got it from their uncle). One kid with a long history of drug abuse overdosed on Valium the day before finals, had a psychotic episode at our high school, and was forcibly confined to a mental institution by police. There are worse cases, but you get the idea. I know this sounds melodramatic and scary, but it's not out of place in extremely affluent communities.

Drug education in this country is very polarized. On the one hand, there is DARE, with police officers scaring middle-school kids, "Go Ask Alice," etc. On the other hand, there is a weird reaction emerging where parents think that, because they did drugs, they can't tell their kids not to.

An example of the latter. The Drug Policy Alliance (http://www.lindesmith.org/homepage.cfm) is an organization that advocates reform in the war on drugs (which I agree with) and wants parents to introduce drugs in a gradient of badness, with the emphasis on safety. "I have news for you. Your kids are going to do drugs," Ayelet Waldman (another columnist at Salon) stated (http://bad-mother.blogspot.com/2005/01/but-pots-so-much-stronger-nowadays.html) in January 2005. Is that really the case?

Unlike sex, recreational drug use does not stem from an instinctive behavior designed to further the good of the species. Although some species and cultures use psycho-affective plants for their non-nutritive benefits, I disagree that treating drug use as an eventuality will do more good than, say, scaring the living bejesus out of youngsters. Treating drug use as a phase might make sense for people who grew out of it and faced no harrowing consequences, but as evinced by your column, prison statistics, the booming market for drug-confessional memoirs, and the thriving alcohol advertising market, for many it is not a phase, and it is significantly harder to grow out of than many in the Bay Area would have you think.

So the question is: What is the most effective stance to take? To the best of my knowledge, recreational drug use has never made anyone happy, but it is rarely as objectively terrible as the moral arbiters would have one believe. Drug use is not sensational, outré or shocking—it's lonely and pathetic. I wish there was a way to explain to young people the degenerative effects of this and other self-destructive behaviors and still be listened to. Is there?

Or am I just trying to prevent the unpreventable?

Clean but Concerned

Dear Clean,

LIKE YOU, I think there would be more happiness and less misery in our little part of the world if fewer teens took drugs. But I suggest that you simply tell your own truth: how you feel about the drug use you have observed, and why you yourself do not do it.

As far as policy goes, I agree with the goals (http://www. lindesmith.org/about/ of the Drug Policy Alliance, with one caveat: When I was a teenage drug abuser, if I remember correctly, well-meaning people did offer me useful information about the drugs I might or might not be taking. I nodded and looked concerned. I made them tea and said, "Would you like to sit on the couch?" But if I was going to not take drugs, there needed to be either A) no drugs around or B) big dogs and men with sticks between me and the drugs.

> Tell your own truth about drugs.

If I had known you at the time, a hip, intelligent young person who did not use drugs, I would have admired you and would have wondered how you could be so cool and yet not do drugs. Maybe I would have thought it was a little sad that you didn't get off like the rest of us. Or maybe I would have thought it was great. It's hard to tell. But I doubt that it would have stopped me. I was too desperately unhappy and too cunning and insincere, too guarded, too aloof, too afraid and too afraid to show that I was afraid.

I was meeting my needs the only way I knew how.

How was a guy like me going to use practical pharmacological data to make balanced decisions about which drugs to take? My main goal was to get so high I couldn't see my shoes.

And therein lies my concern about the realistic, common-sense approach: It seems to assume that the adolescent drug user is a rational actor who can weigh risks and benefits.

I frankly don't know what anyone could have done to help a kid like me. My problem was not a lack of pharmacological data.

It was the problem of how to be a human being, how to live in society, how to experience God, how to grow up and be a man. If somebody had offered me answers to those questions, I might have listened. In other circumstances there might have been a wise elder, healer, philosopher, warrior, priest or some such to help me express and channel those needs. No such luck. Not in that world.

My drug use may have been misguided, but it had at its heart the most noble of desires: the desire to know the universe, to be at peace in the world, to liberate the better self, the true self, to allow what is good in the self to shine, and to know mysteries firsthand, to experience the inexpressible beauty, harmony and complexity of consciousness.

I understand your dilemma: When you say you're against drug use, you seem to say you are against certain noble strains of the questing American spirit—Beats and hippies and transcendentalists and Expressionists and all that.

So I suggest two things: 1) Tell your own truth about drugs. But more important, 2) work to build a culture that meets the needs that people take drugs to meet.

People take drugs to meet legitimate needs: initiation, profound experience, encounter with death, exploration of consciousness, exploration of personal limits physically and emotionally, a certain derangement of the senses, to feel more deeply, to taste the edge of insanity.

Our problem is that we do not know how to collectively actualize the mystery of the universe so that our children can be ushered into adulthood confident that they belong. We need rituals that create vivid experiences of reality, vivid enough to make the drug experience pale by comparison. We need to live in a way that makes drugs irrelevant.

We don't know how to live that way. We don't know how to live vividly enough.

That is what I would pray for: that we learn how to live.

How do I reverse my mother's curse?

For generations the women in my family have been attacking their daughters. Now it's my turn.

Dear Cary,

MY MOTHER COMES from a long line of smart, frustrated women who write venomous letters to their daughters. When I was a child, the arrival of my grandmother's letters to my mother always meant trouble for my siblings and me, who would take the brunt of her anger and hurt. My mother never confronted her mother, aside from not replying. She did, however, swear she would never follow the family tradition of writing poison-pen letters.

Now I am in my 40s, divorced and the mother of a college-age son who is in the midst of a late-adolescent rebellion that consists of not being in college or doing anything much at all. He has argued with his grandparents and, after a physical fight started by my father, no longer speaks to them. My elderly parents, in addition to denying that my father ever punched my son, blame me for the way he has turned out and insist that I have encouraged his behavior, when in fact I have done the opposite. And my mother has just written me a vicious letter—not the first—that puts all the blame for our family's ills on my shoulders.

She demands that I apologize for everything she accuses me of, including my son's behavior; I am not allowed to defend myself.

And despite the fact that she verbally abused me all through my childhood, abandoned me at critical times and told me she wished I'd never been born, I'd be willing to do it, if not for the fact that it would solve nothing. My mother is a champion grudge holder, never forgiving anyone for their transgressions, so why would she change now? And having gotten away from my role as the family scapegoat and found real happiness, I am afraid that caving in to her demands would erase all I have achieved.

Through all of this, I have tried to maintain relations with my father, who I sense is more sympathetic, though ultimately he is on her side. I have maintained communication with both of them, calling them despite the frostiness of their reception. I have invited them to visit and gotten no response. My siblings are at best detached; at worst they side with my parents completely and don't speak to me.

I want to resolve this without betraying myself or my son, but how?

Attacked

Dear Attacked,

YOURS IS THE story of the unjustly accused who will never get a trial, whose crimes are vague. Like all unjustly accused you are thrust out of society, forced to wander seeking justice. Unlike that wandering Fugitive played by David Janssen, however, whose crime was subject to laws of evidence, your crime is an existential one for which there is no standard of proof and no evidentiary defense. Hence you are simultaneously accused and condemned, denied a trial or even the opportunity to speak in your own behalf. And to be put through this ordeal not by a government from which one can dissociate oneself, but by one's own parents whom one cannot condemn because that is like condemning oneself ... what an inescapable trap!

Such an unjust accusation is not a charge but a curse; the source of its power is magical; it cannot be lifted by science; it cannot be satisfied by the payment of a fine or the doing of time or, as you rightly note, by apology.

Since it is a curse, beyond the realm of evidence, its cure can only be magical. Some curses can be reversed by being spoken backward. So tell the story backward: Write the letters that should have been written from mother to daughter. Write the letter, full of pain, that your mother ought to have written to you. In it, writing as your own mother, take responsibility for what she has done to you. And then write the letter her mother should have written to her, taking responsibility for her own crimes against her daughter. Then write the letter her mother should have written to her, taking responsibility, revealing 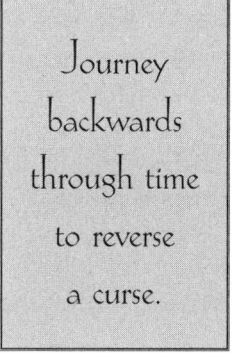 the secrets, exposing the wounds repeated through the generations. Write these letters, going back and back and back until you are out of time and out of this world, until you have gone beyond the farthest grandmother and her travail, until you reach that crime of which no one can speak but which is the foul primordial fountain out of which all this hatred spills.

And what is that crime? Who knows. Perhaps it was something as simple as some spilled milk or a pilfered cow, or something as foul as incest or matricide or some whole family murdered in their sleep, or robbed by their children or set ablaze or burned at the stake or turned in to the state for their beliefs.

That is one kind of journey—back into time—that you must undertake to reverse this curse.

In struggling to reverse this curse you will have to wander, as you will not be accepted in your own home. But your son is your ally. That is why he fought your father. So take him with you as you wander. Do not condemn him for fighting on your behalf. While it may appear that he is doing nothing, he is struggling, like you, with this curse. Until it is lifted he will be stuck; he will not be able to act until this predicament is resolved, until he can see that his mother is safe. Through your magical backward telling of the primordial story, you will free your son from bondage. When he sees that his mother is safe, then he will be able to move on, go to college, do whatever he needs to do for himself.

The other journey you need to take is forward, writing through future generations, a letter to your son, a letter to his children, a letter to their children, explaining to them this awful curse and what to do should they encounter it. Tell them what you have learned about this curse, about its terrible danger, about how it can crop up when they least expect it; tell them how you fought it and felt that you had killed it but one never knows, really, about such things as curses.

When you have done these things, look around you and see if the curse is not lifted. Your mother and father may still act as they acted before, but their power over you should be lessened. That is the substance of the curse: Not their behavior, but its power over you.

Then look at your son. Tell him you are free. Tell him you will be OK, and let him go.

Why can't my mother accept my bisexuality?

Her intolerance breaks my heart.

Dear Cary,

I AM 44 years old and female. My mother is 72. I have always been protective of her because when I was growing up my father was verbally and (sometimes) physically abusive. It always seemed to be my duty to protect her from anything that seemed threatening and upsetting, and to some extent I'm still doing it, which is where my quandary comes from.

Around the age of 5 or 6, I began to realize that I was bisexual. I remember being attracted to both boys and girls. I also learned around the same time that my parents did not approve of my attraction to girls, so I learned, like most queer kids, to keep silent. It was especially necessary because my father was and is deeply homophobic. After I finished college I came out to everyone, including most of my family—except my parents. My relatives actually warned me not to tell them because they would be upset, and since I was living at home, I accepted the bargain. Eventually, however, my father searched my room (he didn't feel that I deserved any privacy in his house) and discovered my porn collection; he wanted to send me for therapy to be cured, whereas I found out the truth of my mother's feelings, which were that I didn't deserve to live or be around children (I was a schoolteacher).

Eventually after my parents separated I fell in love with a man, left home to be with him, and started life on my own. Since then I've been widowed, in love a few times with both men and women, and have had a reasonably happy life. However, because I was born Roman Catholic, the current rulings of the church have caused me to question my long-held silence.

I have worked as a schoolteacher and a college professor, and have been out to pretty much everyone, including students. I'm serially monogamous and I have a decent (though under-paid) life.

Over the years I have told my mother that I've been with women, but every time I've mentioned it, she's acted like it's a horrible secret and that I must be sick in the head or confused, or treated me as if I had undergone some kind of growing phase. Because of her lack of acceptance in the midst of my total support for her emotional needs, we have a rift between us. She says she doesn't understand why I don't invite her over to my home and why I don't tell her about my life, why I seem to be so angry at the Catholic Church. I know I cannot make her accept me, but I feel invisible.

When my best friend and sometime lover died earlier this year, five years after I lost my husband, she was the only person who didn't realize the nature of the bond, even though it was pretty obvious to the rest of my family. Right now I am with a man, but I have nightmares that I may one day meet a woman and fall in love, and that I won't be able to tell my mother and have a full relationship. This is important to me because I am an only child and will probably be caring for my mother as she gets older, and because I truly believe it is a sin to pretend to be what one is not. Because most of the bisexual women I know are in the closet or have completely broken family ties, I'm not sure where to turn for advice; one of my gay male friends called me closeted—even though I've made far more sacrifices by being out at work than he has, and it really hurt. What should I do?

Bisexual and Not Accepted

Dear Bisexual,

WHAT IF SOMEONE told you that your mother will never approve of your bisexuality as long as she lives?

Would that be too crushing a blow? Could you accept that, if it were true? Could you accept the possibility of it, even if no one can ever really know for certain? Would that help you stop hoping for something that, however good and right and just and true it would be, may never happen?

On the off chance that it might, let me say it to you: Your mother is never going to accept your bisexuality.

What might that mean for you? Would it mean that your mother doesn't love you? No, not at all. Would it mean that you are no good? No, of course not. Would it mean that you and your mother are incompatible? No. She accepts you as her daughter; she accepts who she thinks you are, who she is capable of believing you are; she accepts the person she believes to be her daughter. She goes as far as she can go. That is all any of us can do: We can only accept what we can imagine and perceive—what we can let into our heads.

> There are some things your mother might never accept.

But for some reason your mother cannot let this one fact into her head. She can't admit it to consciousness. It is beyond her ability to embrace this thought.

Accepting this will not, in itself, make everything better. The reason to accept it is so you can move on to a deeper, more profound issue.

We all want our parents' approval as children. This wish, if not granted, often persists into adulthood whether we want it to or not. You are 44 years old and you still ache for your mother's approval. I don't think you're going to get it, but neither do I think it is her acceptance today that is important. This is an old, old wish. It seems to be a remnant, in a way, of a broader and more existential childhood wish.

What I think it represents is the phenomenon of your own childhood trauma, a devastating and tragic denial of your personhood. Yes, this happened to you: Your parents, who were supposed to protect you, understand you, respond to you, help you grow, be there for you, instead attacked you for who you are. And that is a devastating thing for a child. Many people never get over it; they limp through life or they burn down buildings or they carry the abuse into their own careers. You didn't do that. You seem to have become a loving and unconventional person of exceptional strength.

I think you have the strength to fully know this. Unlike your mother, you have the ability to admit painful and disturbing knowledge. That is your task: to fully accept and mourn the failure to be fully accepted and loved as a child.

If you can do that, you need no longer be the powerless child asking for permission and approval from your mother—permission to be bisexual, permission to doubt, to be true to yourself, permission, as I have said, that you may never receive. If you can do that, then you regain the power of choice. You. Not the church. Not your mother. Not your neighbors. You regain the choice of what to do. You do not have to support your mother in her old age. It would be a good thing to do but you don't have to do it. If you do so it will be because you choose to do it.

Please do not misunderstand me. When I say accept your mother the way she is, I am not saying things won't change. I have no way of knowing whether things will change or not. I have seen things change between children and parents. It happens. I simply suggest that you stop struggling with the relationship and let it be what it is, flawed and wounded, sad and incomplete, but still a powerful bond between mother and daughter.

I'm a Bad Asian girl

I'm dating a non-Asian man who sleeps over, I almost didn't go to medical school, and I'm a liberal. How can I get my parents to accept me as I am?

Dear Cary,

I GREW UP as the good daughter of two conservative Asian parents. I got into the best college (fulfilling the Asian-American dream) and then came the liberation of me. Now, I swear occasionally, I'm a goddamn liberal, and I almost didn't go to medical school (I took a few years off after college). I learned to drink beer, did pot once, smoked cigarettes, dated non-Asian men, and lost my virginity. Now, I am dating a non-Asian man who sleeps over when he comes to visit from far away. I am not the person of my parents' expectations.

Problem is, my parents had no inkling of my evolution. They still don't know, or want to know, that I drink, although they've caught on to my liberal inclinations. This blindness is no longer tenable for a number of reasons. The main one is the sweet boyfriend who is unfortunately caught in the crossfire of culture. I told my parents about him, they met him once, and they don't approve: You're not compatible, he's too old, he corrupted you, etc. My mother is having a hard time dealing with the fact that I might be sleeping over at his place when I visit (I now evade her questions when she asks where I'm staying). This has meant that my parents treat my boyfriend very coolly. They refuse to see him. He was specifically not invited to come over for Thanksgiving, for example, which really hurt his feelings, and mine, too. From a distance they can still make their feelings pretty apparent. The disapproval is taking its toll, as I feel that I constantly have to choose between boyfriend and family, and both feel that I choose the other.

At the heart of it, I really think my parents would love to see me set up with a nice Asian surgery resident, one who preferably speaks the native language. I want my parents to accept that I've grown up and that they must love me as I am, because I like who I am. I mean, I'm 25 fucking years old, for fuck's sake, but I hate myself for feeling like I'm 15 when I'm talking to them. They don't bring up the subject of boyfriend, or the subject of what I do after 10, unless I do. In fact, they don't really bring up much of anything.

I do love my parents. We have a good relationship. But how do I get them to accept the man who might be The One, and more important, to understand who I am and what that means? Does this mean brutal honesty about everything that I've ever done, or does it mean that I continue to not discuss certain parts of my life (like the part that streaked across the freshman quad my senior year)? Meanwhile, how do I get the sweet boyfriend to understand that the disapproval is no reflection of how I feel or the kind of person he really is?

Why can't everyone just get along?

Bad Asian Girl

Dear Bad Asian Girl,

EVERYONE CANNOT JUST get along because everyone disapproves of everyone else. Which wouldn't matter except we seem to think that a) it matters what the fuck they think about us and b) we must do something about it. The truth is, it doesn't matter and there's nothing we could do about it if it did.

So for your own good, rather than try to get your parents to accept this man, try instead to get yourself to accept your parents. Accept their disapproval. Accept their inability to change. Accept their stolid fealty to ancestral whatever. That doesn't mean obey them. It just means accept their disapproval of your disobedience.

The only way to live serenely is to accept it all, accept the dagger eyes, the haughty deafness, the back turned, the silent treatment, the withholding. Live with it. It doesn't mean they don't love you. It just means that they think you should marry an Asian surgical resident. Don't fall for it. Because if you marry an Asian surgical resident, it won't stop there. Then you'll have to have three children, one a future surgeon, one a future lawyer, and one a future bond trader. And even if you finish medical school as they want you to, now that you have the three little future BMW-driving conservative professionals, you won't be spending enough time with your chil-

Accept your parents.

dren because of the selfish pursuit of your career, which only makes your husband look bad every time you get promoted and your parents look bad every time they have to take care of your kids because you were called away to save the life of some poor Caucasian sucker who was probably unhealthy from not eating enough duck with his family at a big round table.

Their disapproval probably feels like a withholding of love, but it's really the opposite; in a twisted way their withholding of love is their love itself. It's just not a love of your ego. It's a love of you their daughter, the projected avatar of themselves that in their eyes has no ego because it's just a projection of them. Hey, you're Asian: You ought to understand this better than me.

Your parents are being incredibly selfish, of course, and cruel, because all you want is their blessing. But that's the way parents are, and they're much better at this game than you are. As long as you continue to try to get your parents' blessing, you're playing right into their hands. So have fun with your boyfriend and tell him that what your parents think of him doesn't matter. And get back to your studying, because if you're not going to marry the Asian surgical resident, somebody is going to have to make the money.

I used to be funny, but now I'm boring and self-conscious

What happened to me? Are my friends going to desert me?

Dear Cary,

I'VE BEEN PLAGUED recently (last couple of years) by this problem I feel that I'm too smart to have let overtake me like it has: I've become extremely self-conscious, not around strangers—I've always been good at striking up in-the-moment, nothing-to-lose conversations. The problem is with my friends, the very people I should feel most comfortable around (these people have been my friends for years and have stuck by me through all kinds of scenarios).

I used to think of myself as this happy-go-lucky, fun person who was smart and perceptive and could be the life of the party. But now my friends and I are all getting older (just turned 40) and my out-there antics aren't really appropriate anymore. It's no longer cute to be the "crazy one"; now it's about telling a good joke at a dinner party. But this self-consciousness is making me so unrelaxed that I don't know how to hang out and have fun anymore. I've become convinced that everyone can read my mind and that they all think I'm a jerk. I know these problems are all in my head but I just don't know how to shift the focus off of myself and onto others or the conversation that's taking place. It feels as if it's all my fault if the conversation is lagging or there's an awkward silence.

I really want to stop this feeling that hanging out with my friends is some kind of performance (for the record, the people I mostly see actually are brilliant and hilarious). I really do try to talk myself out of seeing it this way. I tell myself to focus on others and not listen to the nagging voice in my head that keeps score of how well I'm doing in the social situation. Then I try harder than I need to by telling some story that sort of flops and makes everyone uncomfortable.

I'm terrified that my awkwardness is going to make them not want to invite me to socialize with them anymore, and so it's this weird self-fulfilling prophecy. It's almost like an OCD disorder that I can't stop from minute to minute wondering how my friends see me, and fearing that I'm going to lose them. I just can't seem to get off the hamster wheel, or whatever the metaphor is. Any advice you have in getting the focus off myself would be greatly appreciated. I have a great trust in your perspective and opinion and hope you can lend some insights.

Self-conscious

Dear Self-conscious,

OFTEN THINGS STRIKE us when we are walking alone that we would like to tell in their full splendor: You wouldn't believe how beautiful it was to see this old rusted iron spike through a piece of square timber driftwood down by the beach this morning, and the color of the sea, a smoky pewter that reminded me of my grandmother's unpolished silver sugar pot ...

Such Proustian meanderings indeed do not make one the life of the party. Maybe that is why I have not been invited to many dinner parties lately. While you are afraid of becoming boring—and perhaps with good reason; you see more deeply into things than most!—I have already become boring, so boring in fact that I am practically intolerable; my wife says I frighten people with the things that I say. When their eyes glaze over it is not just boredom but abject fear, because unconsciously they realize: This is their fate too. We will all become boring.

They see in me, as one sees in a dying man, their future, their inescapable fate!

We went to the ballet last night and I felt like some Russian anarchist, longing to shoot my pistol into the balcony. But I was wearing a corduroy jacket bought mail order from J. Crew! Can you believe that? It was some kind of hideous attempt at a disguise, so that I would not look like an anarchist longing to shoot his pistol into the balcony! All it really achieved, I believe, was to tighten ever so slightly the noose of fatal boredom around my neck. I seriously need to resocialize as a sober non-punk.

This kind of antisocial attitude does not make for sparkling repartee. Nor does my growing preference for the long version. Obviously, most stories have the short version and the long version. Most people when they say they are making a long story short are actually just making a long story boring by taking out the good parts. To truly make a long story short you can usually say something like, "I was shot escaping after a convenience store robbery" or "I did three to five for manslaughter." That is making a long story short. Or you can tell the whole thing. I like to tell the whole thing. That is why I am boring.

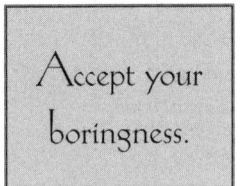

Accept your boringness.

I am interested in the details, is the thing. I like the long, somber narration; I like the bare, unadorned facts beneath which seems to hum a vast incomprehensible mystery. So your grandmother knit you that shawl? Therein rests a universe of pale shiny grandmotherly knuckles (Look at those gnarled old knuckles: as though polished ivory by time itself!) in the window light of an old family home, knitting needles bought at a store that long ago was paved over for Wal-Mart, hands taught by a woman—her mother—who was the first woman ever to cast a vote in her small and unassuming Midwestern town, in the presidential election of 1920, and you know she voted for the socialist Eugene V. Debs, even though he was in prison at the time for advocating noncompliance with the draft in World War I, can you believe that? (This is the moment at which the listener's eyes fasten with great longing on their shoes, unconscious symbols of imminent departure from the boring, over-talkative guest who has collared them in the kitchen and is rambling about the old grandmother in between piercing, revelatory insights into the ingredients of the celery dip—could it really be canned mushroom soup that gives it that richness? But it's the sour cream that gives it the tangy bite, without which, don't you find, it's just a teensy weensy bit flat? Like it needs a little bit of salt or something? And maybe not just plain salt but a seasoned salt, a ... there you have it: Celery salt! Oh, you are the clever one. So you know how many votes Eugene V. Debs actually got in the 1920 election between Harding/Coolidge and Cox/Roosevelt? 913,664! And how did I know that? You know there's this really neat site called Wikipedia? On the Web? Have you heard about the Web?)

So, you know, if the whole idea of being a sparking dinner guest itself just seems kind of lame and 19th century, like you should have a starched collar and knickers or something, you can turn being boring into an insidious and soul-killing form of quiet social homicide; I'm afraid, actually, that that's partly what I do; I cannot stand the silence, and I don't really care, so I fill it with junk, like an old redneck pulling up to the rock pit with a truck full of couches.

I found my dad's gay porn

*My father is very secretive. Should
I confront him with this?*

Hi, Cary,

MY DAD IS very secretive, and I have found his porn that is
man-on-man.

How do you think I should deal with this? Should I talk to
him or tell my mom? I know my brothers would disown him and
I don't want to hurt my dad, but he is killing me.

I have no one to talk to, and I feel like I am doing my mom
wrong. Help me, please.

Lost

Dear Lost,

THIS IS ONE of those situations where there isn't a really great
solution. But you have to do something. You can't ignore this.

You have to have a conversation with your dad about those
pictures. It probably won't be in the top 10 favorite conversations
with your dad. But you can't just let it go.

Do not assume that your dad is gay. Do not assume anything.
Just get out of the house somewhere where the two of you can
have a private conversation, perhaps outdoors where you can
walk while you talk, and tell him that you saw that material. Just
tell him you saw it.

Ask him what it means.

Listen to him.

His first response may be to lie. He may begin a rehearsed performance.

If that happens, it may be very upsetting to you. You may realize that you wanted the truth from him and are not getting it. If what he tells you doesn't sound believable, tell him so. But also tell him that you realize that it may be impossible for him to talk about it honestly with you. Tell him you are not bringing this up in order to pass judgment on him. Tell him it's just that you saw it and you could not ignore it.

It is tempting to say that what your dad does is his business. But it's not that simple.

Suppose it turns out that your dad is gay. Let's think about what that would mean.

First of all, if your dad is gay, he may separate from your mom. That would be upsetting for you. If he were to admit that he is gay, I would ask him if that means he's going to separate from your mom. I would ask him if your mom knows. If she does not know, I think he should tell her. If he refuses to tell her, then it might fall upon you to tell her.

Perhaps he has been deceiving her, possibly for some time.

It also would suggest that he has been deceiving you, the kids. He has been acting as though he is a monogamous heterosexual father when he is not. It is likely you would feel quite angry and betrayed if that were the case.

What else might it suggest?

Since he is your father, it might cause you to question whether you might be gay as well, or potentially gay. Such a thought might not be wholly based on reason, but it could occur to you none-

> Ask your dad the question you want to ask him.

theless; not all our thoughts are rational. It might make you wonder about yourself. It might make you think about some of your father's friends also and wonder if they were not just friends but lovers. It might make you see certain events of the past in a new light. If your mother and father have been fighting, it might make you think that you know now what they were fighting about— that this has been a struggle between them of long standing.

It might also make you fear your dad: If he is capable of hiding this life of his, what else might he be hiding? Might his love for you also be false? Might he harbor a secret contempt for you, as just another boring straight person? It brings a new dimension into your relationship, in which you consider your father in a new context.

Since you indicate that your brothers have strong anti-gay feelings, you might want to take extra caution in considering whether to tell them or not. I would discuss this with your dad. It would be quite a conflict; I would stop short of promising him to conceal it. It would not be right to ask a son to conceal such a thing.

And what of any anti-gay attitudes and feelings you might have expressed within his hearing over the years? Might you have inadvertently insulted or hurt your father by the things you have said? And what about the things he has said about homosexuality to you? Has he said things that now would make him appear to be a hypocrite?

These are just some of the things you might end up thinking about. That is why it's important to talk to him about it.

It may be that the gay porn means nothing. There may be some easy, if unusual, explanation.

So do not go overboard about this. Just have a calm conversation.

And try to have some compassion for your dad. If he is indeed gay, it can't have been easy hiding it all these years. I'm sure he's done the best he could to raise you kids and take care of you.

I got involved with
a married alcoholic and
now I'm all messed up

I always get over relationships quickly, but this one has left me shattered and angry and baffled.

Dear Cary,

I'M A YOUNG (22) city-dwelling woman. A while ago, I sought out a casual, sexy relationship. (I liked—and still do—a lot about being single.) The one I ended up with happened to be with a man who was "getting a divorce." Through a series of revelations, several things became clear to me. He had to keep this a secret from his wife, he couldn't handle a casual relationship, he told me that he loved me and wanted more emotional involvement from me. Finally he told me that he is an alcoholic and can no longer see me, and finally, that he's going to stay with his wife. It seems like a very stereotypical end to things. I know I shouldn't have been involved with a married man, but the shocks came piecemeal, and I found ways to rationalize it.

Since I became attached to him after a while, I was upset, but I know that I'm very resilient. When I get hurt romantically, I grieve, then I rest, and after a while I feel better. I'm not really worried that I won't get over him. In fact, even the other night I came home from work and sighed with relief knowing I wouldn't feel obligated to put in a lot of time composing e-mails to this guy. In some ways, I'm an increasingly solitary person.

Ever since things ended, though, I'm finding I have a particularly hard time coping because I feel like I can't believe anything that happened or anything that he ever said. It's as though I'm stuck in a Rashomon-style nightmare, where different story lines play out in my head. It's like I've become cagey to the point of chronic suspicion. While we were together, I worried that he wasn't telling me the truth about a divorce, but decided to live with the consequences either way.

Now that things are over, I vacillate between extremes of belief and disbelief. Sometimes I can give him the benefit of the doubt, sometimes I feel tremendously naive for doing so. One moment, I'm struck with deep compassion for an alcoholic. I'll become very sad, and I'll be overwhelmed with the memory of my own alcoholic family. I'll hope that he gets help. I'll wish him the best. The next minute, I'm furious for being played the fool. I feel like everything, from start to finish, was a cruel joke at my expense. I feel lied to. I feel bewildered and confused. Sometimes I think he isn't an alcoholic, sometimes I think he never planned to leave his wife, sometimes I think he never meant it when he said anything nice to me. Then I feel like a very bad person for thinking that someone would lie about being an alcoholic. It's very confusing.

I guess what I would like is a little help figuring out how to cope with the fact that I'll never know what really happened, even though I was an active participant in events.

Baffled

Dear Baffled,

ONE REASON YOU are having trouble resolving this may be that you have never been in an intimate relationship with a sociopath before. The behavior of drunks and addicts in relationships is sociopathic.

Sociopathic behavior in intimate relationships causes intense confusion and rage because it consists of deception at a deep, existential level. The deception is baffling and unconscionable; it is not just deception about ways and means, about whereabouts and actions, but about soul and intent. The soul of an addict, to put it plainly, is not there; when you are dealing with an addict, what may appear to be the soul is merely the front for a voracious, amoral hunger.

With a drunk or an addict, the basic relational contract does not hold; the supposition that each person is vulnerable to emotional pain and equally susceptible to pangs of conscience and thus constrained in his behavior is violated from the start. So that's what we feel after such an encounter: violated.

It might help to conceive of this not as a relationship at all, but instead as a gruesome accident, a hit-and-run. You were blindsided. This man was drunk and should never have been given the keys to your heart.

Will you ever get satisfaction from this man? Not while he continues to drink. But perhaps one day you will hear from him after everything has run its course; he will have recently sobered up and will offer you something in recompense. Perhaps what he offers will seem tawdry and thin—a threadbare apology, a few bills he stole out of your purse that you never even missed—but it will be a moral gesture, and you will know that at least his conscience has begun to function.

> Do not feed the addicts.

In the meantime, you will have to get over it on your own. If just knowing what happened is not enough to settle your heart, it might help you to spend some time with a group like Al-Anon. Those are people who really do know alcoholics. They know what it's like to get blind-sided by somebody who never should have been handed the keys.

We're married, but do we have to live together?

I love my husband, but I need my own place.

Dear Cary,

I'VE BEEN MARRIED for seven months to a great man. I'm 43, had never been married and was very happy being single. I enjoy my solitude and autonomy and didn't think I was cut out for marriage, which was fine by me. Then this man came into my life ... totally loving, accepting of my idiosyncrasies, a great partner in every way. I didn't exactly feel fireworks, but I'm mistrustful of fireworks anyway. With him it was a more gradual awareness of the quality of person he was, the way that he loved me and how lucky I was to have someone like him in my life. I approached the relationship with openness and made a very thoughtful decision to share my life with him.

So, I moved out of my little home in an inner-city neighborhood, which I loved. We got a house together that is close to the university where's he's in graduate school. I'm not happy living in the charmless neighborhood and if I'm honest with myself I'm not happy sharing a home with anyone.

I don't want out of the relationship or marriage. I just want to go back to living by myself ... seeing each other several times a week as we did before. I want to be able to come home from work and have the house to myself sometimes, not have him always be there. My husband is open to some unconventional ideas and under different circumstances I would broach the subject.

However, shortly after we married he decided to go back to get his PhD and so financially we can't afford to keep two separate residences right now.

I've had friends tell me this is just a normal adjustment period. If that's the case I'm willing to work at making that adjustment. I also realize that there are sacrifices involved in building any good relationship. I'm making the sacrifices with a pure heart and I'm still not happy, but then I wonder if I need to look at it over the long term. When I get to the end of my life will I be glad I made the sacrifices necessary to build something beautiful with someone?

We do have separate bedrooms, which has helped some. And if I wanted to do more things with my friends or independently he'd have no problem with that. But my gut is telling me that's not the issue and that I'm just not cut out to live with anyone; that I'm always going to need to have my own place to be deep-down-in-the-core happy.

I guess I'd like a little more clarity on the relationship between love, sacrifice, autonomy and happiness.

Reluctant Cohabiter

Dear Reluctant,

IF YOU NEED your own place to be happy, then I would encourage you to look for a way to have your own place and remain married. Since you can't afford it now, you will have to wait until you can afford it. But I suggest that you trust your instincts on this. It's a workable alternative to cohabitation for some couples.

As to the philosophical problem, I, too, would like a little more clarity on the relationship between love, sacrifice, autonomy and happiness. But I cannot really think about that right now because there are people in the kitchen. Well, not exactly in the kitchen. There is no kitchen anymore. There used to be a kitchen. Now there is just an area. In that area, people are working with a radial arm saw and a nail gun.

So I am having trouble thinking.

That's my problem. But my problem relates to your problem: My job is to cultivate thoughts, to grow them from little niblets into fully developed structures. The thoughts take time to develop. They need to develop uninterrupted. They're delicate crystals built in the air, each part suspended by an act of consciousness; they're precarious, like data in RAM, if you will: A crash, or a power outage, or any interruption of the system that holds them in crystalline suspension, and the whole thing falls down and you have to start over.

So if there are people around it can be hard to do the job.

Not everyone is a writer by trade. But many people have the same problem: Identity, or consciousness, or well-being, can be a delicate crystalline structure as well; any interruption and the identity crashes. Consciousness becomes muddled. There are people who are not writers who nonetheless live in the imagination, whose identities and sense of the world are precarious structures. They read books and think about the ideas in the books. Or they wake up from a dream-filled sleep and want to think about the dreams, which hover on the edge of consciousness. So even having to say hello to another person in the morning can make the whole thing collapse.

Try a new arrangement.

Such people can find it difficult not to have control of their own space.

I'm not complaining. I don't think you are complaining either. You're just trying to face the truth and make adjustments. We make these choices. We ask people with nail guns and radial arm saws to come into our area and make it better. We fall in love and move in with someone. We borrow large sums of money and promise to pay it back. We worry the people we live with. They want to talk to us about paying the money back, and we want to live in our little world of precarious crystalline structures.

I'd better go into the office now.

But I say this from the heart: Trust your instincts. I believe you can find a way to have your own place and also have the love of your life near you.

I want vengeance on my narcissistic mother

She didn't pull the trigger, but I blame her for my brother's suicide.

Dear Cary,

MY BROTHER, AGE 45, committed suicide this summer. He walked out into a farmer's field on a beautiful summer afternoon and shot himself in the head. Death is so absolutely final. There is no court of appeal. I cannot talk him out of it—I can't show him that life will get better. He's dead. He'll always be dead now. In his note, he said, "My life has pretty much been a train wreck, and I'm tired of struggling."

Accepting this is hard—really, really hard. He was put in a boarding school at age 14, then mostly spent time in jail from 18 to 34. But he was a kind, generous guy who could make me laugh so hard I'd pee my pants, and he never hurt a soul. I spent a lifetime bailing him out of trouble, and I don't regret a minute of it. He was worth every dime I ever gave him.

I blame my mother, the most narcissistic, self-centered, evil woman you can imagine. Granted, she did not pull the trigger, she did not force him to take crack cocaine, but she was never, ever there for him. Not once in his entire life. She spent a lifetime telling us how much she didn't want children—urged us not to have any because "they're just not worth it." My brother never had a chance in this world.

Seven years ago, she went to his work site to demand that he pay her some money—she almost cost him his job. Then she told lies about him, so that he was pretty much ostracized by the few relatives he had. She hadn't spoken to him in seven years.

When he died, she didn't even miss her regular weekend volunteer gig. I never saw her shed a tear, and found out that many, many of her friends didn't even know she'd had a son who lived nearby.

I'd been there for a visit, seven weeks before he killed himself, and I did not see it coming. My last image is of him waving at me and petting his dog at the same time. I knew his marriage was in trouble, and it scared me. But he'd stayed out of jail for 10 years, and he had a good job and a home. He was a fabulous success story in my eyes.

I'm 49, 17 years sober, happily married and reasonably well employed. I have spent years in Al-Anon and Adult Children meetings; I've done the 12 steps several times. Don't give me platitudes—don't tell me, "If she knew better, she'd do better." That's not true, and I want to hold her accountable.

I want to give her some payback. I want to lock her out in the snow, barefoot. Maybe, if I leave her on her own enough, she'll be raped. I want to pinch her until she cries, then tell her to stop crying or I'll pinch her. I want to hurt her, shame her, lie to her, make her eat her dinner from the dog's dish. I want to steal huge chunks of her life, and as much of her money as I can. I want to beat her with a belt, an egg turner, a switch—whatever will hurt the most.

I'm 3,000 miles away, so she's safe from physical harm. But she's right there on the other end of the phone, or I could send her an e-mail and cc a lot of people she knows. I want to tell her about every sin I can remember—those of omission and those of commission. I want to swear, and rant, and unmask her for the nasty person she is. I want to demand acknowledgment and apologies. I want her to admit her guilt; I want her to feel guilt.

I know, though, that it will never happen. Trying to make it happen will only hurt me—not her.

How do I get over this? He's gone—forever and ever and ever. How come she gets off scot-free?

I have one brother left. At the age of 54 he works as a laborer and barely earns enough to pay for rent, cigarettes and booze. Luckily he lives close to me, not her.

How do I deal with this? Just changing my phone number and cutting off contact doesn't appeal. I want vengeance.

J

Dear J,

WHAT DOES ONE do with this? One takes it to the gods, and then one carries it into battle and battles with it until one is exhausted.

To take vengeance on your narcissistic mother you must find fuel in your own perversity; you must wound her symbolically through your own cleansing of trauma.

You know, of course, that you're going to have to settle for something symbolic, don't you? Not forgiveness, necessarily. It can be vengeance. But it will have to be symbolic.

That does not mean it has to be nice. It just has to be legal.

And you know also that she will never feel what you want her to feel, however much you torture her? All your torture would be in vain; only you would feel it. You'd be worse off. But you can wound her symbolically just by doing well in spite of her.

I won't give you AA slogans, but I will remind you of something: We help others. That's how we get better. So you keep doing that: You help others; and you use your towering lust for vengeance as fuel to drive you forward. You do what you have done up to now, but you do it with a new and powerful energy, with the same fury and desperation that fed your drinking long ago. You use whatever is handy—your own egotism,

> Feel free to want vengeance. Know you can't have it.

your own restlessness, your own doggedness or dogma, your own fear, your own thirst for control, recognition and power. You use whatever you have as fuel. You just keep doing the steps, but with a vengeance.

In that way, your every victory over her tyranny thins her blood; your head held high bows hers down; your free action binds her hands; your proud moment shames her; your sober day makes her drink; your prayer strands her from God; your laugh brings tears to her face; your every step cripples her; your every breath makes her suffocate. Your victory in life is your vengeance. Anything else is a sword in your own eye.

Feel free to want vengeance. Just know you can't have it. Not you. Not real vengeance. You can't afford it. It would blind you and maim you and leave you penniless on the street. You know the conditions of your parole: We can't afford righteous anger. I don't need to tell you about that; everything is permitted but the literal taking of vengeance. You've got to content yourself with a dance, a performance out in the field.

If we were coasting easily along in the current, maybe we could say, go ahead, take a swing at her. But an alcoholic is never coasting; we don't have that latitude. We're eking out each inch with screaming labor, we're rowing against a current of grief swollen with rage and wind-whipped with vengeance, rowing against history, rowing against time, rowing against all that light-devouring narcissism we lived with and cried in and grew up in, terrified, desolate; we're rowing against the towering, tyrannical mother herself, rowing right into her devouring maw, rowing straight up that self-involved gullet and straight out the other side into a freedom in which every conscious action nullifies her tyranny, in which every full breath makes her strangle on its sound.

That is the only vengeance you get, the vengeance of victory over narcissistic tyranny.

So fashion for yourself a stage out in the field where your brother died, a bare wooden stage, unadorned, of dense, dry timber. Build the stage before the noon sun beats down on it, and then, when the sun is setting, take the stage with a spray of wildflowers in one hand and a pistol in the other. Slowly pace the stage, enumerating your grievances, eulogizing your brother and firing occasional shots at whoever passes near. Fire at the stars and the moon and the birds, fire into the earth where he lies buried, fire into the audience that has gathered to see you weep, fire into the trees that surround the field and the highway that runs away toward the city, fire at the house where your brother lived, fire at the past and at the future. Stalk the stage with your spray of wildflowers and your pistol and say what you've got to say about your mother and your brother and this awful thing that's brought you to this place. Tell sun, moon, stars, earth, sky. Whenever you feel the need for silence, fire another shot. If you should feel a sudden tenderness, throw a flower to the audience as it cowers before you. Continue until you're too hoarse and weary and then drop to the stage and sleep with your pistol at your side.

In the morning you can go home. Leave your pistol behind. You won't need it anymore.

The pain just won't end

I lived with an abusive girlfriend for over a year. Now I'm free, but the fear and sadness just won't go away.

Dear Cary,

I'M 24 AND I live in fear and I have no idea how to change it. Last summer I escaped from an abusive girlfriend I lived with for over a year. I still have flashbacks, really intrusive memories of some of the most intense moments, hitting, yelling. It's been over a year and I still have a constant sadness, a constant doubt I can't conquer. I've changed my life immensely since then. I got myself back in shape, I reimmersed myself in school and work and I'm more active now than I've ever been. In short I've done everything I've read I need to do to get past something like this.

But it hasn't helped. I have an enormous desire to meet people, to be outgoing, but I can't break past the fear. I haven't had the nerve to approach women, and when I've been approached I feel like I'm falling apart. I find myself behind a wall I can't break, fearing the impression I leave on people I meet, fearing they will see through my facade of confidence, see that I am an illusion of a person. I speak candidly with family on occasion, but it's rare. The relationship between my best friend and me has become superficial, still strong, but I fear telling him about my depression, or more than small details of my old relationship, knowing how weak it will make me look.

Even though I'm doing more with my life now than I ever have before, I feel more alone right now than I've ever been. Does time heal wounds like this? What can I do to ease the fear?

No Clever Sign-off

Dear No Clever,

TIME DOES HEAL wounds like this. But it takes a lot longer than you expect it to. Just when you think it should be getting better, it seems like it's getting worse. It keeps getting worse for a while. You fight it at first but eventually you resign yourself to a lifetime of misery. You figure that can't last long. But it does. It keeps getting worse. Eventually you get used to walking around in a twisted way like some character in a Francis Bacon painting. And gradually it seems to let up, as though you and your suffering had reached equilibrium, and you think, Aha, you've accepted it, there's grace in the world, it's starting to let up.

> Take as much time as you need.

You relax and take a serene walk in the evening and it jumps on you from behind and wraps its scaly arms around your chest and squeezes your breath out. You think, Hey, I thought we were done. "You should have gotten a receipt," it says. And there's this metallic laughter. You feel this cold breath on your neck as it says, What round is this? I forget. So you figure, I guess it's going to do what it's going to do, and accepting it didn't really work, and neither did fighting back, so you figure maybe you can just put it out of your mind, and concentrate on other things.

And struggling to put it out of your mind magnifies its effect. By this time you're almost dead; you're spending your waking hours crawling on the floor of your little apartment, barely breathing. It hurts to talk. Your ribs are bruised from the squeezing. Trying to concentrate on other things hasn't helped, so you try to really accept it this time, to pray to it, visualize it, meditate on it, and you're almost there but then as you're visualizing it and trying to love it it spits in your face and the spittle runs down your cheek. Now it's personal. So you struggle against it again but this time you're so weakened that you collapse in exhaustion and spend days lying on the floor in a kind of emotional coma. You lose a lot of weight. On the advice of friends, you go to therapy. And that seems to help. Crying seems to help. For a day. But then you wake up on the second day after a good therapy session and it's sitting on your chest taking a big warm shit.

It's like taking a beating from a psychopath. There's nothing you can do. It's addicted to beating your ass. Since it's addicted now, it feels like a victim too. It wants you to feel sorry for it. It's thinking about going into recovery, but meanwhile it just keeps beating your ass in a kind of halfhearted way that's almost insulting. It claims that it's actually painful for it to keep beating your ass, but it can't stop. It hints that it's your fault it keeps beating your ass.

And that, too, goes on for longer than you expected.

If that doesn't sound comforting, well, what can I do? It does end. How do I know? Guess what? That guy lying next to you on the floor, taking the blows right there with you, that's me.

So what's the trick? There is no trick. You just lie there and lie there and one day you get up and it's gone. It just got bored with you and left without even saying goodbye.

Must I have a grand calling in life?

I'm an IT professional. I want to be a mother. Isn't that enough?

Dear Cary,

I AM NOT one of those people who has found a great purpose or passion in my life. I don't love my work or have a hobby or care deeply about this or that cause. In my mid-20s this bothered me quite a bit and I read a bunch of books about how to find gratifying work, but although they all had great advice on how to transform what you love into a job you'll love, they weren't so helpful if you couldn't find what you loved. I even quit my high-paying information technology job and spent a year trying out jobs in various professions and wandering around the city, looking for something I might find inspiring, or at least something that I could see myself wanting to do. I didn't find anything I liked, let alone loved, and left the whole process very depressed. Some days I felt worthless and on the other days I just felt incredibly dull. Eventually I decided to go back to an IT job, since it paid well and I didn't mind it. And really, there are many good things about my job—the people I work with are nice, my boss is flexible, and the work is interesting probably two out of five days. I have a loving husband, a great family, some good friends, a house and a dog, I have a nicer than average life and I am grateful for it. But even still there is a feeling that I am not being who I am really meant to be.

Around the time I turned 30 (almost 32 now) I decided wanted to be a mother. I've always planned on having children, but now I really wanted to be a mother. And it had been a very long time since I had wanted to be anything. It took a year to convince my husband that we were ready for a family and five months to conceive. During that time I watched my refrigerator all but disappear under glossy baby pictures and birth announcements. I smiled happily and watched as my two closest friends had their sons two weeks apart. I listened attentively to their conversations about co-sleeping and breast-feeding and sent them Mother's Day cards. And I was mostly happy for them and only a little bit sad for me, because I felt like I finally knew what I wanted to do and despite my best efforts, I couldn't make it happen.

When we got pregnant and found out the baby would be born in January we were excited and nervous and all the things newly expectant parents are. It seemed perfect that we would start out the new year with a new baby. I planned on quitting my job and staying home full-time. I knew how hard it would be to take care of an infant, but I could hardly wait to finally spend my days doing something that I cared about. And to be quite honest, I was very much looking forward to throwing out project work plans and technology updates and all of that other stuff that currently fills my day.

Three weeks ago I lost the baby. I was nearly four months pregnant and it was totally unexpected. My pregnancy had been normal with all development happening right on schedule. All the doctors could say was "sometimes these things happen." I know that it is very common to miscarry and I know my chances are very good that I will conceive again and have a perfectly fine baby. My husband, family, friends and work have all been supportive and sympathetic, but I am having a hard time. I come to work and stare at my computer doing nothing. I think about continuing with this routine into the new year and I want to curl up in a ball under the desk. I know I should stay at this job. I am planning on getting pregnant again and I have been here long enough to earn a decent amount of maternity leave and I can work my schedule around doctor's appointments, morning sickness, etc., but I really don't see how I can come into this office for another year.

I guess I want to know how do I get through another year of just waiting for the life I want to start?

Childless

Dear Childless,

TO BE QUITE frank and not only that but possibly boring and repetitive as well, the way you get through the year is you do it one day at a time. One day at a time you get up in the morning and one day at a time you go to bed at night. If you are a person of faith you call on that faith every day. Every day, if there's a prayer that you know, you say it. If your doctor says you're depressed, every day you take your medicine. Every day, if there's a posture that you assume, you assume it. Every day you write the book. Every day you notice the minute shifting of light as the earth quietly surrounds the sun. Every day you take note of the precise quality of the miracle of life. Every day you write down your check numbers. Every day you count your change before leaving the counter. Every day you press the button for your floor.

Try it one day at a time.

And never do you let the coming year rise up like a monstrous wave and crush you with unimaginable tedium. Never do you let the dread sink in until you feel cold and dead inside; if you find yourself staring into the abyss you switch seats and think of ice cream.

Aside from that, the interesting thing to me is that you are willing to admit that you have no commanding passion—you don't dream of being on Broadway or becoming president of a cosmetics company; you're not outraged about global warming or the state of coastal wetlands. Not that that's so unusual—on the contrary, I just think you're refreshingly honest. It's so nice to meet someone who isn't faking it. What a crushing burden it is to be required to have a calling. I mean it's nice to think that there is a plan for each of us and each of us matters and each of us is unique, which is what we're told, but what's wrong with living a simple, dignified life, doing what we do, one day at a time, appreciating the good things and accepting the bad? Isn't that enough? Moreover, isn't it your choice alone whether it's enough or not? Why does it even have to be enough?

You're fine. You're refreshingly honest. I salute you. Enough with the dreams already. We're already suffocating in everyone else's destiny. We're up to here in other people's dreams. I say more power to you. Take it one day at a time. Pay attention to the small things. The time will pass more quickly than you know.

My wife's job is
ruining our lives

She's overworked, she's exploited,
and I've had it!

Dear Cary,

I AM BESIDE myself with anger and resentment. My wife works for a large organization. Her first-level boss is a selfish dunce who does not do his job and makes my wife do all of his work in addition to her own. Consequently, my wife works many nights until 9 or 10 o'clock, and weekends. I often stay late to help her, since we work in the same organization. The result: We have no life, and my wife's physical and mental health are suffering.

To make matters worse, the boss of my wife's boss thinks he is wonderful, because he is her lapdog, and she is indifferent to my wife's plight. Worse yet, this second-tier boss is vindictive and petty and routinely harasses and chases away good employees (like my wife).

The problem is several-fold. We need my wife's income, so she can't just quit. She is so busy that she doesn't have time to look for a new job, but even if she could, jobs that pay well (which we need) and for which she is qualified are hard to come by. That leaves us with an intolerable situation from which there seems to be no escape, except retirement which is 20 long years away.

Any guidance you can offer would be greatly appreciated.

Daydreaming Avenging Angel

Dear Avenging Angel,

WHATEVER HAPPENED TO "Screw the bosses"? Whatever happened to workers' spirit of resistance?

How did it become the norm to be exhausted, insecure and unhappy in your supposedly white-collar, middle-class or professional job? Is it the death of unions? The absence of consensus about what is a reasonable amount of time to devote to work? If so, how did we get here? Did an oligarchy rearrange the furniture while we slept? And what do we do about it now that we're waking up—as individuals or collectively?

I have thought a lot about situations such as yours. Although you're by yourself, you're not alone. That is, your same isolated condition is replicated hundreds of thousands of time throughout the system. You are part of a huge class of exploited persons. You just don't talk to each other. Each of you is in your own cubicle worrying about your own boss and your own workload and your own lack of pension.

Strangely, this overworking of people, this destroying of workers' lives, is happening to many hundreds of thousands of people and yet in some sense it is not happening to a group; in every instance it seems as though it is happening to you alone, and it's a problem you alone must solve. No matter that macroeconomic and cultural forces are at work to replicate the same crushing, inhumane circumstances from coast to coast. Still, we think it's we as individuals who are at fault, and it's we as individuals who must solve our problem—even though it is systemic and replicated throughout society! Why do we think that? Because we are stupid? Maybe. We might be really stupid. It kinda looks that way sometimes. Or maybe we're just scared.

Perhaps that is because workers' organizations have become discredited and fallen into disfavor; they are looked upon as old-fashioned and somehow disconnected from reality. But what are we to call it when from coast to coast individual workers numbering in the hundreds of thousands are struggling to make ends meet, working longer hours than any labor board would allow, without overtime ... for what?

I personally think there are some bottom lines we ought to agree about as a society. For one thing: Eight hours is enough. It's plenty. I have at times worked 12-hour days and more, either because I needed the money or because I believed in what I was doing. But really we've got to start talking about what we're doing to people's lives with all this work. Eight hours is enough.

And I think people have to stop knuckling under to bosses just because they're bosses. Where is our democratic spirit? It's surely not in corporations. Corporations are little authoritarian cultures. I do not see how a democracy can survive when its citizens spend all their days under authoritarian rule. How are we to emerge daily from our 10 hours of ritual authoritarian behavior, and devote the remaining four or six hours to democratic self-rule?

We must begin to bring democratic principles into the workplace.

It's time to start refusing to simply perform as many hours as the boss says. It's time to underperform. Who cares if the work doesn't get done? What kind of work is it, anyway? If you take a break, are you going to leave a child gasping for breath on the operating table? Who's going to die if you take an occasional personal day even though according to your boss, or the schedule, or the project timeline so elegantly represented on your project management software, it's not the ideal time for you to be taking a personal day?

Not the ideal time? So what? There is no ideal time. Stuff happens. Deal with it.

And what is going on with you personally? Why do you have to perform so darned well? Why can't you kind of not do such an incredibly great job all the time? Can't you have an occasional off day? And what of us collectively? What is so great about being the most productive country in the world? What has it gotten us lately but war and the well-earned contempt of everyone who is not an American? What is it getting you, this historic juggernaut? Are you vacationing on the Caribbean, are you basking in diamonds and champagne? Of course not. You're just being played.

And how are you being played? You have been conditioned to be the best. You have been taught to do what they say, or you'll end up on the street. But is there really a risk of ending up on the street? And are your capacities limitless? Are you incapable of error and possessed of infinite stamina? Is that what it says on your résumé? Is that what it says on your job description, that you promise to work unending hours and take infinite amounts of crap because you agree, in writing, that as an employee you have absolutely no choice?

I say slack off a little, in the interest of workers everywhere. What are you worried about? Are you worried that if you don't perform like a superstar you will get fired and won't be able to get another job as good as this one? As happy and fun as this one? As personally rewarding as this one? What if you were to start performing as you wish, working the hours you wish to work, try to make your home life a little more pleasant, and see what happens to the job around you. Just wait and watch. Let a ball or two drop. So what? Let the ball roll under a desk. So what? When asked where it is ... How can you know where it is? Somebody must have dropped the ball. Who could that person possibly be? I don't know. How would I know? This office is full of underperformers and incompetents. I can't keep track of them all.

> Bring democratic principles into the workplace.

What will happen? Will your boss berate you? Will that mean anything? Can you handle being berated by someone you don't respect? If you can't handle it, why not? Do you believe what the boss says might be true, that maybe you really don't measure up? Do you believe in undying loyalty to company and country? Do you believe that you don't have the right to put some limits on how much you will do for a company? I say slow down, do what you can, and stop faking it. Stop eating it. Stop trying to be a superstar.

I'm really addressing this to both of you, you and your wife, and to all the other people out there whose lives are falling apart because they are being worked too hard. I say begin a slow and silent revolt. What power do these companies really have over you? They have the power of threats. They can fire you, of course. They can tell you that you're not performing up to standards. They can say they're disappointed! But why not begin to question the whole rationale behind it? What is the meaning of their displeasure with you? Are they the people to whom you look for your deepest values? Is the corporation our only source of moral authority? What has happened to us as workers in America, that our only moral authorities, our only sources of value, are the very forces who would destroy us?

I've got roofers on my house right now. They work hard. It's not fun. They don't get to be interviewed on TV about their opinions. They don't sit down all day. They work. But they show up at 8 and by 4 they're packing up. They don't work all day and all night. And neither should you.

P.S. Don't shoot your wife's boss ... unless he fires first.

I've had it!

I'm surrounded by more stupid, rude, outrageous people than ever—and I have less and less patience with them.

Dear Cary,

I'M IN MY mid-40s and find I have less and less tolerance and patience for the world's vagaries. I've never suffered fools particularly gladly, but these days I find that I can work myself into an irritable frenzy over the smallest things. People talking on their cell phones and not considering anything or anyone around them. Drivers doing 40 in the highway passing lane, then slowing down even more when they know you want to pass. Cashiers who don't even bother to thank you when you've just plunked down $300 at their store. A mother calling her kid a "lying piece of shit" in a department store. Is it just me, or are people saying and doing more outrageously stupid and ignorant things than ever before?

Maybe it's because I live in one of the poorest states in the nation, where there's a huge rate of addiction and lack of education. But something tells me it's not much better in more prosperous places, where people simply manifest their unconsciousness with better liquor and nicer clothes. Lack of civility offends me constantly, and yet I'm living in one of the crassest cultures on earth. Don't get me wrong—I'm not asking for manners à la Letitia Baldrige. But how about just a little common courtesy, respect and decency, bred of realizing that there are other people in the world besides oneself?

Short of moving to a more civilized place (please feel free to specify exactly where that is), do you have any advice on how to cope with the ever present rudeness and crudeness of the modern world? How do I take less offense and have more patience? Or should I just try to live in as much isolation as possible and hope that eventually old age will bring a tired, docile sort of acceptance of humankind?

Ready for a Rooftop and an AK-47

Dear Ready for a Rooftop,

MOVE OVER ON this rooftop, I need to aim. And stop hogging the ammunition.

Like you, I have been giving people a hard time lately. My wife says that I am entering premature codgerhood. I don't approve of how people do things.

But I know this much: You and I and everyone else who can't stand the way other people do things: We're the problem. It's us, not them. There's something wrong with us. We're nuts.

We're like little crazy people going around with secret voices in our heads.

Really it is a form of craziness to walk around thinking everybody should be doing things differently than they do. In most of us it's mild enough that you can't be put away for it. But it's crazy.

It's crazy because it presumes the impossible.

What if, for instance, we criticized birds? What if we looked up at the sky and said, "Those gulls are flying all wrong. Look at them—they're out of formation!" Or the pelicans. Or the dogs. Or the trees, for that matter, the way they grow, so crooked and slow and uneven! What is wrong with them? Don't they know?

Ah, but you say, humans are supposed to know. They're smart. Are they? They've been educated. Have they been? And by whom? Who is supposed to have taught them what they are supposed to know? Did you teach them? Did your mother teach them? Did my mother teach them? In what sense are we to expect

that any kind of uniform instruction has been given, and even if
it has been given, why should we expect that people would con-
form to it? It is equally reasonable to expect that people will do
the opposite of what they have been instructed because they did
not like being instructed, or the instructing was done in a spirit
of intimidation or sadistic control and the person is saying by his
behavior that he will not allow his spirit to be smothered in that
way, that he will be rude and contradictory in a holy way, that
he will fly his freak flag high even though it is the wrong day for
freak flags.

Some people think it's good to drive 40 in the fast lane. I
know that's hard to accept. But if you look at what people do, as
opposed to what you wish they would do, you can only conclude
that our rules are not the only rules. Other people have rules
too. Their rules may not be the rules of consensus, but they have
arrived at them and they believe in them. And so what are you
supposed to do with that?

The problem is that we all have rules but we don't have them
posted. If we carried signs on our chests, things would be much
clearer. Then, when a person with a
sign saying "I think the world is a beautiful place and I hope you do too, and
if you do, then you will smile broadly"
is required to interact with a person
who has a sign saying "The Holocaust
proved that life is tragic and man is a
monster," then they can perhaps each
gauge the proper distance and respect they need to show each
other. Or on the highway, if the person doing 40 in the fast lane
had a sign on his car saying "I believe everyone should go 40 in
the fast lane and if we all did that we'd save gas and the freeways
would be safer" then we could process that. We could say, OK,
that person has an opinion; and as we pass them at 95 they could
attempt to read the sign on our car that says "Have You Ever
Driven the Autobahn? It's So Much Better Than This!"

Basically we are all breaking each other's rules all the time
and annoying the hell out of each other because we pretend that

> Pass the
> ammunition.

our rules are the right ones. So maybe if we could just stop having rules about other people we'd be closer to enlightenment. I would like to get to a point of divine acceptance of all people; I would like to be in love with humankind; I would like to see the divine light in every individual, even the man doing 40 in the fast lane, even the person handing me my change in the wrong order.

But I am far from that.

What I am looking for, unconsciously perhaps, is for others to match me in my discomfort with the world; I want to see reflected back to me in their eyes a little bit of tragic knowledge, a little bit of somber self-reflection, a little bit of acknowledgment of suffering, a bit of gravitas.

I am a cranky bastard, yearning for peace and enlightenment.

And so to you, my annoyed and outraged friend, I say give me some elbow room and pass the ammunition.

Later, I will meditate.

Should I tell the lesbian in the office it's cool that she's gay?

She seems to be hiding the fact, but I think I know the signs and ... that's OK!

Dear Cary,

I WORK AS a manager at a Fortune 10 company, and enjoy both the company and the people I work with. I wouldn't say that I've developed many close friendships with co-workers, but I have some friends and a lot of amicable relationships with people in the office.

One woman that I chat with fairly frequently is (to my mind) obviously gay, though she seems to be making some kind of effort to conceal it when we talk. When referring to her home life, she'll frequently make use of an indefinite "we," has once dropped the word "partner" when describing her life mate, and becomes obviously uncomfortable when someone hears her get a personal call from what I can only identify as a consistent female voice.

Of course, the company has a nondiscrimination policy, and from my personal views I have absolutely no problems with any-one's preference. I'd like for this co-worker of mine to feel com-fortable talking about her home life if she feels like it, but haven't figured out a way to make it obvious that I'm supportive.

Is this something I should be direct about, in the sense of just saying that I both personally and professionally support gay lifestyles, or should I just let her establish her own boundaries even though it seems to me that her desire to conceal makes her uncomfortable? I have no desire to "out" anyone, but I like for the people I enjoy to feel like they can talk to me honestly.

Any tips?

Treading Lightly in the Social Underbrush

Dear Treading Lightly,

IMAGINE HOW IT might feel if someone at work, someone with a fairly high rank with whom you have casual and pleasant conversations at your desk from time to time, were one day to lean down to you and say, in a lowered voice, apparently with the kindest of intentions, "I know we haven't talked about this before, but I just wanted to say, in case you thought it might be some kind of problem here, I can tell you're Jewish, and ... that's no problem!"

If you were Jewish you might feel a certain way. If you were not Jewish you might feel a certain way. Neither of those ways would be particularly good.

So I think you are right to let her establish and maintain her own boundaries. To raise the issue in any way strikes me as unwise.

Even outside the workplace, even if you were not a manager, I simply think that issues of "otherness" are unfathomable.

I have my ideas about why this is. But as one who is anything other than "other"—a straight, white, middle-aged male American—I would be of course on shaky ground in trying describe how it feels to be a lesbian, or, more precisely, a woman whom others take to be a lesbian, in a Fortune 10 workplace. That is a world beyond my experience.

Let people set their own boundaries.

While I do not have the direct experience, I do have powers of empathic imagination. So I will say this: It is my personal belief, based on experience and long thought, that if you are Asian or black or gay or disabled or any other of the multifarious American others, your life must be different in one particular way from the life of a person whom others automatically view as "normal." The difference is that you don't get your social identity handed to you at birth and reconfirmed throughout your life in everyday encounters. On the contrary, you have to struggle to assemble the face you present to the world. You have to struggle to learn just what aspects of that face the world will accept and what aspects it will shun. It gets tiring and frustrating.

If you, my friend, are like me in appearance, that is, an ordinary-looking white male American of average height and build, then you are in fact among an extraordinary elite of men, granted, by dint of history, an astounding array of opportunities, from the ability to go shopping without being followed to the ability to walk into a mortgage broker and be greeted with an automatic smile to being treated as innocent until proven guilty by traffic cops.

This is a case in point: You have determined, based on your observation, that this person is different. You believe that it's OK for this person to be different. That alone—the power to decree that it's OK—is an act of enormous unspoken privilege. There's no way for you and me to escape this. We wield enormous power because we are perceived to belong.

I'm not saying we should feel shame or step aside so that others can take our places. Nor am I saying that history provides an excuse for the inexcusable. I'm simply saying we have a responsibility, as thinking, feeling people, to deeply consider this fact of otherness that describes reality for so many people. For me personally, from that deep consideration, certain advisory postures flow: Caution, for one. Patience. Humility. The never-ending chores of the moral imagination.

All we can do is, as you suggest, tread lightly. Try to pretend that you didn't just win the lottery. Bear your good fortune quietly. Let others control the boundaries of their own existence. Because you and I, my friend, if we try to get over, we're just impostors in the land of the other.

At a crossroads

I've been waiting for his ship to come in so he'll stop being depressed and be with me. Will it ever happen?

Dear Cary,

I'VE BEEN IN a relationship for the last two and a half years, and I now find myself at a difficult crossroads. The relationship has been wonderful at times and a real struggle at other times. My partner is a funny, warm and extremely talented guy. When he wants to be, he is extremely gregarious, and everyone loves him. He is also a writer and has been effectively unemployed for the last two years, though since he's fairly well-known and well-connected he's managed to put together a living by doing freelance work. However, he thrives on stability, and so the constant worry of whether this next paycheck will be his last has put a strain on him and thus on our relationship.

He's currently on the cusp of breaking into Hollywood and is a lot further than most hopefuls ever get. He's extremely talented, and deals are being set up that could set him up for life—but nothing is a definite in Hollywood until the check's been cashed. And so the constant worry and stress have made him self-focused, self-indulgent and self-absorbed. He doesn't ask me about my life, how my day has gone, or how I'm feeling. It just simply doesn't occur to him. For quite a long time, although I've been very clear, open and honest with him about how I feel and what I need, I've been carrying this relationship on my shoulders, doing all the work, going to his house to hang out, and patiently waiting for his sex drive to return.

Because of all this, he hasn't really made an effort to become part of my life. He hasn't made any effort to get to know any of my friends, which they now resent—because after all, one can only go so long before "getting to know the friends and family" is so overdue as to be ridiculous. He balks at coming to my house, preferring to stay close to home in his cavelike environment.

I've brought these things up to him many times, and we have nearly broken up over them before, and every time he asks me to be patient, that this cloud of depression will lift as soon as he is financially stable, that he loves me as much as life itself and that his life would be miserable without me. He doesn't want to go to a therapist because of the expense, as well as his insistence that it won't help him. (He went before because he was abusing alcohol as a means to deal—or not deal—with his depression. He has since stopped drinking, but lately I worry since he's starting to have drinks now and again, he will sink back into it.) He probably needs to be on some sort of antidepressant medication, but he can't afford it, and for various reasons, he doesn't qualify for state assistance.

I am starting graduate school in a month. I have a history of depression (though I've not had problems with it since I was an undergrad about six years ago), and I have been clear with him that our problems have to be sorted out before I start school, or else I can't continue in the relationship. He says that he wants to be supportive, but that I just need to continue to be patient and wait along with him for his break to come. And much as I love him and believe that he's really a good guy in an awful place right now, I just don't know what to do. My friends are telling me that I've given him enough chances and that I should probably just make a clean break before the world of papers and dissertations and all of that swallows me whole and a breakup would be exponentially worse.

He is one of the few people that have really gotten me in my life. I'm reluctant to give up what we do have. We've talked about marriage and kids in our future, which really makes me happy, as I think he'd be a good father. But I just can't carry our relationship on my own shoulders any longer, and there's really no telling how long it will be until he's financially stable, or if that will cure his depression. How do I resolve this?

Philosophically Flummoxed

Dear Flummoxed,

SADLY, I THINK you go. I think you stop carrying the load. If he wants you he can find you. He can win you back. Maybe he'll rise to the occasion. The only way to find out is to stop carrying the load.

He says he cares for you. What the hell does that mean? What does it mean if I say I care for you? Does that cook you dinner? Does that feed your cats? Does that make you warm between your shoulder blades? What if I say I care for Julia Roberts? Do you think she'll come over tonight and read me Shakespeare? I care about the homeless people I step over on the way to work. I care a lot about them. I love them! I care about the dead Iraqi women and children, and the dead soldier boys from small towns in Iowa. I care for you.

> Stop carrying his load.

What the hell does that mean? It means I want you to like me. It means I'd like to keep you waiting around. It means that what you think about me is more important than whether you're happy or sad.

You need more than some guy who keeps you on hold. You need more than a guy who can't get out of his little cave of an apartment to drive you to the beach. You need somebody with a car to put your umbrella in, and your little hibachi, who will drive you to Venice and back just for one of those little corn dogs they sell from a stand.

Sure he needs help. So put him on your health insurance and hook him up with a psychiatrist. But don't hang around and be his girlfriend. You're not helping anybody that way.

I know this guy. I know the kind of self-involved artistic hell he's in, and I know the fear of oblivion and the need for approval and worldly success that drives him to trudge deeper and deeper into that hell. We are brothers in our fear of oblivion and our lust for approval, and we will do anything for it, and it is not pretty, because we are the young dead bodies found by housekeepers at the Chateau Marmont, and we are the overdosed rock stars in fabulous hotels who never got to hear the final mix, we are the writers who burned out after a novel or two because they couldn't take it, we are the critics who wish they had the courage to try it themselves, we are the bitter executives screwing starlets on their leather couches from Pottery Barn, we are the dull, sick soul of television, we are the limp prose of writing schools and the slack-jawed hunger of MFA programs, we are the reason no one respects journalists anymore, we are trudging into hell and we like it, because it proves what we thought all along, that we're really not worth shit and everybody knows it, and we resent you and your graduate school but we don't admit it because we're just trying to keep you around until we score big and then we're going to dump you anyway for Kirsten Dunst, who we're suggesting we cast on our first feature film.

We're just a couple of cheap punks trudging into hell with a film treatment and a card from a cast supervisor at Miramax who said she'd call but never did. Let me warn you, don't follow us; we'll promise to call, but don't count on us.

Maybe he'll stop. I can see him in the distance there, pausing at the gates. Maybe he's turning around. Maybe he'll be rescued. Maybe that's his Lincoln Town Car I see rounding the turn. Or maybe he's going all the way down to the Chateau Marmont for a fabulous party that never ends.

You don't need to go with him. It wouldn't be much fun anyway. And don't wait up. It could be a long night.

Emotional seduction

*My boyfriend let a needy girl crash
in his hotel room, and it bothers me.
Am I being unreasonable?*

Dear Cary,

I HAVE A question about jealousy. My boyfriend and I have
a pretty good relationship. We each have many friends of the
opposite sex, and jealousy has never seriously come up in the
three years we've been dating.

Just this month, he went on an important trip to another city
halfway across the country (he was invited to an arts festival to
perform). No problem there, we've each gone on similar types
of trips.

But a female friend of his—and as far as I know, they're not
real close friends—took a bus 10 hours just to visit him and hang
out, and he invited her to stay with him in his hotel room. Why?
I think he felt bad she came all that way, or he was flattered or
something, but I don't think it was arranged beforehand.

He told me about it (not before it happened though), and he
also told me he was hiding it from fellow performers on the trip
because he thought it looked bad.

I told him it bothered me, and we had a great talk about it,
but I think he's having trouble understanding why I'm troubled
by this—and so am I, actually.

While I have no doubt that he was faithful—I'm sure it had
nothing to do with infidelity or anything on his part—I find the
idea that he would do this disturbing. Part of my distress is that

this girl is 23 and he is 44 (I'm 33). The whole thing just feels dangerous to me.

This person, from what he's told me, seems to get herself into these types of situations with men. She either has abusive relationships with men her own age, or fatherly relationships with older men. And my boyfriend is critical of one friend of his who is quite protective of this girl, and yet he seems to be doing the same thing.

When we talked (and when he told me), she had one more night there before leaving. She'd already been there two days. At first I told him I had to process the idea and that it bothered me somewhat, but I said nothing about what he should do. I didn't tell him to ask her to leave or anything. But he did, and now he still feels guilty. He was worried she would "disappear" as she sometimes does—or go out and do something dangerous. He's being as protective of this girl as his friend he criticizes for doing the same thing.

I feel guilty for telling him that I find the idea of inviting a 23-year-old—one who came 10 hours by bus—back to his hotel room disturbing. But this is how I feel. The way I perceive it is: He's opening the door to a potentially sticky situation.

I know we're both very different socially. He doesn't see how this is different from letting someone crash at your place overnight. I think it's absolutely different. I'm feeling jealous and territorial, something I'm really not used to. Any advice?

Jealous and Threatened

Dear Jealous and Threatened,

OF COURSE YOU feel jealous and territorial. Good for you. That's how you should feel. I don't think you have to understand your feelings in order to trust them and act on them. Nonetheless, here are some thoughts.

Women who act helpless and vulnerable and place themselves at the mercy of men can be emotionally seductive and powerful in their craziness. They can draw men into a world of codependent manipulation where they gain power by appearing weak. They can appeal to a man's fantasy of being the rescuer and protector. Even the lack of sex can form part of a quasi-erotic fantasy: His heroic chastity is in itself a kind of intimacy: He becomes a hero in her eyes and gets off on it. Maybe that's what bothers you. Maybe you sense that he is playing the role of chaste hero, when that's a role he should play for you alone.

Maybe you sense that this woman is using a powerful form of archetypal female behavior to gain intimacy with your boyfriend and to gain some kind of power over him. What you identify as jealousy may be more of a protective impulse—because you intuitively understand what she is doing and how dangerous she can be. Also, you may fear for his dignity because what he's doing makes him look a little foolish.

> Trust the feelings you don't understand.

His fear that she may harm herself if he doesn't let her stay in his hotel room is evidence of her emotional blackmail.

You say that you sense she is dangerous, and I do agree that this situation at least exposes a danger—the danger of the lost woman, the shrieking, vulnerable, "Play Misty for Me" shrew, or the psychotic, or the calculatedly helpless, or the cunning seductress. Or just the danger of your boyfriend appearing to have a blind spot, or to be kind of flaky. Or obtuse.

Because you seem to rely on a lot of talking and analysis in your relationship, I hope this makes you aware of certain emotional depths that lie beyond discussion, of the hidden pitfalls of symbolic behavior, of the limits of talking through things: how beyond the gleaming surface of your relationship lies an ongoing flirtation with hero and devil, which will from time to time force you beyond your own understanding.

Boys leave

*Why was I the cat's meow on the fifth date
and a sex buddy by the sixth?*

Dear Cary,

SO IT'S HAPPENING again: Girl meets boy. Girl likes boy.
Gets boy's number. Girl and boy begin dating. Boy sends all of
the "very interested" signals. Girl responds in kind. Incredible
sex. Eye-gazing. Natural feeling, intelligent conversation. Then
the sixth date: No eye contact, little attempt at conversation,
unimpassioned sex. Boy abruptly, awkwardly leaves that morning, making no mention of weekend plans. Boy insults girl with
small talk. Girl feels used and disappointed. Girl writes Cary.

What's going on here? Seriously. This has happened to me
before. But I didn't expect it from this guy. He's 33. He's in med
school. He's traveled extensively with the military. He's bright
and clever. He lights up a room. He has a zest for life that's dev-
astatingly attractive to me. He's confident.

My male friends tell me that I intimidate guys. I've tried to
tone it down. With this guy I really took it easy. Followed his
lead. Was always very much myself but let a little more of the
softness through. I avoided all the old traps. It seemed to work.
I was pleased with myself for breaking old patterns. Then, sure
enough, with no warning he's gone. Vacant.

Typically this is when I begin to act like a circus clown, jumping all around trying to pinpoint whatever it is that will take him
back to where he was before, and this is when it gets ugly and I
get pathetic, and the whole thing is scrapped (usually with good

reason by then). But I really don't want that to happen this time.
I want to change this pattern. I want to understand what's going
on here.

I really like this one. I do. I rarely meet people that are as
passionate about living as I am, and it felt so nice to not feel
like someone's specimen. He doesn't need my energy to feed off
of—he has his own. I trusted that he wouldn't be another man
who would profess how incredible I am and then in the next
breath tell me that I'm "too much."

I feel hurt and disappointed. How was I the cat's meow on
the fifth date and a sex buddy by the sixth? Cary, can you tell me
what happened at five and a half? I can't think of anything that I
did. I really can't. I'd tell you if I could. Why did he turn off, and
more importantly how should I respond? Typically I would call
and confront him (weirdness ensues), but this time I want to see
what he does, and what you say, before I make a move to unearth
whatever's going on.

How should I proceed? And is there some way I can avoid this
in the future?

A Little Broken Hearted ... Again

Dear A Little Broken Hearted,

AS I GO over your letter, trying to locate you, the image I get
is of a woman spinning wildly like a child on a gleaming ballroom floor, throwing sparks into the night, arranging the very
universe by her dancing, drunk with attractive power. I see a
woman who looks only outward at the shiny, spinning world
full of lights but never inward lest she fall, a woman who sees
around her other shiny, spinning, fabulous dancers and is briefly
drawn into their orbits as they are drawn into hers, forming figure eights as they orbit each other on a great dance floor in some
marble ballroom. It is a fabulous, glittering ball, half-mystical,
and in this ballroom there is no conversation, only dancing and
gesture; nor is there any progression, or any time; there is only

whirling and more whirling and when the whirling stops there is only a dreamless sleep of exhaustion in plush red banquet chairs, and then more dancing. There is no remembering of hard times here in this ballroom, nor is there any self-doubt, nor are any names exchanged. No one can remember the last time the music stopped, and no one can remember the last time a contemplative word was uttered. This is not a place where contemplative people come; it is just a whirling ball, glittering and festive and timeless.

That is how I picture you, as a glittering dancer at a ball, who met another glittering dancer and danced wordlessly until you exhausted him and then he whirled away. But when he whirled away you were sad. You expected something else. But what was it you expected? No one in this ballroom knew that you expected anything else. All anyone does here is dance.

This man who turned away from you and hurt you: What was the substance of your understanding of him? What did you learn about his wishes and desires? Was he looking for a wife, or just a playmate? Was he completely single, or partially attached? Was he what they call "emotionally available"? Do you know how one would go about ascertaining if someone is "emotionally available"? Did you consider that a handsome, worldly, charismatic former military man who is now in medical school might be in some ways not emotionally available? Did it occur to you that in your busy, whirling extravagance of spirit you might have neglected to closely study his eyes, how he reacts to you, whether he's shrinking from you as you expand to fill the room with your fabulousness, whether he might have appeared short of breath as you sucked the oxygen out of the air around him, whether you might have missed any attempt on his part, however subtle and coded, to warn you that he was not the man for you?

Ask your heart if it sees what you see.

It may be that you have great attractive power but only have transactions, not relationships, with men; that would explain why men come and go from your boudoir at will—because although you may dance with them and sleep with them, you have neglected the careful disclosure and attentive listening through which two people establish an emotional narrative. You almost sound like a woman in the last stages of a magical girl phase, when you still have the power, intelligence, vivacity and attractiveness of youth to draw men to you, but find that drawing them to you is no longer enough, that you are groping your way into the world of difficult compromise and self-disclosure that adult relationships require.

If you are ready for that, you will find your way. Here is a tip: The next time you are attracted to a man, try to see him not with your eyes but with your heart. Ask your heart what it sees. It may not see the glittering prince that you see with your eyes. By your heart I mean your intuition, your spider sense, the instant feelings of fear or attraction that you used to rely on as a child.

You're going to have to stop dancing and making love long enough to hear what the next man has to say. What he says may surprise you. It may also bore you. Such is life outside the ballroom and the boudoir.

Only the lonely

*I am divorced and can get women to sleep
with me, but why do I keep sabotaging
real relationships?*

Dear Cary,

I'M A 35-YEAR-OLD professional type, smart and fairly witty
I'm told, apparently not bad looking, and so very lonely. I'm told
it's easy for men in my demographic to meet women, but nobody
ever talks about the flip side of that coin—it's not any easier to
meet the right person.

I'm starting to realize that the problem lies within. This whole
self-awareness project is a relatively new one. I'm still sorting it
all out. Here's what I've figured out so far.

I got married too young. I was 23 years old when I got married. I hadn't dated a lot. I just met someone who felt right and
didn't want to look any further. I truly did think I'd found the
person who was right for me.

Eight years later we'd both changed so much we could barely
recognize each other. The cool hippie girl I'd married had become
an accountant. I'd morphed into what I now am from the dope-
smoking skater kid I once was. We barely spoke, never had sex,
and drifted further and further apart until it was over and I left.
In a lot of ways this was a relatively easy split—we just had nothing to fight over. No kids, mortgages, nothing—but in so many
ways it has extracted a huge toll.

Now I find myself paralyzed by the prospect of relationships
and dating. Not by the terrifying prospect of approaching people.

I honestly don't find that terrifying. It's approaching honestly and openly I'm not so good at.

I'm an astute guy. It doesn't take me long to figure out what people want. Put me in a bar feeling desperately lonely and I can reproduce a reasonable hand-drawn facsimile of exactly what a woman's looking for—at least for the first few hours. So the pattern I've fallen into is basically whoredom.

A female friend of mine put it best. She claims I'm acting like a teenage girl, trading sex for acceptance. I have to agree with her. What I do is trade in whatever fragile bits of self-esteem I've built up since the last time it happened for that close feeling of human contact. For someone who will touch me.

This pattern has varied a couple of times over the past few years, but the results weren't good either time. On both occasions I met what I can only describe as "complicated" women who turned around and delivered me the karmic shit-kicking I probably deserved. I seem to have an inability to let something grow organically between me and another person. If I feel something, it's all or nothing, and I drove both of them away.

Lately I've been trying to fill up what feels like a big empty hole in my life with positive things. I spend time with my friends. I bought a house I'm renovating. I'm learning to play the guitar. All this is good. I have some of the best friends anyone could want. My home is becoming exactly that—a home. Music is opening up a whole new world for me.

But sooner or later it's 2 a.m. and my married friends are heading home. This is generally when the real loneliness hits—and when I wind up the next morning wondering what her name is and how I get her out of my house. And when I do meet someone that offers some possibilities, my heart seems to short-circuit and I mess it up. I'm really starting to wonder why I'm sabotaging myself.

Paralyzed

Dear Paralyzed,

ONE THING THAT happens with men, I think, is that we pretend to ourselves that we're just looking for sex, in order to keep things simple and not be overwhelmed by all our multifarious and complex needs and desires. But we pretend to women that we're not just looking for sex, which is true, except not exactly the way we portray it. We come on a little more heroic and in control than we really are. We're really pretty much a raging ball of confusion, but we don't let on. So we get a little song and dance together that gets us in the door and then once we get in the door, and we can let our guard down, we'd like to be our true selves but we can't because we've already done this other act. So we're trapped in a character we've created.

But if you really laid it all out ahead of time, you figure you'd never get laid, right? Imagine what would happen if you said, Here are my fears, here's my history of being an asshole, here's my meager salary and my secret ambitions to be a rock star, here's my actual opinion of women and love and social bullshit, here's my desire to not ever get married and end up like the guys I went to high school with, here's my possible drinking problem, here's my limited emotional vocabulary, here's my idea of a good-looking jacket, here's my underwear and yes I like it with the holes in it.

I mean, you can't do that, right? So you're trapped.

But you're not entirely trapped. You have to set yourself up with some wiggle room. Picture a scale of 1 to 10. What would be on the scale? Take loneliness and sexual desire, for instance: Need for closeness. Need for sex. Need for quiet talk. Need for sleep. Need for food. Need for exercise. Need for alone time. Need for music and friends. Need for trust. Need to know what's going to happen tomorrow. Just a whole list of things.

Then subdivide them. This loneliness, for instance. There is loneliness that is an aching for someone in particular. And there is loneliness for just people in general, like the need to just walk downtown. That is, there is loneliness that is a longing for intimacy, and there is loneliness that is a longing for just anonymous human contact. Other feelings you think are loneliness might not be loneliness at all, but restlessness, or irritability, or even hunger. You might think you need a woman but you just need a sandwich.

You never know until you start rating these cravings on a scale of 1 to 10, by their intensity and their duration. Likewise, with the need for sex, that could be broken down. What kind of sex do you need? Do you need the kind of sex that involves intimacy with a woman? Or do you need the kind of sex that is more like walking down a street full of strangers, a kind of sex that is more a distraction from yourself than an encounter? You can define all these things for yourself.

What appears to have been happening is that you're feeling various powerful wants but acting on them each time in the exact same way—by seducing a woman. And you're finding that each time you do it the same way, of course it turns out pretty much the same. And so I'd suggest that you start paying attention to the variations in what you feel, and trying to come up with actions more appropriate to what you're actually feeling. Because you're not in it just for the sex. You're in it for a variety of things.

> You might think you need a woman but you just need a sandwich.

That's why it sounds like a very positive thing that you're playing music, and working on the house, and you have this web of friends.

But you're probably still uncomfortable enough in your own skin that you need these periods of, like, emotional blackout, where you just go on autopilot. You're going to have to try to stay awake at those moments where you feel so uncomfortable. Go for that middle zone, where you're a little lonely but also a little tired, or a little attracted but also a little put off. Try to carburet your emotions, get some good healthy mixtures. You've been running too rich, and then flooding and stalling out.

You need to consciously try to change the course of habitual interactions with women. For instance, next time you're with a woman and you can see where it's leading, stop. Say to her that you like her and you sense where things are going but you're trying to change your habits with women. And just see if you can't feel your way along with her in a slightly different way than before. Maybe work her into your life a bit—your life with the house and the music and the friends. Take the time to find out if you really like her or you just want to gobble her like a sandwich. If you just want to gobble her like a sandwich, maybe it's not her, but the sandwich you want to gobble. Maybe then you two could go into the kitchen and put something between two slices of bread.

What's to live for?

I'm 20 and I've seen enough of life.
Why shouldn't I just check out?

Cary,

AFTER 20 YEARS of being told that I have my whole life ahead of me, I already feel like I've seen enough. I don't have it in me to pursue goals for their own sake—I have no motivation to finish college, look for a better job, or do any of the things that keep my contemporaries occupied. I get up and go to work and to class because it's easier than not going, but I know that soon it won't be.

I feel as though I'm broken on some fundamental level. I can't connect to people. The one person I've considered a friend is leaving me soon and has said plainly that she doesn't plan to keep in touch. I've tried dating and met some interesting people, but it's incredibly easy to just let the phone ring when they call. I feel bad, but not bad enough to call back. It's been years since I can remember looking forward to anything. About the only thing that keeps me alive right now is the fact that I don't want someone else to be stuck boxing up my apartment, and there's a lot of packing to do. That, and the vague sense that there's something I'm missing. It sure seems like no one else has trouble finding reasons to get up in the morning.

There's a lot of debate over the rights of terminally ill people to die when they choose, but why is it automatically irrational for a young, physically healthy person to decide that enough is enough? When there's nothing I want to do and no one to be hurt when I go, it's hard not to resent the people who tell me how self-ish and stupid I must be.

I guess I'm still human enough to want to reach out to someone, or be reached out to. For the record, I've been through drugs and therapy without seeing any lasting change, and I'm not inclined to try again. I just want to know why this is so easy for everyone else and so impossible for me.

What's the Use?

Dear What's the Use,

LET ME SUGGEST this to you right now: Think of a happy time. Come on, I know you can think of one. I know it's in there. You may know of it but not want to think of it. Think of it anyway. I know that as soon as I say "happy time" there is at least one that comes into your mind. So go ahead. Stop what you were doing and just think of this time. Remember it. Remember the sounds, the sights, the smells, what you were feeling and saying, who was there. Sit down. Linger on it. Do that for a few minutes. Let the memory suffuse your body. Let it envelop you and flow through you as though it were an expensive perfume or an elixir in your blood. Close your eyes and remember it in as much detail as you can. Take as much time as you need.

When the memory fades and you begin to feel exhausted or sleepy (it's tiring to remember with intensity!), don't do anything for a few minutes. Just let the happy event settle back into your consciousness.

Over the next few days, consider that happy event. Turn it over in your mind. Is there some reason that such a happy event could never occur again? Did it occur in a country that has been blasted off the face of the earth? Are all the people who were there now dead and gone? Have you yourself been maimed or blinded so that you could never experience such a thing? Or might there be a possibility that such happiness might be found again?

Now do something else. Think of more recent times, when you were fully engaged in something and forgot yourself and your many troubles. It may have only lasted a minute or two. Perhaps you were having a conversation with a friend. Perhaps you were finding some information on the computer. Perhaps you were walking along and noticed a bird or a building or a book in a window, or someone passed you whose face reminded you of the face in a book you'd read, or a man reading a newspaper looked like Jack Webb of "Dragnet," or you thought for an instant that was Tobey Maguire sitting at a table, or the cab that passed you gleamed in the rain like a cab in a 1970s television show, or you passed a girl on the street and imagined, with alarming vividness, undressing her in a hotel room in Tokyo.

Stick around for the Buick.

Having thought of these things, consider this: What is to prevent you from filling your life with more events such as the ones you have just recollected, so that your life is charged with such moments? Would that not be the life of a happy man? It's not all that mysterious. String atoms of happiness together like beads, and you can have a happy life.

I'm curious about something. Is there by chance some ugly, frightening voice in you that has utter contempt for the kind of happiness we're talking about? Does a part of you feel that happiness is delusion, unworthy of adulthood, that to be a man is to brood ceaselessly, to be inconsolable and wan, to let your damp hair flap in your face as you sit in a cafe staring at the tabletop, drowning in deep, impenetrable suffering? Is that what it means to be a man?

Did something happen that time you were so happy to destroy it? Was there a father who appeared, telling you you were lazy to be enjoying the sun? Was there a teacher or a disciplinarian who shamed you out of your enjoyment? Did your peers mock you for your transparent joy? What took that happiness away, and what has happened in the intervening years to prevent you from regaining it or experiencing it again?

You have tried drugs and therapy and say that did not work, but there are many kinds of therapy and many kinds of chemicals. If you've been drinking and doing a lot of drugs, or if you're nutritionally unbalanced, your brain may not be working right as of late. Does it feel as though there is a layer of cardboard between your thoughts and your sensation? People write to me and suggest all kinds of things for what you describe—fish oil, for instance, and vitamin B. They write and say, "I was awful and then I started taking these amino acids!" Who am I to doubt them? There are all kinds of reasons why we don't function right. It's amazing what the right chemistry can do. Ask yourself what you need: Protein and vitamins? Salmon and greens and rice. A steak? Some lentils? Whatever pops into your mind. Go take a run. Lift some weights. Take a swim. Go hear some music. Take yourself out of yourself.

Is it worth it, you ask? Would someone be hurt if you were gone? Of course someone would be hurt. But I think you are only asking when dinner will be served, if there will be a game on tonight, if someone will come by to comfort you in your vague but overwhelming sorrow. I am here to say yes, dinner will be served this evening. Someone will appear eventually. You just have to wait.

It is not easy, at 20, to wait. Waiting is what the hunter does, and the poet and the slugger. He waits for the moment of inevitability and fate and then he swings, or shoots, or takes up the pen to put down a line. They don't teach us to wait in America; they teach us to grab. But waiting is what we do when we are looking for something beautiful, when we are looking for an end to our sorrow. Nothing is infinite in life, not even sorrow. You just have to wait.

So maybe you are feeling the sadness of the one who waits. It is a sadness, that's true, but it's tempered by the sure knowledge that eventually a Buick will pull over and a stranger will give you a ride.

Not to be trite, but some people say, "Stick around for the miracle." I would say, if not the miracle, at least stick around for the Buick.

I forgot to tell my wife I have a 12-year-old daughter

I fathered a child when I was a screwed-up loser and kept it secret all these years.

Dear Cary,

BOY, DID I screw up.

About 13 years ago, I fell for a friend of my sister's and got her pregnant. I was at this point in my life a loser. I had no job, no home (I was living with my father), no car, no license (never had it), no complete education, and absolutely no prospects. Her family, predictably, hated me.

After a couple months of unremitting and conflicting pressure from our families, she "realized" that I was a loser and she cut me loose. No contact, no nothing.

The last night that we ever discussed the baby was the night she gave birth. I got raving drunk and never discussed it again. My very WASP-y and remarkably repressed family followed suit (or was it I that was following suit?) Either way, the topic was off limits, that part of my brain and my heart was blocked off with yellow tape, and everyone moved on.

She married and her husband adopted the baby. I turned my life around materially and spiritually (education, wonderful wife, good job, house, etc.). I never tried to contact her or the baby. I told myself that I was only a "donor" and that I would only screw things up for her and the baby. Eventually, my wife and I bought a home not too far from my daughter and her family.

I dealt with the issue alone, fighting the late-night demons and doing everything I could to hold the situation at bay.

Years passed. A mutual friend of the family ran into the woman and told my sister that my daughter is 12 now and asking a number of questions. The resemblance is unmistakable and her parents have done a wonderful job (I am thrilled for them and her). Faced with this, and only because I was faced with this, I decided to tell my wife about the situation.

Predictably, my wife is furious and feels (rightly) that I have violated her trust. We are just about to start a family of our own, and now everything in my life has been thrown into play. I don't know if I would have been able to reveal this if not forced. Now that it is out in the open, the events are painful and crushing.

I'm scared, I'm confused, and I suddenly feel every bit as worthless as I felt all those years ago. I don't think that my wife is going to leave me (we are looking into starting some kind of couples therapy), but I feel like I am still paying for not being good enough all those years ago. I am starting to get angry at those folks who are angry at me.

I have written a letter to my daughter's mother and adoptive father, explaining where I am in my life and that we are very open to contact and a relationship, once rules and boundaries have been established; but my primary concern is my wife. I do not want to lose her (or her respect) over this.

Three days ago I had a normal life, and I feel like I am never going to have that again...

What a tangled web we weave...

Dear Tangled,

I DO NOT think you will lose your wife over this, or that your life will fall apart. You will get into counseling and learn about family systems and the keeping of secrets. You will work out some arrangement with the family of your daughter, and your wife will look at you with unfathomable anger for an indefinite period, and if you are good and do not completely freak out, eventually the normal life you had three days ago will return. But I hope out of this comes some thinking about how you have been living and where the secrets come from and who this person was who so many years ago fathered a daughter and kept it secret from his wife. I detect in your letter perhaps a lack of empathy for your earlier incarnation, and I would like to share a little about how I, who was also a bit of a loser and somewhat out of control, have come in middle age to regard my earlier self.

It has been helpful for me to see that I did some of the things I did because I was trying to do the right thing, strange as it appeared. It has been of great help to me to realize that I have often been an innocent actor, naive and lazy and deluded but not malicious. Like you I was trying to survive. I was doing what I had to do at the time. It has been helpful in considering why certain episodes went wrong to consider what I was running from and why I kept so many secrets and why the truth seemed unsurvivable.

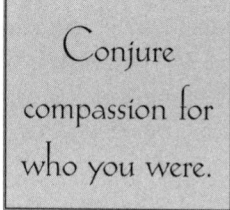

Conjure compassion for who you were.

Was there some knowledge so corrosive that the silence in our household was a kind of insulation, a balm to naked skin?

What truth was so terrible at the time that it could not be uttered in the house? That you had sex without love? Is love a pair of handcuffs that must be worn every time? Is it a sin to do something simply because you really, really want to and it feels really, really good? Was it a sin to make love to your sister's friend? Was there no one else around who could take you by the hand and show you what you then had to do? Was this all up to you? Are you the sole perpetrator of some crime? Must you punish yourself now for rest of your life?

It has been of great help to me from time to time to conjure up this innocent being, this young boy who was simply trying to express love and wonder, and later this young man who seemed to be in trouble but was not robbing houses or hitting people on the head. I suggest you do not hate this younger man, this fuck-up, this version of yourself. I suggest, instead, that you learn to love this nasty little fuck-up that you had to leave behind. I suggest that you offer a hand of forgiveness to this nasty little fuck-up. He was a guy trying to figure it out. He was a guy trying to get along. He was a guy trying to live with whatever it was that hurt. What was it that hurt? Who ever knows what it is with a young guy that hurts so much? We don't talk about it among ourselves, although always there will be a stoned glance or a touch between young men, high on this or that, that says I know the crazy hurting thing too, it's a motherfucker. So you followed the trajectory of your hurting and you got drunk the night your daughter was born.

Fathers have been getting drunk and leaving town for centuries when their babies are born: In spite of our storied propensity for engendering life, we do not always welcome it when it arrives, we kind of wish it would go away, we want to be left to our tools and our greasy hands and our shade trees, our violent metal and brief explosions, our gray primer and rust, our certainty of objects. The birth of a child means more life, more crying, more questions, more hunger, more lying and walking away, more required courses, more questions we cannot answer, more tests, more tedium, more teachers, more classroom sitting, more desolate afternoons, more diapers and howling, more unbridgeable gulf, more rules, more discipline, more silence. We do not like life in a lot of ways. For some of us men we like a few books, we like a little racquetball, we like maybe a sauna and some swimming, we like a long drive down a leafy road in a good truck, but we did not sign on for the entire program and it tires us out, frankly, and after the truck is parked we just want to lie down and go to sleep, and it is like this day after day for many of us men, which is why we father kids and go off into the woods, never to speak of it again until it comes up by a careless word or two in the supermarket, and there we are again, saddled with ourselves, bending under the incomprehensible load of what we have done—given life to a child who now looks out at the world and says, I don't know, man, what you're all so fucked up about, this looks pretty good to me. Just wait, we say. Just wait.

What I mean is, you need to conjure up some compassion for the teenager you once were, this wayward loser without a home or a job. You need to do this in order to stop hanging your head in shame for having been simply young and confused and unsure what to do. My sense of it is that your keeping of secrets arises out of intense shame. You need to replace that shame with some compassion and respect. To do that you need to go back down some of those same old roads and find out what you were really looking for back then.

I can't do that for you. But my guess is that you were looking for a way out of WASPish silence, the long tradition of family secrets, the code your family lived by. You were looking for a more authentic way of feeling and being. Making love and getting drunk seemed like ways to get to something real. But at the crucial moment, when your waywardness truly bore fruit, it was a forbidden fruit it bore, so you turned away in fear. You turned back to what you knew best: the keeping of secrets, the silent bearing of shame.

Now, as an adult man, it's time to pick up where you left off. It's time to finish what you started—not with teenage acting-out but with a sober acknowledgment that wild, untamable passions are as important to your life as oatmeal for breakfast and plenty of life insurance.

You're married now. You've got a house and a job. You're safe. It's time to hold your head up and acknowledge who you were then and who you are now and make the best of a pretty good situation.

I hope you get a chance to tell everything. Sometimes, after a life of secrets, telling everything helps.

I'm pregnant and outrageously horny

*My husband's too busy for sex, but my
also-pregnant girlfriend is looking delicious
and coming on to me. Should I?*

Dear Cary,

I AM PREGNANT with my second child, and the resulting hormones have so ramped up my sex drive that it's hard to get through the day without thinking about sex. As it is, I masturbate at least once a day.

My husband has neither the time nor the energy these days to have sex with me. He works long hours and travels for work, plus we have a toddler whom we both love to pieces and who is, of course, time-consuming. My husband is affectionate and adoring, and in all other respects our marriage is strong and happy. But the fact that I'm not getting any sort of sexual release with him is frustrating me to no end. A girl can only self-pleasure so much (though I'm sure many people disagree with me!). We've talked about it but with no solution, other than his apologies.

Which brings me to the following complication. I have a girlfriend who's also pregnant and who has made a few sexual advances toward me. I am hesitant to say that I'm bi, but I do have fantasies about having sex with other women. A lot. It doesn't help that she's terribly attractive and attracted to me. Thus far we've engaged in some sexy chat only, but I am really afraid that I will cave in because I just want to have sex with SOMEONE, dammit!

I don't want to cheat on my husband, and I wish the masturbation was good enough, but it's increasingly not. Help!

Too Hot

Dear Too Hot,

MY LIMITED UNDERSTANDING indicates that pregnant women often come up with novel ideas best left unacted upon. These ideas sometimes entail the complete dismemberment of strangers in the grocery store as well as the passionate embrace of same-sex friends and hot cyclists in the gym. The principle I would follow here is this: Try not to act on short-term desires in ways that will have long-term consequences. In other words, if it's a temporary thing that could throw your marriage into chaos, try to let it pass. It's basically impulse control only stretched out over a period of perhaps several months.

That's the simple and boring answer. The question, however, becomes slightly more complicated and interesting if you consider that the desire to have sex with a woman may not be simply a matter of hormones and pregnancy. Further, your sexual dissatisfaction with your husband may not soon abate. Then you would have a situation with two young kids, an unsatisfying marriage and a desire to experiment sexually with members of the same sex.

Then a different principle comes into play: Try to act as quickly as possible on long-term needs, because the neglect of long-term needs causes long-term unhappiness. So if you're actually bisexual, get busy. If you're actually dissatisfied with your married life, get to work on it.

The tricky part, it seems to me, is how you tell the difference between short-term and long-term needs. In this case you believe that part of it, at least, is caused by hormones secondary to pregnancy. So my suggestion would be to hold off, if possible, on sleeping with your friend until after you've had the kid. Then, if these desires still persist, rather than live out your whole life with unsatisfied desires, I think you really need to make some serious choices.

And how do you make those serious choices? Well, since they are choices that would shape the rest of your life, you have to assess your life in sweeping terms. You have to ask the big questions. You may find, if you ask these big questions, that you are actually on the right track and doing exactly what you should be doing. Or you may find that your present life is simply incompatible with what your soul requires. That is how you would decide what you must do.

Here are some questions to consider:

What is my purpose in life? Am I working toward that purpose in this marriage? In living as a heterosexual married woman, am I living a lie? Is the self I present to my husband not my true self? What are my obligations to my children? Who comes first, me or them? To whom or what do I owe ultimate allegiance? To myself? To God? To my children? To ideas? To art? To my country? Are the conditions that are causing my dissatisfaction permanent or temporary? If they are temporary, how can I change them? Or will they change by themselves in time? If I were to end my marriage, how would I justify it to an impartial observer? If I believed I had a soul, what would it be telling me to do?

> Ask big questions and try to answer them.

Those are, as I said, rather sweeping and grand questions. But then you are contemplating some sweeping and grand decisions. That one ought to live one's life as though it were a work of art has a certain relevance here, in that a work of art requires an overall design or idea in order to stand as a solitary thing in the immensity of time. So does your life. So ask the big questions, and be guided by the answers.

The other side of the "ex on the shelf" problem

My girlfriend is jealous of my relationship with my ex. Do I have to choose between them?

Dear Cary,

I'M IN A relationship with the "one." She is beautiful, strong-willed, funny, smart and, most important, happy on the inside. We are very happy together, live well together, work problems out openly and disagree about movies we want to see (I want action, she wants drama). The problem is she is very jealous of my ex-girlfriend who I have not seen in two years and have been out of a relationship with for three. I'll admit we talk on the phone every couple months to see how life is, but it is over, I have moved on and I know that she has let me go as well.

In the one's last relationship (also her first serious) she was hurt badly by a very manipulating person who lied, cheated and had an utter disregard for women in general. At one point, he was dating an ex on the sly and the one found out and resorted to spying and confronting him with explosive results. So, now she is hypersensitive to the woman in my past.

I must admit that when I first pursued the one, we talked about the exes a lot. She would tell me how awful he was and I would share the problems I had with my ex (who was also a manipulator). I feel like I've sown the seeds of my own problems, and as I'm getting closer to popping the question I'm worried that being engaged won't diminish the jealousy.

Should I just cut off relations with the ex altogether, something very difficult for me as she is a good friend, which I feel you find few of in life, or do I continue to try to convince the one that the ex is not a threat and has never been one?

Almost Perfect

Dear Almost Perfect,

SINCE THE SUBJECT line of your letter made reference to a recent column (http://archive.salon.com/mwt/col/tenn/2005/04/13/rebound/index.html) in which a young man's photos of his ex sitting on a shelf gave pause to the woman he was going out with, I should tell you that I got a very nice, heartwarming letter from the woman in that column who said that, independently of my advice, before the letter was published, she had done pretty much as I suggested—had a frank and open talk with the man in question about her sensitivities in the matter. And I'm happy to say things worked out fine. They talked about the ex in her boyfriend's life, she felt reassured, and even though she didn't ask him to take down the photos, the next time she visited, she noticed they were gone. Very tactful, very kind of him.

In your case, I would say it's fairly simple: We give things up for those we love. That's the nature of sacrifice. What they want us to give up may seem unreasonable. But if it were easy to give up, or if giving it up made sense, or if you were going to give it up anyway and just hadn't gotten around to it, then it wouldn't be a sacrifice. You'd be doing it for yourself, not for somebody else. Giving something up for someone else means exactly that. We give things up for those we love. We don't hold back. We don't hedge. We go all out. The more dear these things are to us, the better; the greater the sacrifice, the greater our love.

Or so the hypothesis goes.

This may sound old-fashioned and quaint. I prefer to think of it as ancient and heroic. There's a reasonable basis for an ethic of self-sacrifice as well, rooted in a critique of contemporary society as narcissistic, shallow and lacking in realism. You could say that our culture has been conditioned against self-sacrifice because self-sacrifice does not produce the ideal consumer. The ideal consumer believes he deserves everything, because only if we believe we deserve everything will we consent to try and purchase everything. Or that's an argument you could make. Perhaps it goes a little far afield of your particular personal dilemma. But I find it easier to argue for seemingly anachronistic values when they can be seen as a critique of contemporary society!

Besides, doing things for other people is just a good habit to get into in a relationship—the habit of letting go, the habit of thinking of the other. So are you willing to let go of this relationship for her sake? Even if it doesn't make sense to do so? Even if her fears are groundless? It's not a question of is it right or does it make sense; it's a question of are you willing to do something you don't want to in order to please her and make her life more comfortable?

> Identify the spirit of the relationship. Listen to it.

I would think this is the kind of thing that makes the difference between a relationship that's truly heroic, full of difficult but admirable gestures, and one that's constantly being negotiated, full of little holding-backs and selfish hedges. If you want to start off on a good footing, I would suggest that you go ahead and let this friendship go—for now, at least. Show her that you are willing to let it go.

Of course it should work both ways. You shouldn't have to be the only hero. She should be willing to sacrifice things for you, too. Nor am I suggesting that you never, ever talk to your ex again. Relationships change. Right now, your ex seems a threat. In five years everything may seem different. What I'm suggesting is just that each of you be willing to make sacrifices for the other, and that you make the first move, as an example.

It's not a matter of contractual linkage, but of establishing the spirit of the relationship.

Of gender identity,
sexuality, and weddings,
weddings, weddings

*As my friends and I go through our 20s,
will we all abandon our queer ramparts
and begin having babies?*

Dear Cary,

I'M IN MY EARLY 20S, as are most of my friends, and I can hear wedding bells off in the distance for my friends in opposite-sex relationships.

A number of them are now engaged, and a few others are living with partners. Someone who was a close friend of mine in high school, a sharply intelligent woman who has been in a number of relationships that would be classified as unconventional due to the sexuality, gender identity, openness, or number of partners, is now engaged to her straight boyfriend and says that she just wants to be a good wife and mother. Other friends of mine who used to flirt with the boundaries of gender and sexuality are also settling down.

I know in my heart and my head that this will intensify. In a few years, there will be a rash of weddings. Babies will start being born. Most of us will have jobs that require the regular wearing of specifically gender-appropriate clothing.

I'm bisexual and I haven't been in a monogamous relationship, or dated a capital-M male, in years. I was a tomboy and I still sometimes feel that I'm dressing in drag when I put on earrings and a skirt. I'm also into kink. I didn't decide to be any of these non-mainstream things, but now they're part of my identity, both personally and politically. And they've contributed to really interesting and wonderful experiences and relationships over the last few years. Its been scary sometimes, too, and as I've presented in a number of ways to different groups, I think I've learned some things about privilege that as a middle-class white person I wouldn't have learned otherwise.

However, the costs of not presenting as mainstream are going to increase, and I don't know how to work this out. If I wind up with a long-term female partner, I'll have to come out to my relatives. Having more than one long-term partner is even more difficult. I feel no need to "come out" about my involvement with leather/kink/B&D/S&M to anyone beyond close friends, potential partners and other kinky people, but if I wind up being involved with the leather community, there will always be the chance that I'll get outed to employers or relatives. (And finding kinky partners within the leather community is a whole lot less dangerous than looking for them in any other place outside one's circle of friends.)

I'm still in college for a bit longer, so it isn't too late for me to cry "It was all just a phase!" about nearly all of these identities. And academically and career-wise, I'd probably be fine. I'm majoring in something practical that I love, and my grades have been good, so I can pass in that regard. But if I do this, I'll be giving up a lot of who I am, socially and politically, and who I've been for years. And the privileges that go along with being perceived as straight and monogamous and non-poor and basically vanilla aren't fair privileges, anyway. And trying to balance the two—to have a whole identity that your family and your employer can't know anything about—is not a good long-term strategy.

I don't want to be angry at my friends for taking on a whole wad of straight married privilege, but I am. And I'm scared that I'm going to do it, too, eventually (it would be legally impossible with my current relationship status). What do I do before the weddings start coming, and with this whole bigger issue of identification, and how do I not resent my friends for going mainstream, deal with the loneliness of not, or the loss that I'll experience if (when?) I do?

Lost/Delirious

Dear Lost,

SOCIETY IS A gun. Don't point it at yourself. Society is a disease. Wash your hands frequently.

How to live in society without being killed by it? I do not know. It takes a little more out of you every day. It seduces you out of your seductiveness. It coats you with white flour. It makes your voice sound strange. It puts you in a uniform. It wears you down.

> Get used to being alone.

You could live in an apartment full of drag queens and record-store clerks for the rest of your life. There are such apartments to be had, though the rents have gone up.

You could tell your parents all about yourself or you could let them guess. Either way, you will not be understood.

Life is not something you can ace like a test. It's messy, glorious and strange, filled with blowhards like me who say things like "Life is messy, glorious and strange" and "society is a gun" like some 1950s beatnik. (I would march with the beatniks if I could.)

Become friends with queer people in their 60s. Talk to them. Talk to veterans of Stonewall and be prepared for a world as empty of theory as a brick wall. No matter what you say to it, you cannot persuade it.

Rejoice in your singularity. Get used to being alone. Accept that society is out to crush you—but not because it is malevolent! Is the common cold malevolent? That's its nature: to make you sneeze.

Your job is simple, really. It needn't be complicated by tortuous contemplation about what you reveal and what you hide. Neither hide nor reveal. Just be. It's not your job to figure it out. It's the job of society, that ravenous beast of sameness, that gravel-crushing machine.

And one day, like me, assuming you survive, you will say to people in their 20s: You know what's really terrifying—more terrifying than the deadening effect of society? It's that, bit by bit, completely of your own accord, you eventually become so boring that you want to stomp yourself in the face with a boot.

Which you cannot do because your knees are too stiff.

My family treats
my dad like dirt

*I can't believe the cruelty and I don't
know what to do.*

Dear Cary,

I HAVE BEEN living in New York City for the past 12 years. I originally come from a small, unimposing town in Massachusetts and, like many people, I usually spend some part of the holidays visiting my family. This year was no different. But I am finding that every time I visit, however short and infrequent those visits may be, I just get more and more enraged.

Here's a little background for you:

My dad is 70 years old and a recovering alcoholic. He hasn't had a drink in approximately 25 years or so but, having never attended 12-step meetings, he still displays the "dry drunk" behavior that comes with such a disease. He's never been a great provider, which has caused my mother a great deal of frustration over the years. At heart, however, he is a good man and an extremely loving father. He's also the son of two alcoholics himself and came from an extremely fucked-up family situation that no one could have gotten out of without some amount of damage.

My mom, on the other hand, has always been the center of the family. She was the one who somehow managed to pay the bills on time when my dad was bingeing, keep the children clean and well fed, and, basically, keep things from falling apart.

Obviously, this created much anger and dissatisfaction for her over the years.

However, as tough as my mom has always been, there was another side to her. She was (and is) fiercely controlling. When it came to her home and her children, it was understood that she was in command. She was the disciplinarian and many of us lived in a certain amount of fear should we do something wrong—however slight.

Along with that control came a burning desire to always be right and always be needed. Her opinions were accepted as gospel. In addition, her children were taught from an early age that they could only get so far in life. College was out of the question (We don't have the money for that!) as was any kind of success whatsoever. We also had to suffer her angry mood swings. God help us if she came home from work in a bad mood. She would go from one of us to the other and rip us all to shreds with her words. In the end, all of her children were left with a troubled sense of self and very low self-esteem. I am the only one who moved away to achieve a modicum of success, although I have always been haunted by towering self-doubt.

As things are now, my mother and father are still living in the same house I was born in along with my oldest sister and only brother (both in their 40s). My siblings have no idea of the world outside of their little circle and are dangerously enmeshed with my mother who is, perhaps, even more controlling than she used to be. She has also managed to enlist my brother and sister against my father. This has resulted in my father becoming a literal shell of the man he once was. He is all of 100 pounds and spends most of his time being screamed at and verbally abused by my mother, my sister and my brother. His only respite is to smoke endless amounts of cigarettes out on the back porch, and drink coffee incessantly—actions that only seem to provide fuel for the fire. He eats little, is very unhealthy and, if I didn't know any better, I'd say he wants to die.

Whenever I return to Massachusetts (as I did for Christmas) I am enraged at their behavior. It is almost as if my mother has spent the last 25 years or so getting back at my dad for his drinking. She screeches at him, insults him and has made him her lackey. My brother, who is himself a mountain of anger, does nothing but bully him and my sister does the same. They believe my mother is an angel, possessed of nothing but generosity, kindness and selflessness. But they refuse to see the other side of her personality: that of a verbally abusive, controlling martyr/monster. My dad has been stripped of every ounce of power, dignity and self-respect. And I don't know what to do.

Tired of Dad Bashing

Dear Tired,

I SEE YOU coming up the steps with your suitcase, the son who left, the son they fear, the son they find a little uppity now with his education and his job and his ideas, coming up the old steps you used to play on, carrying your suitcase into this haunted house, a little lost and blind in the sudden darkness after the winter sun, everything so incredibly dark and so incredibly the same after so many years, and you tug your suitcase a little tighter, your suitcase, your ticket to goodbye. And there's your father on the back porch smoking and drinking coffee, taking it and taking it and taking it because after all he was a drunkard all those years so it's his job to take it now, whatever they can dish out. After all he made them out of his own flesh and blood so whatever they've got, bring it on, he's got his coffee and his cigarettes, he's got his place on the back porch. He drank it all away so now he absorbs the blows, the insults, the daily onslaught of unrelieved resentment and fury and loss. There he is, killing himself, killing off his feelings with every puff, living on coffee and cigarettes till the end. And there you are carrying your suitcase through the house and finding him on the back porch and thinking, What in God's name am I going to do?

Maybe he'll say something like, "At least I'm keeping thin, son. Looks like you put on a little weight down there in New York City."

What in God's name can you do? Where do you even begin? And what do you say when your mom comes out and tells you not to bother with the old man, he's not worth it, and the old man chuckles like it's a fond old joke.

You could take him to a meeting, you know—those 12-step meetings he never went to enough of. You could call up and find out. Call AA, for heaven's sake, it's in just about every town on the planet, and ask if there's someplace for an old alcoholic to come and get some kindness and coffee—coffee no better than the stuff he's drinking now, and possibly worse, but free.

That's the only thing I can think of. He could go and spend some time with his kind—not his kin, who are eating him alive, but his kind, who will nod and say, Yeah, I know what you mean. Even once a week if he could just sit with other old guys who've blown it in perhaps far more spectacular ways than your dad—guys that have killed children on the highway in blackouts, guys that have awakened on desolate roads in unknown towns with inexplicable bruises, and guys that have just lived miserable little medicated lives of dim depression and unvoiced despair but who are now, amazingly enough, pretty much happy and OK!—if he could just spend some time with guys like himself maybe once a week, and maybe chuckle or just laugh out loud at it all, and let go, and learn how to live as an old alcoholic, maybe it might help.

Back slowly away from the hope.

But you're thinking, If only there was a way I could fix this awful family of mine—the way they treat him! Well, listen, my friend: Back slowly away from the hope. You're not fixing your family. Nobody is fixing anybody's family—not today, not any day.

The one guy you're concerned with is your dad. There are things you can do for your dad. I'd leave it at that. But that's plenty right there.

The sex is great,
but he's not my type

He's coarse, crude, temperamental, testy ...
and great in bed.

Dear Cary,

WHERE DO I begin? I've been in this off-and-on-again relationship with a man who is 20 years younger than me (I am a month
shy of 50). What's so extraordinary about our relationship is
that the sex is nothing short of transcendent. We read each other
like a book, his touch sends me to the moon and we love each
other's smells. Oh, it's tantric and dare I say mystical at times,
and agonizingly slow when it needs to be and just plain lusty and
a bit rough at others. He is the most thoughtful, kind, generous
lover I could ever hope for. We trust each other implicitly, we
don't take ourselves so seriously in bed, we laugh at the body and
bawdy sounds we make.

We also love to spend hours talking about God and the world,
Nietzsche and Chomsky, American Republicans and Canadian
liberals. I love his articulate views on things although they tend
to be rather different and more conservative than mine. He challenges me on my belief systems, I learn from him, he loves to hear
me talk of my adventures when I was young and foolish. We enjoy
listening to music together, and the crossword puzzle in the Sunday
New York Times is our weekly denouement to the sleepover.

So what's the problem here? He's not my type, not just physically (I tend to prefer the English bicycle type and he's built more

like a refrigerator), but also socially. Truth be told he embarrasses me in public with his rather bullish ways. He tends to be suspicious of others before any suspicion is warranted, and you can almost see the hairs on the back of his neck start to bristle, ready to pounce on a poor unsuspecting individual who accidentally bumped into him while in the grocery line. He has appointed himself the platonic form of the alpha male, and although I find it rather lovely to be enveloped in his big burly arms, I tend to cringe when I see the alpha part in action in a public forum. My mother and two daughters don't particularly like him. They find him vulgar and crass. I don't disagree with them.

We've known each other for three years, but for the last year and a half we've seen very little of each other as the relationship broke off on less than amicable terms. The time we spent together was tumultuous. He was ready to marry me one minute and told me a baldfaced, hurtful lie the next. I couldn't deal with his jealousy. I felt I couldn't be me when I was in public with him. We've reconnected lately. He seems to have learned a few things during our hiatus and right now things are easy and relaxed between us. And then there's the sex, of course, which is pretty much as grand as it always was.

My question is, is it possible to be addicted to a person, because it sort of feels like an addiction. I don't think I'm addicted to sex per se. (Although I love sex so very much, you won't find me skulking around in bars trolling for a one-night stand.) It seems more to do with him. I can't say I love him (I do care for him, however), but I do love the time we spend together as long as it's in his apartment.

For some reason I always thought if the relationship was good, the sex is good, but based on my past experience with him the relationship sucked but the sex is great. What does this mean exactly?

Part of me is looking for someone I can spend the rest of my life with. I can't imagine it being him, but I also can't imagine having sex with anyone else. Am I weird?

A.

Dear A.,

I SUPPOSE IT'S possible to be addicted to a person in a meta-phorical sense. You're not cooking him up in a spoon and shooting him into your arm I hope. That would be a weird high. But there may be aspects of your relationship with him that resemble aspects of an addiction, like the secrecy part, the shame part, and the sense in which you may be using him for a sexual high rather than relat-ing to him as an individual. Also, you may feel a little out of control about seeing him, as one does when one is addicted. You might not consciously want to see him and yet you find yourself seeing him anyway. You may also be hiding him from your family, as one hides an addiction. And you may feel guilt and shame about what you do with him, as one feels about what one does when one is high. In these ways, I suppose it might be helpful to say you're addicted.

But there the usefulness of the metaphor ends. I don't see how calling it an addiction will help you figure out what to do. When you have a drug addiction, usually the only thing to do is to quit using. Sometimes a drug user may not consider herself addicted per se, and yet still wants to quit—because the drug use is clearly harmful in a behavioral and/or a medical sense. I do not get the sense that your activities with this man are harmful per se. I do not hear you ask-ing "How can I stop seeing this man?" I only see that you feel confused about some aspects of this relationship. That seems normal. This is a passionate relationship. There is some conflict in this relationship. There are specific differences of opinion. You disagree about politics. You don't like some of his behavior. Your mother and your daughters don't like him. You don't feel comfortable with him in public because he does not act in a refined manner. You're not able to relax because you fear he will embarrass you. And yet you are intensely drawn to each other.

At the root of this relationship seems to be something rare and wonderful. Conflicts can be solved. You can make decisions. You

> Accept the imperfection.

can come to agreements. You have control and discretion, which would not be true if you were addicted.

However, while this relationship does not seem to be pathological, part of the sexual excitement may lie in the private abandonment of those very social codes that you insist must be observed in public. That conflict takes place within yourself, rather than between you and him. There may be an allure that has to do with perceived transgression, and that may be another way in which you suspect this is an "addiction." It is possible that what you have is the classic secret lover of whom society disapproves, the noble savage, the one who satisfies you in private but not in public. Again, this is a conflict that can be managed. It's not out of control. But it's an internal conflict.

There is a possibility, though, that solving these conflicts may take some of the forbidden allure out of it. If you make this relationship more adult, more rational, he may lose some of his potency, metaphorically speaking. He may become less interesting if less exasperating.

Your choice appears to be whether to abandon this relationship, confine it to the sexual, or broaden it to a partnership in life. I don't see why you should abandon it. Though you say he has a temper and is often disagreeable, I don't get the sense that he is violent or coercive.

It seems to me you could solve it like this: If each of you could say to the other, "I want to make this work. I want to be committed to you. I want to find ways to resolve our conflicts so we can live together," then you might have the basis for a lasting relationship. If, however, one or the other of you is unwilling to make such a commitment, then you still have the basis for a satisfying sexual friendship, if you can accept it as simply that.

My family gives me no respect

*I'm accomplished and responsible
but they treat me like a loser.*

Dear Cary,

I HAVE A great job, own my own home, car, dog and medium-size 401K, have put myself through college and law school. I am not a loser! So why does my whole family treat me like one?

My family is not a normal set of folks; we are in a whole new category of dysfunctional and it would take 20 hours' worth of couch time to even come close to describing the crazy things below the surface. Anyway, the issue is that I want to be loved and respected. I am loved by some but respect is just not there.

My youngest sister is forever telling me how poor my judgment is, how bad my understanding of people is and how unprofessional I am, despite the evidence of my high-powered job at an internationally renowned organization. I have a résumé to die for. That is not just a boast but a statement of fact (OK, a boast, too. I need to bolster myself since I am not getting it from outside sources). She tells me that she has no faith in me, in my judgment or in anything about me, that my house is awful, my neighborhood sucks, my dog is poorly trained, etc. And this is the sister I get along with best.

My mother makes it clear that a woman of 39 (me) without a husband and without children is a loser by definition. I had a husband, a drug-abusing, foul-mouthed yet charming brute who almost bankrupted me, stole from me and my friends, cheated on me with other women and possibly men, and verbally abused me in public and private. Dumping him after seven years of marriage was the best decision of my life. I feel lucky that any of my self-esteem survived that one. Yet, here we are five years later and my mother still criticizes me for not keeping that guy! Her current advice: Find a man who wants American citizenship and trade my bed for a green card!

My father barely speaks to me because I dated a guy he did not like a year ago. Two of my sisters do not speak to me at all. I honestly do not know why but both claim to be angry at me. My brother thinks I am an irresponsible idiot. My last sister, who is the only one who acknowledges me as a fully grown and responsible adult, still tells me that my divorce from an abusive ex is a sign of my inability to keep a commitment!

For God's sake, what is it going to take to get these people to admit that I am fine as I am and why the hell do I care! Are these people overly judgmental or am I insane?

Dissed by My Family,

Dear Dissed,

YOU ARE FINE as you are. I know that. You know that. It's the truth.

But your family is never going to give you what you want. That's also the truth.

You will never be at peace with your family until you stop wanting what they will never give you.

It is easy to say, "Accept the way things are."

But exactly how do we accept things? What is this action called acceptance? I would say that acceptance is knowing rather than wishing. You studied law. You committed many laws to memory. You may wish they were one way but they are the way they are. If you go into the courtroom and expect the laws to be different from the way they are you will not succeed. You must accept that the law is the way it is. You must know the law.

The same is true with your family. You must know your family as it is. You must study your family and know it thoroughly.

That is your route to acceptance. Regard your family as a fact, immutable as the law. They are what they are. They behave in a certain way. The facts are unpleasant. But they are facts.

What happens to people who do not like the law and so do not obey it? They get their asses kicked.

You may not like what you know about your family but you must accept it or you will get your ass kicked. You will step into the ring expecting a kiss and get slapped. Don't do it. Don't let them kick you around.

You may find it hard to accept your family as it is. There are reasons for that. One reason is that in accepting your family as it is, you have to give up, or mourn, the ideal family that never was. You may have to go through a sort of grieving process. You may have to feel the hurt, the lifelong ache of wanting a family that is loving and kind and supportive and never getting it. It hurts. It hurts a lot. It hurts for a long time. But that is the price of knowing the truth.

> Allow your family to withhold the one thing you most want.

I think the truth is worth it.

Here is a consolation: This other family, this ideal, imaginary family that you always wanted, this family that really gets you, that supports you, that appreciates you as you appreciate yourself: It is a real family, too. It is real in your mind. You can keep it, in fact. You can keep this imaginary family in your mind. This dream family is your family, too. It's the family you deserve. It lives on a different street in a different neighborhood where only you can go.

Here is another consolation. Sometimes if you leave something alone long enough it begins to heal on its own and one day long after you have given up even thinking about it a gift arrives in the mail that is so delightful you break down right there on your doorstep because you had given up all hope of such a thing ever, ever happening.

I'm just saying it's possible. Maybe one day if you leave this alone it may fix itself. But don't hold your breath. Let it be.

Your family today is sad and difficult and dangerous. Remember that. Accept it. Don't give them the opportunity to kick you around anymore.

Get what you need some other way. Get it from people who have it to give.

My boyfriend dumped
me and I'm desolate

*Though we had some problems, I didn't
see this coming, and don't know how
to get up off the floor.*

Dear Cary,

I AM WRITING because I am so utterly heartbroken and lonely
that I don't know if I can go on.

I am 29, and my boyfriend and true love of 3.5 years just
dumped me on my ass. I always considered him my soul mate,
my husband, my partner. I always thought he considered me in
the same light. (He told me he did constantly throughout the
years.) Our families were completely intertwined—his siblings
were like my siblings, and vice versa. We were beneficiaries on
each other's life insurance policies. We owned a dog together,
cosigned our lease together. Then, almost out of the blue, in bed
one night while casually bringing up a topic we have talked about
constantly over the years with mutual enthusiasm—becoming
domestic partners—he mentioned that he didn't think it was a
good idea. He then went on to say that he has been unhappy with
our "lack of passion" for a while. (I am on libido-crushing Prozac
and have a terrible body image problem, low self-esteem, etc.)
After a desperate night of many tears, I said that I would work
on it—the very next day I called therapists, made appointments,
bought books, talked to friends and started channeling my passion for him by having more sensual, playful sex with him.

Flash-forward: two weeks later. I bring up the topic of my progress with my self-improvement campaign. "How do you think I'm doing?" Basically, then, we start a talk that goes into the next morning, which concludes with the following: "It's too late. Problems that I've kept inside me for too long about our relationship have festered and overcome me, and now I realize that I have fallen out of love with you, and I will never love you again. I want to break up with you."

Everyone, everyone, was shocked. His closest family and friends (not to mention me) were all clueless as to any problems. Maybe twice in the past 3.5 years we had minor talks about our sex life—he wanted more. I tried, but didn't deliver. I suppose that I should have taken that more seriously, even though I had no idea how serious an issue it would end up being. Otherwise, our relationship, I thought, was literally perfect. Every night we slept in each other's arms after laughing together all day long. Held hands, said "I love you," etc. So there wasn't enough sex, enough passion—I was getting help.

I know I should probably feel like I deserve better than a man who didn't love me enough to put any work into our relationship, or to open up his mouth and communicate with me about our problems, which I deserved as his partner of so many years. But all I am is devastated, utterly hopeless, heartbroken, totally crushed. I have had no contact with him since. I moved in with my parents. Even though I desperately want him, want to see him, talk, get information … what's the point? He looked me in the eyes and said, "I cannot love you." Good riddance, right?

After this tirade, my question: How the hell do I get over him? I know it's been done before: People get their hearts broken every day. At least there were no kids (neither of us wanted kids), but we had such a love (I thought), plans for a future together, a life to look forward to. He was "it" for me, absolutely and joyfully. Now I live in a tiny town where everyone knows everyone (I can't relocate because I own a store here), and cannot possibly conceive of ever getting over him, ever moving on, ever finding love again, ever being happy again.

I just need some advice—what do I do with myself? I am now, ironically, in therapy with a great professional. But I need more.

I need steps to take to help me get over my pain. I wish some days I had the guts to kill myself, but instead I soldier on, miserably. I feel like my entire life is shattered and destroyed. I love a man who just let me go, so easily, after so many years, with no warning and hardly an explanation.

Please write to me, say something wise, give me some hope. I am so desperately hopeless and abysmally sad.

Joanna

Dear Joanna,

OK. I WILL take this on. But I will not offer you hope because hope is a fragile thing, easily dashed. You might better reach for other qualities of more enduring purpose—skepticism, anger, determination, knowledge of your situation. You need strength and protection. Where will that strength and protection come from? It won't come from hope. It will come from fierce determination never to be blindsided like this again.

Something died. That is what happened. Something died and everyone who loved what died is sad. What died is this thing that you and he had been keeping alive, this wonderful thing that was not you or he but a luminous third being, whose breath was your breath, whose blood was your blood, whose being was like filtered starlight that came through your bones, a twinkling thing that would catch your eye, a twinkling thing that came with a tune, like a tune you hear in a dream that seems to mean everything.

It was this that died. It died and now everyone who loved it is sad.

This thing died and everyone is sad and asking why. Why indeed do things die? Children ask this question. Why? Why do things die? But who is supposed to answer that question?

It would be comforting to have an answer. We could say love is a gift from the gods that is occasionally snatched back.

The truth seems too cruel to say.

So we go on talking just to calm your nerves, to make some music you can listen to as you grieve.

We don't say that the reason for your misfortune is that the gods are bitchy and full of shit, that they are crazy, sick mother-fuckers, that the gods spit on us when they're drunk and curse us when they're mad. We don't mention what is actually known to be true, that although sometimes in some places the gods inter-vene on our behalf, just as often they get lost and don't show up, that they fight among themselves instead of attending to our wishes, that they look at us with interest and sometimes with lust but only rarely with pity, that instead of offering us protection they scheme to have us for themselves no matter what havoc it causes down here! They couldn't care less! They are gods!

We tend to think only of the good gods, the ones that offer us bountiful harvests and invent intricate bees. It's a habit from childhood, when we were taught to think of one good god, when although we dreamed of monsters we were told that god was watch-ing out for us, that there weren't really any monsters there in the closet, that they weren't really crawling around up there in the space between ceiling and roof. No responsible adult would have thought to teach us that among the gods are horrible nasty fucks that would just as soon sprinkle cancer seeds in a womb as devise a per-fect delivery of a perfect little baby.

> Get some toughness.

So we grew up with fairy tales, misunderstanding the nature of power, thinking power came with the good. Ha!

So these sick motherfuckers like to screw with us all, and they wait until we're pretty soft and trusting because it amuses them no end to see our horrified expressions when the things we love are crushed in impossibly strange ways, when our cells turn against us and buses lose their brakes, when sisters collapse in warm Hawaiian waters for apparently no reason, when strong minds go amok like frayed, sparking wires. They love it.

We live on the fragile edge of annihilation, imperfectly shel-tered from the void, open to the sky and to the asshole motherfucker gods who fuck with us night and day for their own amusement. We pray to a kind and loving insurance god who sometimes provides coverage but who just as often excludes on technicalities the calamities that befall us, looking the other way when he should be watching out for us. And this too amuses the asshole motherfucker gods, who may be many things but are not stupid or naive.

It isn't even so much the dying that we can't handle, it's the surprise, the betrayal, the way you think you'll be OK until they yank the rug out and laugh.

So what do we do? We toughen up. We quit playing patty-cake patty-cake give a dog a bone, we season ourselves, we take the bit in our teeth, we flog ourselves with birch branches, we bitch and moan and howl at the moon and give up our illusions of a soft loving god who hears our prayers and answers them. We board the windows and doors. We wise up and face the fuckers, we quit lying down and taking it, we let go of our prettiness, we prepare for the battle ahead. We say never again will we be caught off guard, never again will we pretend, never again will we believe that this thing we have created cannot be poisoned in an instant by a shit-head god on a bender, fucking up our paradise for his shallow and grim amusement.

Never again will we believe in fairy tales.

We were taught a lot of silly things as kids. Only later would we learn what pleasure the gods take in disrupting our plans; only later would we learn how minuscule are our options, how puny our plans of defense; only later would we learn there's not a whole lot we can do except rub stone in our eyes, interrogate our lovers mercilessly, place fierce guards at entrances and exits.

That's no consolation, really, is it. It's just the truth. You're wiser now though black and blue, sobbing in the firelight, waiting for dawn.

Do I have to?

She broke up with me and I still love her.
Should I keep my word and try to be friends?

Dear Cary,

A FEW WEEKS ago my girlfriend broke up with me. This was the first truly serious relationship for both of us and one that lasted for over five years. The breakup came with relatively little warning; as recently as a few months ago, we were both talking about spending the rest of our lives together.

A little while before she ended things, we had a minor fight during which I, out of frustration, raised the possibility that we might eventually have to break up. She was understandably upset by this and asked me to promise that if it ever happened, I would remain friends with her. I agreed, since I realized that the threat of breaking up with her was just something I had said out of anger and didn't really mean.

Since then, I've tried to stay true to my word. I've spoken with her fairly regularly and even met with her a few times since we broke up. The problem is, these meetings have only reminded me how much I am still in love with her. Every time I see her feels like our relationship in fast-forward; I start out incredibly nervous, settle down and feel comfortable with her, become sublimely happy just to be in her company, and when I leave, feel like she's dumped me all over again. When she's not around, I'm more accepting of the fact that we're no longer together, but when I'm with her I have to keep myself from trying to hold her hand or telling her that I love her.

I don't want to go back on my promise, especially if it would look like I'm doing it out of spite, but at the same time I realize that it's probably not a good idea to spend a lot of time with someone whom I still love. Is this devotion to my ex (and my promise to her) dangerous? Can there be some happy medium between living in denial and cutting her out of my life?

More Than Just Friends

Dear More Than Just Friends,

IF YOU DON'T want to be friends with her after your breakup, you don't have to. It's good to keep promises, but certain kinds of promises are a kind of wishful thinking nourished by the euphoria of love. When the love ends, the promise seems strangely inappropriate and out of context—because it is. It's a little like

Mow your own lawn.

if you were married and had promised to mow the lawn every week and then you got divorced but you're still mowing her lawn.

Here is the logic of this: She broke up with you. Along with rejecting you, she rejects your promises and your obligations. She probably made lots of promises to you. If I read you correctly, she even gave you reason to believe that she might like to spend the rest of her life with you.

Maybe that says something about what kinds of promises we should make when we're in love. A breakup is in itself a kind of broken promise. So if you don't want to be friends with her, if it's too much of a pain, I think it would be OK if you just told her so. In fact, it might do you some good to put your own feelings ahead of this sense of duty for a while.

So take back your mower. Mow your own lawn.

It looks like my niece is autistic

*Could you offer some words of advice
to her mother?*

Dear Cary,

WELL, I'LL JUST jump into it. My sister's 2-year-old daughter
has just been diagnosed with both mental and physical disabilities and my sister is going through a pretty rough time of it right
now. I think she's had this idea of what her family life was going
to be like—you know, the husband, the dog, the two kids and
love all around. But that seems like a distant dream now that
she's faced with the possibility of having to care for her daughter
for, quite possibly, the rest of her life.

We all sort of assumed that my niece was just taking her time
to blossom. The first warning sign was that she hadn't learned to
walk when she was a little over a year old. They attributed that
to the broken leg she suffered when she was about 8 months old.
But suspicion turned to worry turned to actual testing, and the
doctors found my niece to be mentally at a 10-month-old level.

Now, my sister's feeling pretty devastated. She's reading all
these blogs about parents with autistic kids and what their life
is like. And for sure it's rough, but I can't help thinking that she
likes to envision all these worst-case scenarios.

Compounding the problem, she's in a place where she doesn't
have much family support and she's sort of a self-proclaimed
introvert (although I don't believe that at all). Also, she's a stay-
at-home mom, and basically bears the brunt of my niece's long,
hard and tedious therapy work.

I know she's a big fan of your column and I think your words provide a sense of comfort for her. I was wondering if you could say something to her. I know she'd appreciate it. Thanks.

Brother of a Worried Mother

Dear Brother,

IT'S VERY KIND of you to write to me on behalf of your sister. I think I understand what you are asking. You are not really asking me to solve her problem. You are asking me to send her a little gift on your behalf. I think I can do that.

But first, if you are the sister in question, please know that you have a very loving and thoughtful brother, and that is a very cool thing. Please also bear with me while I talk to your brother just a little bit more:

Your request makes me pause to consider how I work. Most days I'm like a guy in his workshop. People bring me things and I try to figure them out and repair them, or suggest how they might be repaired. But also I make stuff, little boxes, little songs, in which I try to hide some delight.

The truth is—and you don't need to know this, but since you have come into my shop and asked for something to be sent to your sister, and I am in a talkative mood now, leaning across the counter with my coffee, I will confess to you: What I am doing here is I am trying to produce art. While it may seem perverse that I would do so in such a venue, this cheap little workshop of mine, or hopeless that such a form as this could support those intentions, or that the results of this endeavor fall so short of being art as to be laughable ... nonetheless, I confess to you, a customer, that is what I am trying to do, in my way. I am trying to produce little pieces of art.

So it is a welcome delight to have such a commission as yours: to simply send uplifting greetings, a few practical hints, and a reminder of my convictions.

But I try to do more, too. I also try to sing the song of how what we are required to do is always a gift. I am singing that song right now, standing under your sister's window in the snow.

It may be a gift we don't like—and now I am singing to you, sister—but we feel obligated to act grateful. I don't know if you believe in God or not, or a benevolent force, or anything beyond yourself, but in cultivating this feeling I am talking about it helps to live in the conscious presence of something beyond yourself, something that you are in essence working for, so you can say, "I'm doing this for you, whoever you are. I'm lifting this burden for you."

Because otherwise at times it's: Why lift this burden at all? Why not put it down in the snow and walk away?

I also know that when things like this happen it is good to look around for support—as though you suddenly felt dizzy and sought a shoulder to lean on, or a fencepost to steady yourself during an earthquake. That's natural and good. What looks like support, however, is not always support; it may be rotten. Pay attention to how you are standing, lest the earth shift again. And don't put all your weight on something until you know it is secure.

It is also good to do the things that are not practical but are important. For instance there may be research you need to do or a friend you need to see. You might think the research is more important, but sometimes choose the friend. You need to understand what is going on not just with your child but with you; you need to live through this thing or nothing will be good. So seek out other people who have gone through the same thing, and hang around them doing nothing much of value, sitting and talking and wasting time.

Allow reality to live with you.

Don't so much try to live with reality; just try to let reality live with you. It will do what it needs to do, reality will; it doesn't need your help. It doesn't even need your permission. Just make some space for it so it doesn't crowd you out.

Now this is a thought that is perhaps a bit far afield: It might help to get out in the woods a bit—to get away from the built environment in order to be reminded how vast the woods are. Something has come into your life that you did not expect. It may seem that everything was going swimmingly until this occurred. To place our natural resistance to surprising and unpleasant occurrences in perspective, it is helpful to be reminded how small our little world of competence and predictability is. The woods will often remind you of that.

People who are born different also have much to teach us. I go to the Y and work out and then I sit in the hot tub. There is a young guy there who is not like the rest of us. He asks me if my family is with me. I say no. He asks me if I have kids. I say no. He asks me if I have pets. I say yes. He asks me how many pets. I tell him. He asks me what kind of pets. I tell him. He asks me their names. All these things I tell him: The names of my pets. The ages of my pets. What movies I like. What movies I own. What my favorite movie is. Whether I like Robin Williams.

He makes lists: Here are all the Robin Williams movies that he owns. We make lists together. There is no weighing and jockeying, nothing tiresome, nothing of the ego. It is pure delight in the things that are: DVDs owned and watched, family members and pets.

It is exhausting, though, to talk like this.

Perhaps this is why it is exhausting: It is much easier to talk about reality in general terms than to actually make even a partial list of its many constituent parts. How many string quartets did Dmitri Shostakovich write, and how many of them have been recorded, and how many of them do I own, and how many times have I heard them performed, and in what cities, by what soloists, in what weather, in what seats? How many times did Charlie Christian enter the studio, and how many times was he recorded live? There are many ways to arrange reality. That is what the people who are different teach us. (You know, speaking of Charlie Christian, a musician friend recommends the book "Expecting Adam," by Martha Beck; I haven't read it but you might give it a look.)

I don't know how your 2-year-old daughter will arrange reality to suit her, or what problems she will have in learning to live on this planet, but I suspect it will teach you much even as it requires much from you. I can't think of any more noble calling. Those of us born into the vin ordinaire of human consciousness, whose brains all work in the same rather mundane, predictable but no less arbitrary fashion, as we trot along in the epistemological mainstream and lounge in the warm lobby of consensus: I'm sure we have no idea. All we can do is salute you.

My boyfriend was a sexual control freak

*He is making amends, but I'm not sure
I can forget his past.*

Dear Cary,

THREE YEARS AGO I met a wonderful man in his early 30s. I was always disappointed when dating men who kept little black books or lists of women they had slept with. This guy was different. I was pleasantly surprised to find out that he was relatively sexually inexperienced (e.g., he had trouble unhooking my bra). However, the longer we dated the more information I found out about his past. To make it short, my new guy was a date rapist for seven years before we met. His victims were mostly older, unattractive women whom he met in clubs and bars. They were weaker and liked the attention of a younger man. He would manipulate them by telling them lies and by staying sober while buying them drinks. He also had a one-year "relationship" with one woman who was six years older and going through a divorce. She was never interested in sex, but he would pressure her and cause her to feel guilty in order to get what he wanted. At times when he was not able to convince her, he would tell her that she could just lie still while he had his way. According to him, she had obvious mental problems.

He told me that the reason he appeared so sexually inexperienced is because he had never really had sex with anyone except me. He says that the reason he manipulated those women was

362

not for sex, but for control, and he felt the highest level of control by being able to perform the most intimate acts. Physical pleasure was never a factor for him, and he was often confused as to why others would say that sex felt physically good. For him, the feeling of being in control was the best part.

When I put it all together from his stories he did not attempt to deny it. Since admitting to having been a rapist, he has been actively trying to change his attitude toward women and sex. He is a volunteer at a rape crisis center and he came clean about his past to the directors of the organization. They sent him to a psychiatrist to make sure he was fit to be a volunteer and now they support and encourage him. He says that the only reason he was capable of changing anything was because he fell in love with me.

My problem is me. I know that love can change people. I know that he is a different man now. I know that he would do anything to stay with me. I know that I'm not one of his victims. But I still can't seem to get over his terrible past. Sometimes I start asking him questions just to prove to myself how wrong and bad it was and how different it is now. Why am I trying to prove things that I already know when I'm thinking rationally? At other times I think that I should just look for someone else who does not have a criminal past. Wouldn't that make it easier for me?

I love him. I want to stay with him. How can I get over his past?

Help, Stuck in the Past

Dear Stuck,

BEFORE WE TALK about your boyfriend's past, we should talk about the extraordinary power of the words you use to characterize that past. You call your boyfriend a former date rapist with a criminal history. You have the right to characterize the situation as you see it. So I let your words stand. But I think we should acknowledge that those words will not be understood the same way by all readers.

Some will agree that the coercive methods you describe do constitute rape, plain and simple. Others will note that none of his victims, over a seven-year period, ever lodged a criminal charge against him; they will ask how he can be considered a criminal if he has never been charged with a crime, much less convicted. Readers will also note that except in one instance of mild force (as you have conveyed to me privately), no violence was ever used. Nor did he, as many date rapists have been known to do, covertly administer any drugs (again, as you conveyed to me privately). His victims chose to drink in his company, while he chose to remain sober. As one person with whom I shared your letter commented, "He seems to have stopped short of forcing women to have sex with him, which is what I think of as rape. Instead he manipulated them into having sex with him, which is different."

Without turning this column into a disquisition on language, those seem to be important points.

For much of my life, the word "rape" has been used in the press mainly in cases of flagrant, violent assault on women by strangers. We did not talk about husbands raping their wives. We did not call it rape when athletes or college students coerced women into having sex with them on dates. We did not talk about a whole range of unspoken, tacit coercion of women in everyday life. So I see today's open and abundant use of the word "rape" as, in part, a corrective to a history of secrecy and suppression in which rape flourished unacknowledged. If, to counter that history of silence, some women use the word to tell a personal and emotional truth rather than one currently prosecutable in a court of law, I do not see much wrong with that. And it may be that many of these acts will eventually be prosecutable.

Nevertheless, for the moment, if we cannot all agree about the meaning of a word, its usefulness decreases. So we will agree that when you say "rape" you mean the lying and manipulation your boyfriend engaged in, and when you say his "criminal past" you mean the inexcusable way he objectified and victimized women to gratify his own obscure desires—acts that may be or ought to be crimes, but crimes for which he was never charged.

Not to belabor this further, but I have one more point: To get the full story, we must tell both what was done and what it felt like. Words not only tell what is, but how it feels. In that sense, rape is the perfect word for what he did. To express one's outrage, one needs a word that says, "This is what you did, you criminal! By deception and manipulation you robbed a fellow human being of free choice in the most intimate of acts! You reduced her to the status of a prisoner or a slave, you degraded her, you violated her humanity!"

But also, in understanding the fact of what we have done, it is important to describe it in cool precision, to say, I told her I was an airline pilot and had once killed a man; I told her I had played guitar for David Bowie's band; I told her I had a bank in Reno that would cash my check when we landed.

> We also choose the dark side.

Together, these two ways of describing someone's actions can, I think, help one integrate it, make a story of it, which is what you need to do. My intuition tells me that one does not ever simply get over someone else's past in a case like this. Not in the sense that one forgets about it or that it ceases to matter. What one does, I think, is transform that past into a story that one can make sense of, a body of knowledge about the world and about oneself.

For instance, one falls in love with a former torturer. Only after one has loved him for many years does one learn that he was a torturer. One then has to make room for this new knowledge. Perhaps one calls it evil. Perhaps one calls it the intergenerational transmission of a traumatic history of abuse. Perhaps one calls it the evil of the state and the will to power. Perhaps also one has conflicting feelings about it: While horrified by the intentional infliction of extreme pain, one may also experience fantasies involving power and restraint.

So one gains knowledge and is humbled, because the world does not appear as simple as it once did. Before meeting a person like this, one might have disregarded any such behavior as beyond the pale. Then one comes to love a person who embodies irreconcilable facts of past and present and comes to some new knowledge. When someone says they cannot imagine how anyone could do anything like that, you think to yourself, Well, yes, I not only can imagine it, but I know how it can occur.

To create this new meaning might require extraordinary emotional and spiritual strength—the kind of strength sought and sometimes possessed by artists and intellectuals who regularly wrestle with the incommensurable facts of existence. If you were a committed artist or intellectual with the time and the psychic energy to wrestle this phenomenon into expressive, comprehensible form, perhaps you could deal with it on your own. But few souls are granted the setting in which to pursue such problems, much less the fortitude to tease meaning and form out of them. So I would recommend that you seek help from a competent psychotherapist, psychoanalyst or the like. I would say to this person: I need to make meaning out of this.

In an intimate relationship, everything is connected. At least that's what I think. We choose people for their positive traits, but we also choose their dark side. There are many kinds of dark sides—there is the dark side of a person that is emotionally dead, tragically wounded, that is exuberant and power-hungry, narcissistic, hateful, etc. Why should it be only the positive traits we choose? While we consciously choose the bright smile and the record of achievement, our dark side is meanwhile choosing the history of abuse or the uncontrollable ego. Good citizens that we are, we name these attributes "faults." But the dark side likes them. It is mirrored by them. It finds connection. It is perhaps even healed by them. They remind us of something long forgotten; we feel comfortable with them, like with a family member. Out of all possible kinds of darkness, we choose a darkness that we know, a darkness we can get around in.

Isn't it odd that you were seeking innocence, and you saw innocence in his inability to unhook your bra? But it wasn't innocence of sex at all, but innocence of intimacy. This is the kind of question you might explore with a therapist. He is anything but innocent about sex. And he is not at all innocent about power.

It is also interesting that in your search for a man who was not obsessed with power—i.e., a man without a black book, a man not boasting of his conquests—you found a man far more obsessed with power than any of the other men. Power is probably a prominent theme in your relationships with men. Perhaps you are consciously attracted to acceptable kinds of power—mastery, competence—but not other, darker kinds of power—domination, control. You might explore with an expert how your fantasy life may be affected by your knowledge of this man's previous activities.

I would also, from this expert, seek to understand what the scientific community knows about him as a member of a class of persons. What is his diagnosis? Is he a sociopath? What are the chances of relapse into past behavior? What are associated antisocial acts that a person like him might need to guard against? Are there dangers too great to bear?

Learn as much as you can. Know yourself. Know him. Be on guard. Accept that he may be, in certain ways, not only damaged but dangerous. Recognize that you cannot take this relationship for granted, that in spite of all you do it may simply not work; it may come to a place in the road where it can go no further; he may balk and be unable to move forward. There may be ways in which he will never love you in a mature, adult way. Realize that if you reach that point, you may have to make the decision to leave him. And if you aren't ready to take that chance, and to do all the work required, it might be time to leave him now.

Help! I'm insanely jealous and full of contempt

People who don't think things through but get what they want anyway are driving me insane.

Dear Cary,

I AM NEARLY 30 and my husband and I are both trying to establish our careers and buy a home that will accommodate the children we plan, in two to three years, to have. I come from a (very) tenuously middle-class household and want to guarantee my hypothetical children a college education and every tool for adult happiness and success. I plan to stay home with them during their early years, if I find it suitable and possible, and return to a family-friendly career, if this also proves suitable and possible. We are vigilant about birth control because before we conceive we must undergo testing to ensure that we do not pass on a severe genetic deformity that runs in my husband's family. We plan to have this done soon. I am a mite disturbed by the possibility that I, too, carry this gene, but my husband and I have always planned to adopt at least one child. I have an adopted sibling, and the idea of adoption always seemed very natural to me. Somehow, it also seems less wasteful.

The problem is that I have developed almost biblical feelings of jealousy and resentment toward people with children, particularly younger people with children. I realize that part of my problem is my background: I went to a high school plagued by teenage pregnancy (every year at least one girl in my homeroom was pregnant, and the principal had to announce that students were not permitted to bring their children to class). Also, my older sister was a teenage mother. While I love my nephew and am glad he was born, I can't help correlating my sister's dismal incompetence as a mother (she no longer has custody) with her decision to go ahead with the unplanned pregnancy. It isn't hard to pick an effective method of birth control (or two) and use it (or them) correctly and consistently. If you can't even be responsible for your own body, I think it portends badly for your abilities as a parent.

When I go to the grocery store I'm not troubled when I see a mother with one or two well-behaved children, but when I see a mother with a grubby or rambunctious brood a storm cloud appears over my head and it thunders, "It's not like shitting! It has to be planned!" When people self-righteously complain about the burden of raising their children I want to shout, "You chose to have children! Shut the fuck up!" I always thought that you should work toward creating a stable environment before having children, and I feel that young parents have selfishly skipped all the hurdles I'm going through to create what I hope will be a healthy, happy family.

Of course, I know that it's really none of my business whether other people choose to reproduce, and I'm sure that most parents are less cavalier about the decision than I usually assume them to be. How can I let go of this?

Thus Far Childless by Choice

Dear Thus Far Childless,

WHAT I SAY may sound crazy. But a little craziness may be what you need.

You can let go of this by loving the world and everyone in it. That's the only way I can put it. We could chip away at your attitude. We could agree that you're no better than the people you are mentally criticizing. But that wouldn't fill your lungs with fresh air. I prefer to sing: Love the assholes you hate. Love the cocksuckers you judge. Love the idiots. Love your dismally incompetent sister. Love the numbskulls too lazy to roll on a condom. Love the zeroes who shouldn't be parents. Love Vice President Dick Cheney (love your enemies out of sheer perversity). Love all the babies in vitro and otherwise, love all the sperm donors jerking off in sterile rooms, love all the unwed parents in their blithe unconcern, love the children blooming on the roadside like wildflowers, love the one-eyed mistakes, the legless mistakes and the heartless mistakes because they too are perfect, it's only our vision that is flawed, love the woman in line before you at the grocery store with the unruly children and the woman behind you with no children and the atheist at the checkout counter and the Greek Orthodox bookkeeper in the manager's box and every other ethnic and religious designation too numerous to mention, love them all, love every category that serves to divide, love the atom and the chromosome of indivisible creation, love the falsehood for its beauty and the truth for its fragility, love all social classes and economic classes and love all the prisoners in all the prisons and all the soldiers in the sand and all the babies emerging into the cruel light of day every day and every night and love your own hatred and your own bile and your own contempt.

> Love the assholes you hate.

Love, love love. In place of contempt, bring love. In place of anger bring love. In place of judgment bring love. The uglier the baby, the stupider the baby, the ranker the baby, the fouler the baby, the more love. Extend your love to those with whom you disagree, those who do not come up to your standards, those who burn churches, those who burn bridges, those who burn with nothing but stupidity and those who burn with woman-hating righteousness, those who burn with passion and those who burn with dullness, those who burn with a dumb repudiation of everything you believe, those who burn with renunciation of everything they themselves believe, those who burn their valuables and everything they own, those who hoard their newspapers in piles to the ceiling, those who do "the wave," those who shit on street corners, those who piss in doorways, those who sleep on our steps, those who break into our houses and rob us, those who call us to sell us mortgages and trips to Reno, those who look down on us as we look down on them, those who see through us as we find them opaque, those who despise us even though we love them, those who would murder us if they could only get out of jail, those who follow us down dark roads hoping to do us harm. Love them all. Cast them into the sea and love the sea.

It's the only cure I know. It's not even a cure. It's just a little song I sing, blinded by my own cruel eyes. I sing, I pretend, I beat my drum, I dance, I wiggle, I run away, I fret, I breathe, I play, I sing. I sing this little song and try to fill my heart with love.

It helps. It's dumb, but it's the only cure I know.

I'm not sure I have a self. How do I get one?

Things are fine, but when I look inside, I don't see a coherent, durable person. Is that normal?

Dear Cary,

THERE ARE A lot of things I love about my life. I like my job; I like my home. In a few months, I'm marrying a wonderful man whom I love deeply and who I know loves me just as much. I just sent out a stack of invitations to a couple of dozen wonderful friends.

The thing is, though, when I really think about it, I'm not sure why my fiancé thinks I'm so great, or why my friends like me at all. At my best, I tell myself there must be something there to attract so many good people into my life. At my worst, I believe they are all just being nice, are desperate, or are friends by association. (I tend to be reserved and introverted, but I often get close to one dynamic person with a lot of friends.)

At the moment, my friends are scattered all over the country (and a few in other parts of the world), and none of them live in the city where I live. I've been here for a year and have made a few attempts to reach out locally, but I haven't made any real friends nearby. I also tend not to be very good at keeping in touch with friends who are far away, and that's been an issue for years. I've gotten into arguments a few times with friends who felt very hurt by this, and by now I feel like a terrible friend who doesn't deserve to have friends at all. Which, of course, may be the underlying reason why I don't keep in touch in the first place: I don't think I'm important enough to be missed.

I know I have some problems with self-esteem. I grew up with a mother who numbed the pain of her past with alcohol and a father who called me immature, selfish and spoiled. As an adult, I can recognize that name-calling is immature, that insulting someone when they don't do things your way is selfish and that children don't get spoiled by themselves. But after years of that, it's hard to switch off the internal tape player now.

Still, it's more than just the self-esteem. How can I like myself when I don't really know who I am? I'm happy in my relationship, and I like what I do, but I know there's a deeper element of self beneath action and ties to others. What is a self, really, and how do I find mine? My lack of self-worth and self-concept, I guess you could call it, is affecting not just my relationships with others but also my ability (or willingness) to take care of myself physically and emotionally, to be productive with my creative work, etc. How can I be centered enough to do these things when I don't even know where or what my center is?

Missing in Action

Dear Missing,

IN REFERENCE TO your anxiety and uncertainty about having a self, I think you should think about postmodernism. Check this out. (http://webpages.ursinus.edu/rrichter/essayfive.html)

I actually started getting into Fredric Jameson when I discovered that people who are younger than I are really, really, fundamentally different in how they process what we call "reality." I'm a relic. I'm surfing the very last, crumbling, feathering tip of the crashing modern wave. Culturally, I'm dead or almost dead. I have a self. Sure. But I'm a relic. What I'm doing is high modernism. I don't even know why anyone can understand what I'm doing, except that we are so slow to become what we are—that is, we still understand this dead language because it's what our parents spoke.

Read Fredric Jameson where he talks about the depth model of self versus the postmodern self. Maybe the self you're talking about—the self that you're worried about not having—is the old-fashioned high modernist self. Maybe you don't need that kind of self. Maybe responding and sorting and processing are enough. Maybe there isn't a static self to discover.

But more concretely, you're very anxious now. You had trouble with your parents. You've got a wedding coming up. But there's your anxiety and then there's your anxiety about your anxiety.

Where's the anxiety coming from?

A good cure for postmodern dizziness is meditation. In fact, the meditative state is maybe a great metaphor for how we must proceed through the postmodern cornfield, all grown high and strange.

Meditate. There doesn't have to be anything down there to find. But meditate. It may calm you down. Just calming down is a good thing. There doesn't have to be a self to discover.

Now here is the thing. As I said in my letter to readers, I have been dealing with a lot of family stuff lately. Some of the family stuff required spending time in the Florida Panhandle. So I was sitting outside on a hot July night in Florida recently, thinking about your question and writing about it in my journal.

So I am transcribing from the journal now:

There are many ways to describe a self: As a set of memories, for instance. You are the storehouse of all that has occurred; you are the repository of and expert on all events occurring to you, a curator of memories, a collector.

Then there are your talents and abilities, the things you do with particular relish or style. Most interesting to me, though, is your collection of incidents of maximum impact, moments of insight, life-changing events: Two roads diverged in a yellow wood, the thing that has made all the difference. Some of these things involve unknowing knowledge, unsayable understandings. Certain things work for us: certain painters, certain tunes. That we can know dependably what works for us is also a measure of self.

Consider what others see when they see us: A kaleidoscopic procession of tiny performances. We are a canvas, too, a movie screen upon which others shine their light and, recognizing themselves or thinking they recognize themselves, love their own images seen on our blankness—on what we feel to be our lack of existence and which may really be our lack of existence!

What else do others see in us? If we have ever been kind, or laughed at a joke, or smiled a certain way or paid a compliment, or looked into another's eyes with piercing intensity, then we have given something. As a consequence, people may feel that we are generous and kind. What we have given them may have been done in secret, unbeknown even to ourselves: We cannot always know what we are giving people; they get things from us we don't understand. We help people without knowing it. We may have simply responded naturally, but it is taken as a gift, an act of kindness.

Also: We magnify others with our attentions. Have you ever been with someone whose interest in you seems inexhaustible, who can drink up as much of your blather as you can dish out, who never tires of your shovelfuls? Your shoulders tire of the shoveling and your eyelids grow heavy but ... she glistens, mesmerized; you are unable to bore her no matter how dull you feel your words to be: You are the only person in the room and are thus magnified and so feel royal royal royal.

> Don't worry about your self. Meditate.

That is how it is with some people who don't necessarily know us but have felt our effect and thus feel they know us, even if we feel that we do not know ourselves.

What do they know really? They know our kaleidoscopic sequence of tiny performances. They are familiar with our work. They know what we show them.

So there are many things that might constitute a self. But the interesting and somewhat contrary view is that the self is bondage, that our happiness can be attained only through losing self—by merging or acquiescing in something higher beyond us.

Which comes first, the something higher or the freedom from self? One way to approach it is to focus on losing the self.

Whatever lies beyond will come naturally once the self dissolves like a shell, ushering one into the world beyond.

Another approach is to declare belief in something beyond the self and try to thus break free—what I would think of as a Protestant evangelical Christian approach: I accept Jesus as my personal savior; now let's get on with the transformation of self!

But what is this thing that happens, this spiritual awakening that is a loosening of the bondage of self? For me it was at first literally a formal recognition of an altered spatial relationship, the admission of a third entity that was not me and not other, like ...

A possum just sauntered by me as I sit outdoors at midnight in the warm air of the Florida Panhandle—that possum appearing on cue as if to illustrate my point precisely: There is me, there is not me, and then there is this little possum that is walking by, evidence of the indifferent but connected other toward which we can only respond with silent awe and amusement!

O possum, relieve me of the bondage of self that I may be of greater use to my fellows. I am here in the scrub pine backwoods redneck land of my beloved people: My fatherland and motherland where my grandparents are buried. Bless me, O possum.

Meditate.

The Index

A NOTE ABOUT this index and the organization of this book:

The columns in this book appear in no particular order—or, if you like, in a very particular order whose principles of organization are undiscoverable to any save the authors and designers.

But this index provides untold delights.

It lists not only the page numbers on which certain subjects and columns appear, but also various memorable phrases or clauses such as "At birth everybody gets a sweater" and "Every campaign of abuse begins with a period of seduction." These are clumps of words that may have stuck in your head as you read one of the columns in the past, or they may strike you afresh as strange, interesting-sounding word-accumulations, as you peruse the index.

For sheer delight of reading we especially like the "Index of Similes," which is a listing of almost all the phrases in the book that begin with the word "like." Most of the phrases were created by the author, but quite a number of them come from the letters submitted by people hoping for some advice. (As you will notice, the letters asking for advice are quite literate and discerning.)

To be honest, not all the phrases that begin with the word "like" are true similes; in some instances, the words simply form an expressive phrase of some sort. But what we really like about the "Index of Similes" is that it can be read aloud, starting from just about any point, with great hilarity and enthusiasm. For that reason, we think that this index is more fun than most indexes, and we hope that henceforth other book writers will follow our example when they are faced with the task of compiling such an important but often boring addendum.

Enjoy the index!

INDEX

INDEX

INDEX